REVISE EDEXCEL GCSE (9–1)
Religious Studies B
CHRISTIANITY AND ISLAM

REVISION GUIDE

Series Consultant: Harry Smith

Author: Tanya Hill

A note from the publisher

In order to ensure that this resource offers high-quality support for the associated Pearson qualification, it has been through a review process by the awarding body. This process confirms that this resource fully covers the teaching and learning content of the specification or part of a specification at which it is aimed. It also confirms that it demonstrates an appropriate balance between the development of subject skills, knowledge and understanding, in addition to preparation for assessment.

Endorsement does not cover any guidance on assessment activities or processes (e.g. practice questions or advice on how to answer assessment questions), included in the resource nor does it prescribe any particular approach to the teaching or delivery of a related course.

While the publishers have made every attempt to ensure that advice on the qualification and its assessment is accurate, the official specification and associated assessment guidance materials are the only authoritative source of information and should always be referred to for definitive guidance.

Pearson examiners have not contributed to any sections in this resource relevant to examination papers for which they have responsibility.

Examiners will not use endorsed resources as a source of material for any assessment set by Pearson.

Endorsement of a resource does not mean that the resource is required to achieve this Pearson qualification, nor does it mean that it is the only suitable material available to support the qualification, and any resource lists produced by the awarding body shall include this and other appropriate resources.

> **For the full range of Pearson revision titles across KS2, KS3, GCSE, Functional Skills, AS/A Level and BTEC visit:**
> www.pearsonschools.co.uk/revise

Published by Pearson Education Limited, 80 Strand, London, WC2R 0RL.

www.pearsonschoolsandfecolleges.co.uk

Copies of official specifications for all Pearson qualifications may be found on the website: qualifications.pearson.com.

Text and illustrations © Pearson Education Ltd 2017
Typeset and illustrated by Kamae Design
Produced by Out of House Publishing
Cover illustration by Miriam Sturdee
Picture research by Alison Prior

The right of Tanya Hill to be identified as author of this work has been asserted by her in accordance with the Copyright, Designs and Patents Act 1988.

First published 2017

20 19 18

10 9 8 7 6 5 4 3

British Library Cataloguing in Publication Data
A catalogue record for this book is available from the British Library.

ISBN 978 1 292 14882 3

Printed in Italy by Lego

Acknowledgements
The publisher would like to thank the following for their kind permission to reproduce their photographs:

(Key: b-bottom; c-centre; l-left; r-right; t-top)

123RF.com: 123RF 11tl, Ramzi Hachico 86; **Alamy Stock Photo:** age fotostock 54, Alistair Linford 22, Art Directors & Trip 70, Artepics 4l, david pearson 64, Don Johnson_ON 75, dpa Picture Alliance 47, 83, GoGo Images 21, Graham Prentiss 40, Gregory Wrona 19, Jim West 67, jozef sedmak 52b, OJO Images 13, Peter Barritt 5, Peter Maclaine 50b, Peter Titmuss 65, Pictorial Press Ltd 46, PRISMA ARCHIVO 73, REUTERS 18, Robert Herrett 26; **Creative Commons http://creativecommons.org:** 87; **Fotolia.com:** angelo.gi 35, dglimages 11bl, Getmilitaryphotos 50t, Ingrid HS 72bc, rock_the_stock 11bc, Sasanka7 31, szeyeun 79; **Getty Images:** DEA / G.Dagli Orti 4r, DEA / M Seemuller 48, Noah Seelham 78, Print Collector 52c, Time Life Pictures 52t; **Pearson Education Ltd:** MindStudio 11tr; **Shutterstock. com:** bestjeroen 10, fizkes 28, Getideaka 72tl, Image Zebra 29, Jasminko Ibrakovic 68, Jurieta 82r, Monkey Business Images 11br, Nickolay Khoroshkov 34, Valery Sidelnykov 82l, welcomia 72cr, 72bl, yusoffjalil 89, ZouZou 76, Zurijeta 7; **© The Metropolitan Museum of Art:** 72br

All other images © Pearson Education

We are grateful to the following for permission to reproduce copyright material:

Figures
Figures on pages 58, 75, 78, 121, 122 from *Revise Edexcel: Edexcel GCSE Religious Studies* by Tanya Hill, Pearson Edexcel, 2012, pp.5, 7, 14, 32. Reproduced by permission of Pearson Edexcel.

Text
Surah extracts on pages 69, 70, 72, 73, 75, 78, 82, 84–86, 88, 90–106, 108–112, 116–120, 122–124, 126, 127, 129–131, Sahih International, The Qur'an: English Meanings and Notes, Riyadh: Al-Muntada Al-Islami Trust, 2001–2011; Jeddah: Dar Abul-Qasim 1997-2001; and Surah extracts on pages 81, 87, 113, translated by Mohsin Khan, Dar-us-Salam Publications, March 1999, https://dar-us-salam.com, 713.722.0419. Reproduced with permission.

Contents

1-to-1 page match with the Religious Studies Revision Workbook ISBN 9781292148816

The Trinity

The **Trinity** is used by Christians to express their belief in **One God** who has made himself known in three different ways – **Father, Son** and **Holy Spirit**.

The nature of the Trinity

- ✓ Christians believe in One God. It is a **monotheistic** religion.
- ✓ Christians believe that there are **three equal, yet distinct, persons in One God** – the Father, the Son and the Holy Spirit.
- ✓ The word 'Trinity' comes from 'tri-unity', meaning **'three-in-one'**, showing belief in One God, but three separate and unique roles.

Golden rule

Remember: the Trinity is not the idea that Christians believe in three gods.

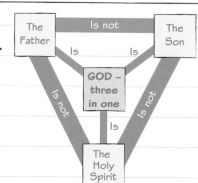

The diagram of the Trinity demonstrates how the three parts are interlinked, while also remaining three separate ideas.

The Trinity in worship and belief

- Christians **bless themselves** by making the sign of the cross and offer prayers 'in the name of the Father, Son and Holy Spirit'.
- **Prayers** such as the Lord's Prayer, Nicene Creed and Apostles' Creed refer to the Trinity.
- Some Church **hymns** refer to the Father, Son and Holy Spirit.
- The belief in the Trinity is intended to be at the centre of each Christian's individual daily relationship with God.

The importance of the Trinity

The Trinity helps Christians understand the three ways that God can be understood – Father, Son and Holy Spirit. Christians can understand God better by relating to these three aspects.

> Then Jesus came from Galilee to the Jordan to be baptized by John… As soon as Jesus was baptized, he went up out of the water. At that moment heaven was opened, and he saw the Spirit of God descending like a dove and alighting on him. And a voice from Heaven said, "This is my Son, whom I love; with Him I am well pleased." (Matthew 3:13–17)

Christians believe that each part of the Trinity is equally important.

The Trinity and the Nicene Creed

The Nicene Creed is an important statement of belief about the Trinity and the different characteristics of each role. It states that:

- the **Father** is the powerful creator of everything – 'maker of Heaven and Earth, of all that is, seen and unseen'
- the **Son** is Jesus Christ, who came to earth as God in human form (incarnation) and was crucified to redeem humanity's sins – 'For us and for our salvation he came down from heaven'
- the **Holy Spirit** is the invisible power of God that works within the world today to guide and inspire us – 'the giver of life, who proceeds from the Father and the Son'.

Now try this

Outline **three** beliefs about the Trinity.   **(3 marks)**

This style of question asks you to describe three separate beliefs about the Trinity, so you should aim to write three separate sentences – one for each belief.

Interpretations of Creation

Christians may hold different understandings of the Christian Creation story. For example, Christians may interpret the story of Creation in a literal or a non-literal way.

Literalists

Literalists (also known as Creationists) believe that:

- the Creation story as it is told in the Bible is **literally true** because the Bible is the literal 'word of God'
- God created the world in six 24-hour days.

Literalists do not accept scientific explanations about the world such as the Big Bang theory or the theory of evolution. They think these **scientific explanations are wrong.**

Non-literalists

Non-literalists believe that:

- God created the world but **not exactly** how the story in the Bible says (the story is **metaphorical**). The Genesis story of Creation is more myth than fact, e.g. the word 'day' in the Creation story is a **metaphor** for a much longer period
- science and religion together explain the Creation. There is no conflict between religious and scientific explanations – the Bible explains **why** Creation happened and science explains **how**.

Word of God

> In the beginning was the Word, and the Word was with God, and the Word was God. (John 1:1)

This Bible passage introduces the idea that the universe was created at a command from God – at his 'Word'.

Spirit of God

> In the beginning God created the heavens and the earth. Now the earth was formless and empty, darkness was over the surface of the deep, and the Spirit of God was hovering over the waters. (Genesis 1:1–2)

This biblical quote shows the power of God in creating the universe and the role of the Spirit of God.

Worked example

'The story of Creation still has a purpose for Christians today.'
Evaluate this statement, considering arguments for and against.
In your response you should:

- refer to Christian teachings
- refer to different Christian points of view
- reach a justified conclusion. **(15 marks)**

There are three extra marks for SPaG.

As the Creation story appears in the Bible (e.g. Genesis), which Christians accept as the Word of God, many Christians would agree with this statement.

The Creation is seen as an important gift from God showing that he loves us. It also shows the power of God, as he created the universe in six days, resting on the seventh.

While literalists dismiss the idea of the Big Bang, other Christians believe that it simply describes how God made the universe – that it was part of his plan. Although different Christians interpret this story differently, all Christians see the final result of Creation as 'proof' that God exists.

Christians believe the Creation story also sets out the role and place of humans within the world – as 'stewards' of his creation.

This is the first part of a student answer. It starts well and offers some reasons why Christians would agree with the statement. The student needs to continue by offering reasons why Christians may disagree with the statement and then give an overall conclusion.

Now try this

Explain **two** ways the biblical account of Creation can be understood.   **(4 marks)**

Make sure you **explain** rather than just state beliefs. You need to show awareness of why different beliefs may exist.

The Incarnation

The word 'incarnation' means 'becoming flesh'. It is used by Christians to explain how God **took human form** through Jesus and lived and died within the world.

The importance of Jesus

Jesus is seen by Christians as the incarnate **Son of God** and is given great importance within Christianity.

- His birth fulfilled the prophecy of **Christ** coming to earth as the **Saviour** who was promised by God – so God took human form to be present within the world.

- Jesus is the 'Son' part of the three ideas (the **Trinity**) that make up the Christian understanding of God.

Gospels in the New Testament

✓ Information about the life of Jesus is found in the Bible in the first four books of the **New Testament** – Matthew, Mark, Luke and John. These books are known as the Gospels.

✓ Accounts in the New Testament describe Jesus' birth, life and death.

... the Word became flesh and made his dwelling among us... (John 1:14)

... He appeared in the flesh, was vindicated by the Spirit, was seen by angels, was preached among the nations, was believed in the world, was taken up in glory. (1 Timothy 3:16)

Jesus as Divine

Though Jesus was human, he was **Divine**, which means he was God. Christians believe the Bible shows us examples of how Jesus is Divine.

1. Jesus is **omnipotent** (Matthew 28:18) and **omniscient** (John 21:17).
2. Jesus **forgave sins** (Mark 2:5–7).
3. Jesus **performed miracles** (for example, John 21:25).
4. People **worshipped** and **prayed to** Jesus (Matthew 2:11).
5. Jesus was **resurrected** after death (Mark 16:1–20).

Jesus as human

It is easier for Christians to understand and relate to Jesus, as he was human and experienced the same problems we do.

1. He was **born to a human** mother – Mary – as a 'normal' baby (Luke 2:7).
2. He had a **human body** (Luke 24:39).
3. Jesus got tired (John 4:6), thirsty (John 19:28) and hungry (Matthew 4:2).
4. He showed **human emotions** such as amazement (Matthew 8:10) and sorrow (John 11:35).
5. He **prayed** to God (John 17).
6. He **died** (Romans 5:8).

Worked example

Explain **two** reasons why the Incarnation is important for Christians today. **(4 marks)**

It is easier to understand God in human form as it is easier to relate to him. Jesus lived and suffered and prayed as humans do, and showed the same emotions – even anger, for example when he overturns the traders' tables in the Temple.

Jesus went to heaven after he died and this gives Christians today hope as he is viewed as the Saviour, dying to save the sins of the world. It tells Christians there is an afterlife and provides hope that they will also to go to heaven.

Here, you are asked to provide two reasons. For each reason, you will need to state what the reason is and then develop it in order to access both marks available. Try to use references from the Bible to support what you say.

Now try this

Outline **three** Christian beliefs about Jesus.
(3 marks)

3

The last days of Jesus' life

'The Passion' is the phrase Christians use to describe the last few days of Jesus' life. It is made up of a number of key events.

The Last Supper

Jesus shared his last meal with his disciples, where bread was broken and wine drunk. Jesus predicted that one disciple would betray him.

'... I will not eat it again until it finds fulfillment in the kingdom of God.' (Luke 22:14–16)

Betrayal and arrest

Soldiers came for Jesus while he was in the Garden of Gethsemane. Judas had betrayed him by telling the soldiers where he could be found.

Then Jesus went with his disciples to a place called Gethsemane … (Matthew 26:36)
While he was still speaking, Judas, one of the Twelve, arrived. With him was a large crowd armed with swords and clubs. (Matthew 26:47)

Ascension

The resurrected Jesus ascended to heaven 40 days after his resurrection.

After the Lord Jesus had spoken to them, he was taken up into heaven and he sat at the right hand of God. (Mark 16:19)

The Passion

Resurrection

Jesus was brought back to life three days after his crucifixion.

… the men said to them, "Why do you look for the living among the dead? He is not here; he has risen!" (Luke 24:5–6)

Crucifixion

Jesus was sentenced to death on a cross as he was accused of blasphemy, tried and found guilty.

Carrying his own cross, he went out to the place of the skull, (which in Aramaic is called Golgotha). (John 19:17)

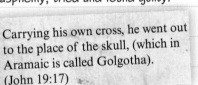

The importance of the Passion

- The events of the Passion provide **evidence** that Jesus was the Son of God and came to Earth in human form. They show that Jesus was special and is worthy of respect and obedience.
- They demonstrate the Christian belief in **life after death**, which offers hope to Christians.
- They show the relationship between God and Jesus. Christians believe that through the death of Jesus, **God saved or redeemed humanity**, and it is through following Jesus' example that God can forgive them.
- They help Christians to understand the **sacrifice** Jesus made and reinforce the importance of Jesus within Christianity.
- The **Eucharist** (bread and wine) is taken from the Last Supper – a tradition at the centre of Christianity today.

This question requires you to state three things that happened to Jesus in the final few days of his life. Make sure you write three separate points to achieve the marks available.

Now try this

Outline **three** events in the last days of Jesus' life.   **(3 marks)**

Salvation

Salvation for Christians refers to being saved from sin through belief in Jesus. **Atonement** is the idea that humans are reconciled and forgiven by God, and **redemption** is how Christians believe this can be achieved.

The role of Christ in salvation

Christians believe that through God sending Jesus to Earth, the sins of humanity are forgiven. Jesus, who was perfect and without sin, offered redemption for humans through sacrificing his life.

Jesus is "the stone you builders rejected, which has become the cornerstone." Salvation is found in no one else, for there is no other name under heaven given to mankind by which we must be saved. (Acts 4:11–12)

For God so loved the world that he gave his one and only Son, that whoever believes in him shall not perish but have eternal life. (John 3:16)

Atonement is understood by Christians to be the mending of the relationship between God and humanity, which was broken when Adam and Eve disobeyed God in the Garden of Eden.

Different understandings of atonement

1. Jesus' death as a divine sacrifice represents God's love for humanity.

2. Jesus' death was a sacrifice – an offering to God to mend the broken relationship.

3. Jesus' death is the victory of good over evil, as Jesus was used as ransom to stop the devil having any hold over humanity.

4. Jesus' death represents the price being paid for the forgiveness of humanity.

Significance of atonement and salvation for Christians today

Atonement and salvation are important because they:

- ☑ restore the relationship between God and humanity
- ☑ confirm belief in an all-powerful and loving God
- ☑ allow humans to understand the importance of being reconciled with other humans
- ☑ give humans hope that they can follow the example of Jesus, to be rewarded in the eternal afterlife.

Worked example

'Outline' questions require you to **state** three beliefs about the given focus.

Outline **three** beliefs about the role of Christ in salvation. **(3 marks)**

Christians believe God sent Jesus to repair the relationship between humanity and God that was damaged when Adam and Eve disobeyed him in the Garden of Eden. Jesus is free from sin and able to take the role of being sacrificed. The Bible states that God sent Jesus to atone for the sins of humanity and allow humans to be reunited with God in heaven.

Now try this

Explain **two** reasons why atonement and salvation are important to Christians today. **(4 marks)**

Remember to give **two different** reasons, then develop each one to show you understand it fully.

Life after death

All Christians believe there is an afterlife for those who believe in God. **Eschatology** is the word used for 'end times'. It can refer to the end of a human life or the end of the world.

Christian beliefs about:

① Resurrection

Christians believe that death is not the end. They believe that the resurrection of Jesus – when he came back to life from the dead – proves life after death.

> I am the resurrection and the life. The one who believes in me will live, even though they die. (John 11:25)

② The soul

- Death is only the end of the body; the soul is immortal.
- Souls that have been saved either go to heaven or to **purgatory** (which is the Catholic idea of a 'waiting room', where souls go to be cleansed before entering heaven).
- Souls that have not achieved salvation will go to hell.

③ Judgement

Christians accept God is just and it is God who will decide the destination of every human's soul after death. They believe that Jesus is also involved in judgement and will offer every human the opportunity of salvation. Those who refuse will face the 'Last Judgement'.

> For we must all appear before the judgment seat of Christ, so that each of us may receive what is due us for the things done while in the body, whether good or bad. (2 Corinthians 5:10)

④ Heaven

Heaven is mentioned in the Bible, yet it is rarely described. Some Christians believe heaven is a physical place, but most think it is a spiritual state of being united with God. The Bible teaches there is no sin, sadness or suffering in heaven.

> He will wipe away every tear from their eyes. There will be no more death or mourning or crying or pain. (Revelation 21:4)

> For we know that if the earthly tent we live in is destroyed, we have a building from God, an eternal house in heaven, not built by human hands. (2 Corinthians 5:1)

⑤ Hell

The Bible teaches that hell is where unrepentant sinners go after death if they have not accepted God's offer of forgiveness and salvation through Jesus. It is a place of pain and suffering, without God.

> Do not be afraid of those who kill the body but cannot kill the soul. Rather, be afraid of the One who can destroy both soul and body in hell. (Matthew 10:28)

The 39 Articles of Religion

The 39 Articles of Religion, written in 1563, are statements from the Church of England to make clear the position of the Church on key teachings.

> Christ did truly rise again from death, and took again his body, with flesh, bones, and all things appertaining to the perfection of Man's nature; wherewith he ascended into Heaven, and there sitteth, until he return to judge all Men at the last day. (39 Articles IV)

Divergent understandings

All Christians accept the belief in life after death, however some Christians:

- understand heaven and hell as physical places, while others accept them as spiritual ideas
- believe members of all faiths have a place in the 'Kingdom of God', while others believe those without faith who have lived good lives will be rewarded
- believe in the Second Coming or return of Jesus from heaven to Earth.

Some Christians see life as a test for the final judgement, while others see belief in God as more important.

Now try this

Explain **two** beliefs about heaven for Christians.

(4 marks)

Evil and suffering

Evil and suffering cause a problem for people who believe in God, as well as non-believers. It may lead some to question their faith in God or even reject God's existence altogether.

Types of evil and suffering

There are two main types of evil and suffering:

1 **Moral evil/suffering** – actions carried out by humans who cause suffering, e.g. murder, rape, war and theft.

2 **Natural evil/suffering** – things that cause suffering but have nothing to do with humans, e.g. famine, disease and natural disasters.

Does God exist?

Christians may question:

- how a loving and righteous God would allow people to do evil things
- why people need to suffer
- whether, if God does exist, he is all-powerful, as he should stop evil and suffering.

The problem of evil and suffering in the world, such as a brutal terrorist attack, can lead some people to reject the existence of God and question their faith.

The problem of evil and suffering

If God is **all-good**, he would want to remove evil and suffering as he cares for his creation

omnibenevolent

If God is **all-knowing**, he would know how to remove evil and suffering

omniscient

GOD

If God is **all-powerful**, he would be able to remove evil and suffering

omnipotent

Use the diagram above to help you answer this question. Make sure you explain any terms you include in your answer, such as **omnipotent**, **omniscient** and **omnibenevolent**.

The Bible

The Bible says God is benevolent and cares for his Creation. Christians believe that God would want to help his Creation if it were suffering.

The Lord is compassionate and gracious, slow to anger, abounding in love. He will not always accuse, nor will he harbor his anger forever. (Psalm 103:8–9)

And the heavens proclaim his righteousness, for he is a God of justice. (Psalm 50:6)

You answer us with awesome and righteous deeds, God our Savior. (Psalm 65:5)

Refer to quotes such as these, which demonstrate what Christians believe the nature of God is like.

Now try this

Explain **two** reasons why evil and suffering raise problems for Christians about the nature of God.   **(4 marks)**

Solutions to evil and suffering

The existence of evil and suffering challenges the Christian belief in an all-loving and all-powerful God. Christians respond in a number of ways, with some maintaining that God did not create evil.

What does the Bible say about evil and suffering?

☑ Genesis says that God created a perfect world.

☑ The Fall: Adam and Eve used their free will in the Garden of Eden to disobey God (the Fall), which allowed evil and suffering to enter the world.

☑ Christians believe God sent Jesus to Earth to overcome the evil in the world and die for the sins of humanity on the cross.

☑ Some Christians accept that evil came into the world through the devil, for example when the devil tempted Adam and Eve in the Garden of Eden.

Christian responses to the problem of evil and suffering

1 Book of Psalms – this offers reassurance that evil and suffering have a purpose in the world: that they give people the opportunity to follow the example set by Jesus in order to live as God intended.

> God is our refuge and our strength. (Psalm 46.1) Teach me knowledge and good judgment, for I trust your commands. Before I was afflicted I went astray, but now I obey your word. (Psalm 119:66–67)

2 Job – the Bible describes how Job endured many examples of suffering, including losing his family and physical pain, yet he did not lose his faith. He trusted in God and believed that suffering was part of God's plan for him. Christians believe that they may not understand why they suffer, but they need to trust in God and will be rewarded for doing so.

> In all this, Job did not sin by charging God with wrongdoing. (Job 1:22)

3 Free will – God gave people free will and Christians recognise that humans sometimes choose to turn away from God. This explains the presence of many acts of moral evil. Theories such as this are contained in St Augustine's *Theodicy*. For more on moral evil, see page 7.

4 Vale of soul-making – this is the idea that evil and suffering have a purpose, even if we do not know what it is. Suffering can make a person stronger and help them appreciate the good things in their life. So evil may not always be a bad thing. The philosopher John Hick put forward this theory.

5 Prayer – many Christians respond to evil in the world by prayer, so that God will give them the strength to cope with the problems they are facing. Christians believe that even if their prayers are not answered in the way that they want, God has a plan for everyone.

6 Charity – many Christians have been inspired by the suffering in their own lives to try to help others. For example, Chad Varah established the Samaritans as a result of the suffering he witnessed in his community as a priest working in London.

Now try this

3 SPaG marks are available.

'It is not possible to believe in God and accept evil and suffering in the world.' Evaluate this statement considering arguments for and against. In your response you should:

- refer to Christian teachings   • reach a justified conclusion.

(15 marks)

Marriage

Marriage is an important rite of passage in Christianity. For Christians, marriage is traditionally accepted as being between a man and a woman, and is seen as the correct context in which to have a sexual relationship and children.

What the Bible says

The Bible states that marriage should be **monogamous** between a man and woman and **for life**.

> But at the beginning of creation God made them male and female. For this reason a man will leave his father and mother and be united to his wife, and the two will become one flesh. So they are no longer two, but one flesh. Therefore what God has joined together, let no one separate. (Mark 10:6–9)

The Christian purpose of marriage

1 To provide companionship, friendship and support between husband and wife.

2 To enjoy a sexual relationship within marriage and have children and raise a family.

3 To make a lifelong commitment to another person, establishing a permanent and stable relationship, thereby also providing stability to society through the teaching of good moral and social behaviour.

Marriage is an important bond between a man and a woman.

Christian beliefs about marriage

1 Most Christians believe marriage is a **sacrament** – a ceremony in which God is involved. Vows, such as being faithful, are made between the man and woman and also to God, showing marriage is sacred and binding.

2 Marriage is believed to be a **gift from God** – it is part of God's plan for men and women to live together as stated in the Bible.

3 Marriage is seen to provide **security** and a **stable environment for children** to be raised as Christians.

4 Although marriage is important, some Christians believe that God doesn't want everyone to be married. Jesus himself wasn't married and some Christians believe they have a **vocation from God** (for example, being a monk or nun) where marriage is not a requirement.

Non-religious attitudes

Humanists do not use religion in their lives; instead they rely on their use of reason. They do not accept marriage as a religious institution blessed by God, but they do accept marriage in a secular sense as a couple making a **commitment** to each other.

It is possible to have a humanist wedding, although this is not accepted legally and a civil ceremony would also be required.

Cohabitation

Today, not everyone wishes to get married. Some couples prefer to **cohabit** – to live together without being married. With many believing marriage is expensive and unnecessary, they may choose not to get married.

Christians, however, argue that marriage provides stability, the basis for family life and involves sacred vows made in front of God, so they do not support cohabitation as an alternative.

Now try this

Explain **two** reasons why marriage is important to Christians. In your answer, you must refer to a source of wisdom or authority.
(5 marks)

Remember that you have to refer to a quote in your answer.

Sexual relationships

Christians hold some key beliefs about sexual relationships, including the belief that a sexual relationship should only take place between a man and woman who are married to each other.

The nature and importance of sexual relationships in Christianity

Christians believe sex is a gift from God intended for **procreation**, therefore they believe that sex should take place only within marriage. They believe that sex is an important way for a man and woman to show commitment to each other. All forms of sexual activity are forbidden outside of marriage.

Alternative Christian views of sexual relationships

Some Christians believe that, in modern society, some ideas about sexual relationships are outdated. They believe that love is important and should be celebrated in whatever form it occurs. This may allow them to accept cohabiting couples who have a sexual relationship as well as homosexual couples who are in a permanent and stable relationship.

1 Corinthians 6:1–20 can be interpreted to mean that the body is sacred and sexual relationships should not be abused, or that a sexual relationship is a way of honouring the body, with sex being a gift from God.

Non-religious attitudes

Humanists believe that consenting adults should be allowed to share a sexual relationship provided it does not harm anyone else. Atheists are unlikely to have a problem with sex outside of marriage or with homosexuality.

Sexual relationships in the Bible

① Casual relationships are wrong – marriage is intended for sexual relationships.

② Adultery is forbidden in the Ten Commandments, which are rules from God.

③ Married couples should be faithful to each other as spoken in the marriage vows.

④ St Paul in the Bible condemns homosexual acts, stating that they are 'shameful'.

⑤ Being sexually pure is advised, and many Christians take a vow of chastity before marriage.

Marriage should be honoured by all, and the marriage bed kept pure, for God will judge the adulterer and all the sexually immoral. (Hebrews 13:4)

Flee from sexual immorality. All other sins a person commits are outside the body, but whoever sins sexually, sins against their own body. Do you not know that your bodies are temples of the Holy Spirit ... Therefore honour God with your bodies. (1 Corinthians 6:18–20)

God blessed them and said to them, 'Be fruitful and increase in number; fill the earth and subdue it'. (Genesis 1:28)

You shall not commit adultery. (Exodus 20:14)

Christians believe sex is a gift from God that should take place only in marriage.

Now try this

Explain **two** Christian teachings from the Bible about the nature of sexual relationships. **(4 marks)**

You need to give **two different** teachings from the Bible for this question. State what the teaching is, then develop your answer using quotes and explain what they mean.

Families

The family unit and family life is important to Christians. Family life has changed significantly over the past 50 years as society has modernised, and so have views about what constitutes a family.

Types of families

There are different types of family within society today.

Nuclear family:
two parents (man/woman) and their children living together

Blended family:
stepfamilies that have joined together through remarriage

Types of family

Family with same-sex parents:
Two same-sex parents and children

Single-parent family:
one parent and children

Extended family:
parents, children, grandparents, aunts, uncles and cousins

Purpose of the family

Christians believe the family was God's intention for humans when he created them. Christians believe the purpose of the family is:

1. to provide the right place for a married couple to have children

2. to provide stability and security for society, as children can be raised in the correct social and moral setting

3. to teach children the difference between right and wrong

4. to raise children as Christians and introduce them to the Christian faith.

Children are a heritage from the Lord, offspring a reward from him. (Psalm 127:3)

Children, obey your parents in the Lord, for this is right. 'Honor your father and mother'—which is the first commandment with a promise—'so that it may go well with you and that you may enjoy long life on the earth.' Fathers, do not exasperate your children; instead, bring them up in the training and instruction of the Lord. (Ephesians 6:1–4)

Parents do not embitter your children, or they will become discouraged. (Colossians 3:21)

These quotes show the roles within the family that parents and children are given. Try to use quotes from the Bible such as these when you are explaining key ideas in your exam.

Now try this

Outline **three** purposes of family for Christians.   **(3 marks)**

Make sure you write **three different** sentences to answer this question. Each sentence should have a different idea contained in it.

Roles within the family

Family is important to Christians. Each member within the family is seen to have a specific role that they believe God expects them to fulfil.

Christian teachings about the importance of family and roles within the family

Parents

- Most Christians believe they have a responsibility to get married and have children if able, as this is what God intended.

- Parents have a responsibility to love, support and care for their children and keep them safe.

- Christian parents raise their children as Christians – getting them baptised or christened and introducing them to the Christian community, Church and religious teachings.

Importance of family today

- Family strengthens society, providing structure and support.

- Family is where people feel safest – with the people they love.

FAMILY

Children

- The Bible teaches that children should honour, obey and respect their parents.

- Children are expected to care for their parents in their old age, just as their parents once cared for them.

Social environment

- Within the family, children are introduced to Christianity – attending church and celebrating festivals as a family unit. Children are also baptised, attend Sunday School and learn about Christianity.

Church teachings

- The Church is seen as a family that Christians belong to wherever they are in the world.

- The Christian community can provide support to the family unit when it faces problems.

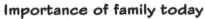

Divergent Christian responses to types of family

Christians believe that family is important in ensuring children are raised correctly. Most Christians prefer the traditional family unit of a nuclear family, as they feel this reflects the idea of family first shown in the Bible with Adam and Eve. Yet today, many Christians are realistic about the changes to family in society and would accept the differing kinds of family that provide a stable upbringing for children.

Explain **two** reasons why family is important to Christians today.
(4 marks)

Christians consider that the example of Adam and Eve in the Bible is the first family and so they think it is important for this to be followed where possible, as this is what God intended.

A second reason is that family unites people and provides a support network for both parents and children. The Bible teaches that parents and children have different roles within the family – parents are expected to raise their children as good Christians, guide them in their understanding of Christianity and keep their children safe. Children are expected to obey, respect and learn from their parents.

This student has successfully given two reasons to explain why family is important. In the first sentence, they have stated the reason and then they have gone on to develop it by adding more detail.

Now try this

'Family is very important to Christians today.'
Evaluate this statement considering arguments for and against. In your response you should:

- refer to Christian teachings
- refer to different Christian points of view
- reach a justified conclusion.

(15 marks)

The family in the local parish

Christians believe it is their duty to do all they can to support both their own and other families. They can offer pastoral care to other families who need help in the local parish.

How can the parish help families?

The parish can help families by:

- ✓ supporting couples who are expecting children, e.g. by organising classes and social events
- ✓ organising family events and special family worship services
- ✓ running parental support classes
- ✓ being involved in rites of passage, e.g. christenings or marriages within the family
- ✓ encouraging children to attend Sunday School and special services, e.g. crib services
- ✓ providing counselling support.

Christians believe the family provides stability, so children can be brought up in the right moral and social way.

Worship

- ✓ Local churches will hold **family services**, to allow families to worship together. This could involve having a shorter service or involving children within the service.
- ✓ In **Sunday School**, children learn more about the Christian faith.

Christian teachings

Christians believe it is important to follow the teachings of Jesus, who showed humans how to **care for each other**. They believe that this includes the family as well as all Christians worldwide.

A new command I give you: Love one another. (John 13:34)

Anyone who does not provide for their relatives, and especially for their own household, has denied the faith and is worse than an unbeliever. (1 Timothy 5:8)

Rites of passage

Rites of passage celebrate key points in a person's life. They include occasions such as a birth or marriage.

The Church recognises the importance of celebrating these events as a family. Relatives and friends may attend baptism or marriage ceremonies, as well as members of the wider Church community.

Counselling

Many Christian communities will offer counselling services such as the Marriage Care or the Catholic Child Welfare Council. They will discuss issues and offer solutions.

Ministers or vicars may also counsel couples if they are experiencing conflict or struggles.

The first question is an 'outline' question, for which you have to state **three** pieces of information. The second question is an 'explain' question. This requires you to state a reason and then develop it to explain it fully.

Now try this

1 Outline **three** ways in which the local parish can support families. **(3 marks)**
2 Explain **two** reasons why the local parish believes it has a responsibility to support families. **(4 marks)**

The family in the parish today

The family is given great importance in Christianity. Church communities believe they have a responsibility to support families in their area. This belief can have a positive impact.

The importance of support given by the parish today

The parish provides **practical, emotional and spiritual support**.

The parish allows Christians to **socialise** with others who share their faith and beliefs.

Support given by the parish

The support of the parish **demonstrates the love of God**, as family was part of his intention for humanity.

The parish provides a sense of **Christian community** and strengthens the Church and the people within it.

What the Bible says

Then people brought little children to Jesus for him to place his hands on them and pray for them. But the disciples rebuked them. Jesus said, "Let the little children come to me, and do not hinder them, for the kingdom of heaven belongs to such as these." (Matthew 19:13–14)

This passage is taken by Christians to mean that children are important to God. Some Christians believe it means that they should take their children to church in order to learn about God and Christianity. Others interpret it as the Church having a duty or responsibility to provide for families, including parents and children.

Worked example

'Support given by the Church community and parish would be useful for all families.'

Evaluate this statement considering arguments for and against. In your response you should:
- refer to Christian teachings
- refer to different Christian points of view
- reach a justified conclusion. **(12 marks)**

Christians would agree with this statement, as they believe that support given by the local parish is invaluable to all families within the parish – Christian or not.

The Church offers pastoral support like counselling, the opportunity to talk through their problems with either others in the same situation or with the vicar or other authority. This can be useful to all families, because families of all religions face similar problems in their lives, for example difficulties communicating or struggling to cope with the demands of family life.

The Church can also offer social opportunities, perhaps for people who are lonely, or old, or who are wanting to meet others like themselves – or even just clubs for people with similar interests. This is again useful for all families.

The Church can also offer guidance for families who would like to understand the faith better. Families who are already Christian can attend family services to pray together, while other families might have the opportunity to find out more if they wish to.

This is the first part of this student's answer. It has started well, giving a Christian view, and has offered a number of reasons and examples that relate to the question. The answer needs to be developed by adding an alternative viewpoint and then an overall conclusion.

Now try this

Outline **three** reasons why support given by the parish to family is important today. **(3 marks)**

Family planning

Contraception is the intentional prevention of pregnancy and different Christians hold differing views about whether or not it is acceptable.

Types of contraception

- **Natural** methods of contraception include the rhythm method, which is when a couple has sex when the woman is not fertile (ovulating).
- **Artificial** methods are human-made objects designed to prevent pregnancy. They include the condom and the birth control pill.

Christian teachings about contraception

Contraception is a challenging issue for Christians. There are no direct teachings in the Bible, since it is a more modern issue, but Christians rely on their Church teachings.

As for you, be fruitful and increase in number; multiply on the earth and increase upon it. (Genesis 9:7)

Christians understand this to mean they have a responsibility to procreate.

Catholic beliefs about contraception

- Every sexual act should be open to the possibility of a child, so artificial methods of contraception should not be used.
- Contraception prevents one of the main purposes of sex – having children.
- Contraception could encourage promiscuity or casual sex, which could lead to sexually transmitted infections (STIs).
- Natural forms of contraception are acceptable as procreation is still possible.
- Pope Paul VI's **Humanae Vitae** (1968) affirms that contraception is not acceptable.

Protestant beliefs about contraception

Some Protestants agree with using contraception because:

- the main purpose of sex is procreation, but sex is also for pleasure as an expression of love between a husband and wife
- contraception is a sensible method of family planning
- using artificial methods of contraception does not go against God's teachings.

Atheist attitudes to family planning

Atheists might argue that each person's situation should be taken into consideration. They believe that people may use contraception because:

- they want to plan when to have a family
- they are not ready to have children
- a couple's lifestyle may not be compatible with having children
- pregnancy could be harmful to the mother
- they want to be safe from STIs
- the couple carry genetic disorders.

Humanist beliefs about contraception

Humanists generally have no issue with the use of contraception. The British Humanist Association argues that if contraception 'results in every child being a wanted child, and in better, healthier lives for women, it must be a good thing.'

Now try this

Explain **two** reasons why there are different Christian attitudes to contraception.   **(4 marks)**

Christian responses to these beliefs differ. Some, such as Catholics, maintain that the use of contraception prevents procreation, which is a key purpose of sex. Other Christians, such as some Protestants, may agree with some of the views, although for religious rather than any other reasoning.

Divorce

Divorce is the legal termination of a marriage and different Christians hold different views about it. Attitudes to divorce have changed significantly in recent times.

Marriage for life

Marriage is intended to be for life – symbolised by the ring given in the wedding ceremony being an unbroken circle. Christians believe that if divorce is needed to end a marriage, the couple should have first tried everything possible to reconcile. If one of the couple dies, the marriage is effectively ended and the partner is free to remarry.

Bible teachings about divorce

Different Christians may hold different views about divorce.

> Therefore what God has joined together, let no one separate. (Mark 10:9)
>
> Jesus replied, 'Moses permitted you to divorce your wives because your hearts were hard. But it was not this way from the beginning. I tell you that anyone who divorces his wife, except for sexual immorality, and marries another woman commits adultery.' (Matthew 19:8–9)

The Bible teaches that marriage is for life.

What Catholic Christians believe

- Divorce is not recognised because marriage is for life.
- Jesus said divorce is wrong.
- Marriage is a sacrament and divorce would break the promises made with God.
- The marriage bond is not broken even if a couple receives a legal civil divorce.
- Remarriage is not accepted. If a divorced person remarries, the ceremony cannot be held in a Catholic church.
- A legal separation may be accepted in some cases, e.g. where care of children is needed.

What Protestant Christians believe

- Divorce is not to be encouraged, but may sometimes be necessary.
- Divorce must be acceptable as UK law allows it.
- People can make mistakes and God is ready to forgive sins.
- It is up to the individual minister to decide whether a couple is allowed to remarry in their church.

Humanist and atheist views

- **Humanists** believe that the breakdown of a marriage can cause problems within the family, but they accept that divorce can sometimes be necessary. They do not associate marriage with religion, so do not feel any promises to any sort of God are broken.
- **Atheists** may hold similar views. They may adopt an ethical standpoint similar to that of **situation ethics**, where they consider the best action in each individual situation in order to make a decision. If, for example, the marriage is causing arguments and disagreements, especially if children are involved, the best action in this situation may be for the marriage to end through divorce.
- Christians will respond differently to these views, depending on their own beliefs.

Now try this

1 Outline **three** reasons why some Christians may be against divorce.
(3 marks)

2 'Divorce is always wrong for Christians.'
Evaluate this statement considering arguments for and against. In your response you should:
- refer to Christian teachings
- refer to different Christian points of view
- reach a justified conclusion.
(15 marks)

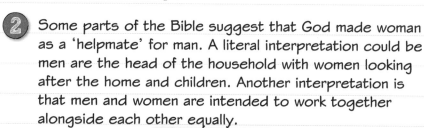
Men and women in the family

In today's society, equality is an important idea. Men and women are seen to be equal.

Roles of men and women in the family

1 Men and women were both made in the image of God. God made humans to be different from all other creations.

2 Some parts of the Bible suggest that God made woman as a 'helpmate' for man. A literal interpretation could be men are the head of the household with women looking after the home and children. Another interpretation is that men and women are intended to work together alongside each other equally.

5 Other Christians today may argue that men and women are equal and either can provide or take care of the home and children.

> It is not good for the man to be alone; I will make a helper suitable for him. (Genesis 2:18)
>
> Then the Lord God made a woman from the rib he had taken out of the man, and he brought her to the man. (Genesis 2:22)
>
> Submit to one another out of reverence for Christ. Wives, submit yourselves to your own husbands as you do to the Lord. (Ephesians 5:21–22)

4 Catholics accept men and women were created in the image of God but were given different roles: man was created physically different to work the land; while woman was designed to assist him. Yet, they are seen to have complementary roles.

3 Many Christians today may feel that a traditional understanding of men as providers and women as carers is outdated.

Humanist and atheist views

Humanists and atheists are likely to accept more modern interpretations of the roles of men and women within the family unit. They believe in the equality of men and women and support their roles, as long as they are happy in them.

Many Christians agree with this view of equality today. Some Christians may, however, hold on to the traditional views.

Worked example

Outline **three** Christian beliefs about the role of men and women in the family. **(3 marks)**

Christians believe that men and women were made equal by God but given different roles. Some Christians believe that men are the providers and women are the home-keepers. Some Christians may also believe that women should submit to their husbands in their roles.

Use the content above to help you answer this question. Offer different reasons why someone may agree or disagree with the statement. Always check that you have included a Christian viewpoint and supported your arguments with evidence, as well as a conclusion to sum up your thoughts.

Now try this

'Men and women should have equal roles within the family.'
Evaluate this statement considering arguments for and against.
In your response you should:
- refer to Christian teachings
- refer to different Christian points of view
- reach a justified conclusion. **(12 marks)**

Gender prejudice and discrimination

While Christian teachings state that equality between males and females is very important, there have been examples where gender equality was not fully encouraged. This includes where men have traditionally been given higher status than women, for example in roles of authority.

Definitions

- **Gender prejudice** is when a person is judged on their gender to be superior or inferior.

- **Gender discrimination**, also known as sexism, is when a person is treated differently from another person as a direct result of their gender. This could be positive (in their favour) or negative (against them).

Gender discrimination in the Church

Catholic Christians only accept men to hold the positions of bishop, priest or deacon and pope. They believe that these roles represent Jesus, who was male, and follow the teaching in the Catechism of the Catholic Church, which states that only a baptised man can hold these positions.

Libby Lane was made the Church of England's first female bishop in 2015.

Bible teachings

There is neither Jew nor Gentile, neither slave nor free, nor is there male and female, for you are all one in Christ Jesus (Galatians 3:28)

This verse states that all humans – male and female – are equal before God. Yet gender inequality still exists in the world.

Promoting gender equality

Many Christian organisations promote gender equality, including Christian Aid and Tearfund, which believe gender inequality goes against issues of human rights. They work in partnership with communities to try to tackle inequality. They use Christian teachings such as those of stewardship and all people being cared for to support their views.

Atheist and humanist attitudes

Atheists and humanists are likely to share the view that men and women are equal, albeit for different reasons. Humanists and atheists may argue that it is a matter of principle that all people are seen to be of equal value and worth. They may argue that everyone, of whatever gender, should be given the same opportunities. Christians would respond to these views by arguing that it goes beyond simply being a matter of equality that men and women are the same, but that it is a teaching from God (as in Galatians 3).

Now try this

Explain **two** reasons why Christians believe gender discrimination is wrong. In your answer you must refer to a source of wisdom and authority. **(5 marks)**

You need to state a reason and then develop it by adding a second sentence to explain what you mean. This style of question also requires you to refer to a text or source of authority for Christians, such as the Bible, in your answer.

Christian worship

Worship in Christianity is when Christians show respect and appreciation towards God. It can take different forms, including liturgical and non-liturgical forms of worship. Different denominations in Christianity worship in different ways.

Liturgical worship

Liturgical worship is when Christians worship according to a set pattern on a regular basis (e.g. on a Sunday). There will be set prayers and readings, often using the Book of Common Prayer. Catholics and Anglicans often follow liturgical worship patterns.

Non-liturgical worship

Non-liturgical worship is less formal than liturgical worship, as it does not follow a set pattern and can involve more unscripted or improvised forms of worship. Methodism and Pentecostalism are denominations that have more non-liturgical worship services.

> Come, let us bow down in worship, let us kneel before the Lord our Maker! (Psalm 95:6)
>
> ... the true worshipers will worship the Father in the Spirit and in truth, for they are the kind of worshipers the Father seeks. (John 4:23)
>
> It is very meet, right, and our bounden duty, that we should at all times, and in all places, give thanks unto thee, O Lord, Holy Father, Almighty, Everlasting God. (Book of Common Prayer)

Examples of Christian worship

1 **Eucharist/Holy Communion/Mass** – most Christians have a formal liturgical service each Sunday, when bread and wine (representing the **body and blood of Jesus Christ** as stated at the Last Supper) are distributed among the congregation. There will be hymns, a Bible reading and a sermon.

2 **Charismatic worship** – Pentecostal churches often have non-liturgical worship involving clapping or dancing as well as the use of music, emphasising the importance of spreading the Gospel. It can also include **speaking in tongues**. This form of worship represents being filled with the Holy Spirit.

3 **Personal/private prayer** – this can take different forms, with a person **spending time alone praying** praying quietly as a group or simply reading the Bible. It could involve meditation on God. Some Christians perform this as part of a **retreat**, where they withdraw in order to focus on prayer.

4 **Silence** – some Christians, such as the Quakers (or Religious Society of Friends), follow **no set pattern of worship** or services. Instead, followers sit in silence for significant periods of time. It is not understood to be private worship, as they are collectively sharing worship together. Some may feel prompted to speak, read aloud or share personal experiences.

Different Christians worship in different ways because of the denomination they belong to. They may believe that certain practices or rituals bring them closer to God or form a closer bond with him. Some give more significance to liturgical forms of worship, while others prefer more non-liturgical forms. Although they are all united under the heading of 'Christianity', they choose to practise and recognise their faith in different ways.

Make sure you offer **two different** ways.

Now try this

Explain **two** ways in which Christians worship. **(4 marks)**

The role of sacraments

A **sacrament** – or ordinance – is a rite of passage or ceremony where the grace and the power of God can be received. Sacraments recognise important milestones in the life of a Christian.

The 39 Articles

Sacraments ordained of Christ be not only badges or tokens of Christian men's profession, but rather they be certain sure witnesses, and effectual signs of grace, and God's good will towards us. (39 Articles XXV)

The 39 Articles state that the sacraments are important as signs of God's grace and evidence of being a Christian.

Most **Protestant Churches** recognise two sacraments (baptism and the Eucharist).

Some **non-conformist Churches** recognise two sacraments; some recognise none.

Different views of the sacraments

Catholics recognise seven sacraments: baptism, confirmation, penance and reconciliation, Eucharist, ordination, marriage, and anointing of the sick (extreme unction).

Infant baptism

Most Christian groups have a ceremony to welcome a baby into the Christian faith – a christening or baptism.

- The baby is baptised in the belief that it will cleanse the child from original sin.
- Parents and godparents make promises on behalf of the child.
- A sign of the cross is made on the baby's forehead and water is poured on their head from the font in the church.
- A lighted candle is given to represent the light of Jesus.

Adult/believer's baptism

Some non-conformist churches, e.g. the Baptist Church, prefer adult baptism as they feel only an adult can fully make the choice of belonging to the Church.

- Each candidate is asked questions about their faith and makes a personal testimony about why they wish to become a Christian.
- They are baptised through full immersion.

Then Jesus came from Galilee to the Jordan to be baptized by John. (Matthew 3:13)

Therefore go and make disciples of all nations, baptizing them in the name of the Father and of the Son and of the Holy Spirit. (Mathew 28:19)

The Eucharist and its meanings

1. The Eucharist is the re-enactment of the Last Supper that Jesus shared with his disciples.

2. The bread represents the body of Jesus and the wine his blood.

3. The service is given different names: Catholics call it 'Mass'; the Church of England calls it 'Eucharist' (from the Greek word meaning 'giving thanks'); and Baptists call it 'The Lord's Supper'.

4. Catholics believe in transubstantiation – that the bread and wine become the body and blood of Jesus.

5. Protestants accept the bread and wine as symbolic of the body and blood of Jesus.

Now try this

'The Eucharist is the most important sacrament.'
Evaluate this statement considering arguments for and against. In your response you should:
- refer to Christian teachings
- reach a justified conclusion.

(15 marks)

The nature and purpose of prayer

Prayer is when a person tries to communicate with or talks to God. In Christianity, there are different types and forms of prayer including traditional set prayers, spoken prayers and silent prayers.

Purpose of prayer

There are four main purposes of prayer for Christians:

1 to get closer to God and communicate with Him

2 to praise God or thank him for what he has done

3 to ask for God's help

4 to say sorry to God when a person feels they have done something wrong.

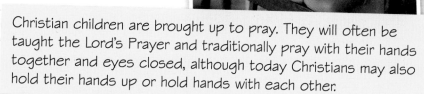

Christian children are brought up to pray. They will often be taught the Lord's Prayer and traditionally pray with their hands together and eyes closed, although today Christians may also hold their hands up or hold hands with each other.

What the Bible teaches about prayer

Therefore I tell you, whatever you ask for in prayer, believe that you have received it, and it will be yours. (Mark 11:24)

But when you pray, go into your room, close the door and pray to your Father, who is unseen. Then your Father, who sees what is done in secret, will reward you. (Matthew 6:6)

The Lord's Prayer

Our Father in Heaven, hallowed be your name, your kingdom come, your will be done, on earth, as it is in heaven. Give us to day our daily bread. And forgive us our debts, as we also have forgiven our debtors. And lead us not into temptation, but deliver us from evil one. (Matthew 6:9–13)

Set prayers

Some Christians have a prayer book that is used in their Sunday services of worship. Many prayers reflect key Christian beliefs, which may praise or thank God for what he has done and provided.

Types of prayers

Informal prayer

This is when people pray by themselves privately. It can include praying silently or aloud. Sometimes Christians use the Bible to help them understand the prayer they are offering to God.

The Lord's Prayer

This is the most famous prayer, which it is believed Jesus taught to his followers. It contains many of the key Christian beliefs about God.

Importance of different types of worship

• Christians feel different types of prayers and forms of worship suit different occasions.

• Having different forms of worship reflects the many different denominations within Christianity and shows the various words and actions they use as part of their communication with God.

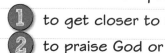

Now try this

The question asks for **three different** examples, so make sure this is what your answer gives.

Make sure you give **two different** reasons and develop each one by explaining what you mean.

1 Outline **three** different types of prayer. **(3 marks)**
2 Explain **two** reasons why prayer is important to Christians. **(4 marks)**

Pilgrimage

A pilgrimage is a journey religious people make to a special or holy place. Many places of Christian pilgrimage are associated with the life of Jesus or other religious figures.

A history of Christian pilgrimage

- Christian pilgrimage has its roots in Jewish pilgrimage. Jews used to travel for religious festivals such as Passover.

> Every year Jesus' parents went to Jerusalem for the Festival of the Passover. When he was twelve years old, they went up to the festival, according to the custom. (Luke 2:41–42)

- Christian pilgrimage was first seen when early Christians visited places of historical significance related to the life of Jesus – Bethlehem (his birth) and Jerusalem (his death).

- Other popular sites of pilgrimage are those with which saints are associated or where visions supposedly occurred.

> Some Christians may feel there is no need to participate in a pilgrimage, as religious faith and practice is a personal thing.

Pilgrims are able to take time out from their normal everyday lives in order to concentrate on their religion.

Places of Christian pilgrimage

1. **Jerusalem** – Jesus celebrated the Last Supper, was arrested, crucified and resurrected in Jerusalem. Christians may visit the Garden of Gethsemane, where he was betrayed and arrested, and the Via Dolorosa, the path he took to his crucifixion. They think about the sacrifice Jesus made in dying for the sins of humanity.

2. **Iona** – this island off the coast of Scotland is considered to be sacred as many saints lived there. Christians visit Iona to spend time in prayer and reflection. A special 'pilgrimage walk' takes place every week to visit areas with spiritual, religious or historical significance.

3. **Taize** – many Christians visit Taize in central France to join the monastic order or to experience and share in the community's way of life. Taize brings together Roman Catholic and Protestant monks and pilgrims to spend time in meditation, prayer and silence, and live a simple life.

4. **Walsingham** – in 1061, a woman in Walsingham in Norfolk, England, received a vision of the Virgin Mary, who showed her Jesus' home in Nazareth. A replica was built in Walsingham, as it was difficult for many to make the journey to Israel. Today, this is a popular place of pilgrimage, where Christians pray to Jesus.

Worked example

Explain **two** reasons why Christians go on pilgrimage. **(4 marks)**

Christians go on pilgrimage to visit places that are significant to the history of the religion, to trace the religious roots and become closer to God. One example is Jerusalem, as this is where Jesus died and was resurrected, so it is a place where key Christian teachings were founded.

Christian pilgrims also share their faith with other Christians on a spiritual journey. Many pilgrims go to Taize to experience the monastic order and share in the community's way of life.

Now try this

1 Outline **three** purposes of pilgrimage in Christianity. **(3 marks)**

2 Explain **two** reasons why pilgrimage is so important to Christians. **(4 marks)**

Celebrations

Christmas and Easter are two of the main festivals celebrated and recognised by all Christians.

Christmas

1 Christmas celebrates the **Incarnation** and **birth of Jesus** – when God's son came to Earth in human form. It is celebrated on 25 December, although this is not believed to be Jesus' actual birth date.

2 **Cards and presents** are given, houses are **decorated** and special **church services** such as Midnight Mass are held. Carols are sung and nativity plays put on. Families come together to share a **special meal** and Christians attend a special Christmas Day service.

4 The festival of **Advent** marks the beginning of the Christian year and the **countdown to Christmas**. It takes place four Sundays before Christmas and is a period of preparation. Advent calendars and candles are used to count down the days.

3 Many Christians express the **meaning of Christmas** by helping others and sharing with them.

And she gave birth to her firstborn, a son. She wrapped him in cloths and placed him in a manger, because there was no guest room available for them. (Luke 2:7)

For to us a child is born, to us a son is given; and the government will be on his shoulders. And he will be called Wonderful Counselor, Mighty God, Everlasting Father, Prince of Peace. (Isaiah 9:6)

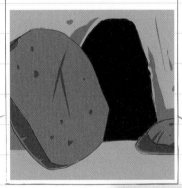

Easter

1 Easter is the festival that remembers the **crucifixion** and celebrates the **resurrection** of Jesus. Good Friday is when Jesus was crucified and then on Easter Sunday the sadness at the death of Jesus is forgotten and his resurrection is celebrated.

2 **Special services** are held. There may be a re-enactment of the crucifixion on Good Friday, and hot cross buns may be eaten to remind people of Jesus' death on the cross. Cards and presents may be given on Easter Sunday, along with Easter eggs to represent the empty tomb of Jesus after his resurrection.

4 **Holy Week** is the final week of Lent leading up to Easter. It commemorates the last week of Jesus' life, from when he entered Jerusalem on Psalm Sunday to the Last Supper and crucifixion.

3 The story of Jesus' resurrection helps Christians find **faith in eternal life** and confirms their beliefs about God.

For God so loved the world, that he gave his one and only Son, that whoever believes in him shall not perish but have eternal life. (John 3:16)

Jesus said to her, "and the life. The one who believes in me, will live, even though they die." (John 11:25)

But if it is preached that Christ has been raised from the dead, how can some of you say that there is no resurrection of the dead? (1 Corinthians 15:12)

Now try this

Give **two different** reasons and develop each reason by explaining it fully.

1 Explain **two** reasons why the festival of Christmas is important to Christians.   **(4 marks)**

2 'Easter is more important than Christmas for Christians.'
Evaluate this statement considering arguments for and against. In your response you should:
- refer to Christian teachings
- reach a justified conclusion.   **(15 marks)**

The future of the Church

The Christian Church has worked hard to continue to grow in society. Many Christians feel they have a responsibility to share their faith with others and provide a ministry of service through education, medical work or social justice.

Church growth

The Christian Church has responded to the changing nature of society by trying to **unite people** and **bring them to the faith**. Education programmes, charity work and missionary work attempt to bring Christianity to all people.

The first quote is instructing the Gospel to be shared and the second demonstrating how the Holy Spirit is present within the world. In the third, Jesus asks fishermen to help him save people by telling them the message of God.

Many Christians feel that by completing **missionary** or **evangelical** work, they put these Bible teachings into practice and help allow people to be saved from their sin through Jesus.

Missionary and evangelical work

- A **missionary** is a person who is sent out on a **religious mission**, especially to promote Christianity in foreign places. **Evangelical work** refers to the **spreading of faith** by missionaries.

- Christians who undertake missionary or evangelical work are sent into an area to **share their faith and the message of the Bible**, and to provide a **service to others**.

- There is a long **history** of missionary work within Christianity. Prominent Christian missionaries include William Carey (1761–1834) and Eric Liddell (1902–45).

- Missionary work can take place within local communities as well as across the world.

He said to them, 'Go into all the world and preach the gospel to all creation.' (Mark 16:15)

Again Jesus said, 'Peace be with you! As the Father has sent me, I am sending you.' And with that he breathed on them and said, 'Receive the Holy Spirit.' (John 20:21–22)

'Come, follow me,' Jesus said, 'and I will send you out to fish for people.' (Matthew 4:19)

Divergent ways churches grow locally, globally and nationally

Locally	Nationally	Globally
• Local churches fund projects to spread God's word, e.g. via grants to community projects or to help the elderly. • Events open the Church to non-believers and introduce them to Christianity. • Local churches are involved in **ecumenical** work – they all work together to serve the community. • Local churches provide community support, e.g. through local food banks or events for children.	• Many churches may be linked across the country and involved in national faith-based events, e.g. conferences, summer camps for children, educational projects or charity events. • Special event days may be held where Christians from different denominations share their faith. • Many churches in different areas may work together on community projects, e.g. to help the disadvantaged or by providing a play area or allotment.	• There may be opportunities to study or create links with Christians in different countries and to be involved in spreading the Christian message globally through missionary projects. • People can choose to go to underdeveloped areas and help with building work, education or shared projects.

To answer this question you will need to give **two different** reasons. For each, state your reason then develop it by giving further information and explanation and supporting it with evidence from Christian teachings.

Now try this

Explain **two** ways in which evangelical work helps others.

(4 marks)

The church in the local community

The local church has always held an important role within society. In the past, it was where key messages were communicated and information was shared. Today, it helps to bring people together and unite them within communities.

Role and importance of the church community

The local church community is important because it:

 unites the local community

 provides support and comfort when needed

 can give advice from sources of authority, such as the minister or vicar

 gives identity and belonging to people in a community.

> Just as a body, though one, has many parts, but all its many parts form one body, so it is with Christ. (1 Corinthians 12:12)
>
> For where two or three gather in my name, there am I with them. (Matthew 18:20)

---

1 Centre of Christian identity

The local church will organise events to bring together people in the community and create a sense of Christian identity. These include:

- clubs for children, such as Sunday School or youth groups, to educate and introduce them to the Christian faith
- social groups, such as coffee mornings to create social opportunities for Christians to share in their faith together
- Bible study groups where Christians can understand and discuss their faith together

How the local church community helps

2 Ecumenism

Ecumenism tries to break down barriers between different Christian denominations, reminding all Christians that they are followers of God and believe in Jesus.

- Groups of Christians may visit each other or hold events to help achieve unity.
- Some ecumenical church communities may share buildings or hold joint services.

3 Outreach work

Many Christians choose either to volunteer or to work in positions that involve them going out into the local community. This is known as outreach work. Examples include:

- working with families to resolve problems
- visiting those in prison or hospital
- organising and running community activities.

4 Worship through living practices

The local church community will celebrate special events, including festivals such as Christmas and Easter and rites of passage such as baptisms, marriages and funerals. These help to mark important milestones in the lives of those within the community.

> Be shepherds of God's flock that is under your care, watching over them…not lording it over those entrusted to you, but being examples to the flock. (1 Peter 5:2–3)

This suggests the importance of supporting each other within the local community by being an example and role model to others.

Now try this

1 Outline **three** ways the local church community helps the individual believer and local area. **(3 marks)**

2 'The local church community is important today.'
Evaluate this statement considering arguments for and against. In your response you should:
- refer to Christian teachings
- reach a justified conclusion. **(15 marks)**

The worldwide Church

Although Christians worship in many denominations and many individual churches across the world, they are all united by the fact that they are part of the worldwide Christian Church. Charity is a key Christian practice of caring for all Christians all over the world.

Importance of the worldwide Church

✓ Gives a **global identity** to Christians.

✓ Promotes **unity**.

✓ Provides **support** when needed – to Christians, other religious believers and non-religious individuals.

✓ Shows how Christian **teachings** can be put into action globally.

> A new command I give you: Love one another. As I have loved you, so you must love one another. (John 13:34)

Reconciliation and facing persecution

- Christians sometimes face persecution, including verbal and physical abuse. They can be prevented from practising their faith or made to feel isolated.

- Christians believe they should work to overcome persecution and break down barriers.

- Some Christians support those being persecuted, for example by educating people about Christianity.

- The worldwide Church emphasises the shared nature of faith to unite all Christians.

Christian teachings about charity

1. Christianity teaches **compassion** and treating other people fairly: 'Love your neighbour as yourself' (Mark 12:31).

2. Jesus taught about **helping others**: e.g. the Parable of the Good Samaritan (Luke 10:25–37).

3. Christians believe God made all humans in his image, so all people should have **equality** and dignity: 'God created mankind in his own image' (Genesis 1:27).

4. Christians believe they will be **accountable** to God for their actions in this life: the Parable of the Sheep and the Goats talks about how humans will be judged according to how they helped others (Matthew 25:31–46).

Christian Aid

Christian Aid is a Christian charity that works globally to end poverty. It campaigns against injustice and seeks to change government policy.

It believes:

- in treating people with compassion

- that every human deserves respect and dignity

- equality and justice are achievable

- all humans are accountable for their actions.

> Love is patient, love is kind. It does not envy, it does not boast, it is not proud. It does not dishonor others, it is not self-seeking, it is not easily angered, it keeps no record of wrongs. (1 Corinthians 13:4–5)

 Agape love (unconditional love towards everyone) is an important teaching in Christianity.

Now try this

Explain **two** reasons why the worldwide Church is important to Christians today. In your answer you should refer to a source of wisdom or authority. **(5 marks)**

Divergent Christian attitudes to charity

Some Christians will tithe, which means giving a set amount – often 10 per cent of their salary – to charity each month. Others believe a person should give what they can afford and that Christian teachings about charity teach the importance of piety (being devoted to Christianity) and helping others in any way possible.

Origins and value of the universe

The main scientific explanation for the origin of the universe is the Big Bang theory. Christians today have different responses to this theory.

The Big Bang theory

- The scientific Big Bang theory is the belief that an enormous explosion started the universe around 14 billion years ago. It suggests that all matter was concentrated into a great mass, which then began to expand to form the universe.

- Georges Lemaître is thought to be the first person to write about this idea, in 1927. He proposed the theory of the expansion of the universe, which was later called the Big Bang theory.

- The expansion that started with the Big Bang is thought to continue even today.

Scientists believe that everything within the universe – planets, stars, matter – is the result of the cooling and gathering of matter as a result of the Big Bang.

Christian responses to scientific explanations for the origins of the universe

Christians believe the story of Creation found in Genesis, the first book of the Bible. They believe the world is a gift from God, created over six days with the seventh day being a day of rest.

Some Christians **reject scientific theories** of Creation, instead believing that the Creation story in the Bible is true in all detail. Where there is conflict between religion and science, they believe science is wrong.

Some Christians believe that there is **no conflict** between science and religion. They believe the Big Bang did cause the universe to exist and evolution is correct, but that the Big Bang and evolution are part of God's plan.

Worked example

Explain **two** reasons why Christians believe the world shouldn't be used as a commodity. **(4 marks)**

Christians believe the world is a special gift created by God and that humans were given the duty of stewardship.

Christians also believe God will judge them after death on how they treated the world. This will determine whether they go to heaven or hell. Therefore, we should take care of God's gift and not use it as a commodity.

This answer offers two different reasons and each one is developed and includes a good explanation.

Christians use Genesis 1–2 to back up the arguments given in this answer, explaining how God created the world in six days, creating something different on each day. For this reason, the universe is not a commodity to be abused by humans but should be treasured.

Now try this

Make sure you explain **two different** Christian responses.

Explain **two** ways Christians could respond to scientific explanations for the origins of the universe. **(4 marks)**

Sanctity of life

Christians believe human life is special and holy – this is known as the sanctity of life.

Why human life is holy

There are important passages in the Bible that show life is special.

Christians believe human life is holy and sacred because it is a gift from God and therefore belongs to him.

Then the Lord God formed a man from the dust of the ground and breathed into his nostrils the breath of life, and man became a living being. (Genesis 2:7)

… your bodies are temples of the Holy Spirit… (1 Corinthians 6:19)

You shall not murder. (Exodus 20:13)

Image of God

So God created mankind in his own image, in the image of God he created them; male and female he created them. (Genesis 1:27)

The Bible teaches Christians that God made them in his image. This does not mean humans look exactly like God – rather, it refers to the idea that humans are special and different from the rest of Creation: God breathed life into them in a different way.

Importance of sanctity of life today

The sanctity of life teaching is important to Christians today because:

1. it will determine their **beliefs about issues** such as abortion and euthanasia

2. they will **value human life** and this will impact on the way they live

3. it will guide them when making **moral decisions** and determine how they treat others.

Worked example

Explain **two** ways the Bible shows life as special. **(4 marks)**

In Genesis 1:27 God made man 'in his own image' as the final part of Creation. This means that God made humans to be different from every other creation, as he wanted to show they are special.

The Bible also states that humans were made as a 'Temple of the Holy Spirit' – humans are given a soul that connects them to God.

These points support the sanctity of life argument.

Two reasons are given and each is fully explained. The answer is also supported with relevant quotes from the Bible and shows good knowledge as well as understanding of what the question requires.

Remember to offer arguments from more than one viewpoint in your answer. When complete, read through your answer to check for mistakes.

Now try this

'Human life is special as it was created by God.'

Evaluate this statement considering arguments for and against. In your response you should:

- refer to Christian teachings
- reach a justified conclusion.

(12 marks)

Human origins

Christians hold different responses to scientific and non-religious explanations about the origins and value of human life, such as evolution and survival of the fittest.

Theory of evolution

The theory of evolution is based on Charles Darwin's theories that the origin of human life was through the gradual development of species over millions of years. Individuals who were better adapted to the environment (fitter) survived to pass on their genes to the next generation. This is known as the '**survival of the fittest**'. Over time, this meant life **evolved** so only those beings with the characteristics or features that were strongest survived.

Charles Darwin proposed that people evolved over time from more simple life forms.

The problem of evolution for Christians

Some people believe that the theory of evolution conflicts with what Christians claim about God creating everything in the universe. Also, it could be used as evidence that God does not exist, as evolution suggests it is due to chance that things have evolved to their current forms.

So God created mankind in his own image, in the image of God he created them; male and female he created them. (Genesis 1:27)

Then the Lord God formed a man from the dust of the ground and breathed into his nostrils the breath of life, and man became a living being. (Genesis 2:7)

Christian responses to evolution

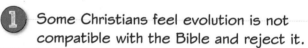 1 Some Christians feel evolution is not compatible with the Bible and reject it.

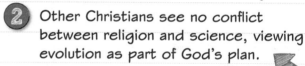 2 Other Christians see no conflict between religion and science, viewing evolution as part of God's plan.

These responses could cause conflict among Christians today who hold differing views.

The Special Agenda IV Diocesan Synod

This document attempts to bring together ideas of evolution and traditional Christian teachings on Creation. It aims to show they are not in direct conflict but can work together.

Now try this

Explain **two** ways in which Christians respond to scientific explanations about the origin of human life.

(4 marks)

Remember that science and religion can be seen to complement each other or be in conflict with each other. Your answer needs to show awareness of this.

Christian attitudes to abortion

Christians may hold different views about abortion that refer to different teachings.

The nature of abortion

Abortion is the deliberate termination (ending) of a human pregnancy so that a child is not born. Currently in the UK, it is legal to have an abortion up to 24 weeks of pregnancy with the consent of two doctors.

Divergent Christian teachings

Pope Paul VI in 1968 issued the *Humanae Vitae*, which said abortion was wrong:

> … all direct abortion, even for therapeutic reasons, are to be absolutely excluded as lawful means of regulating the number of children. (*Humanae Vitae*)

Arguments Against abortion (pro-life arguments)

Some Christians (such as Catholics and Evangelical Protestants) believe the rights and life of the foetus are important and they do not support abortion because:

- life is a sacred gift from God
- life is believed to begin at conception
- all life has value, even if a child may be born disabled
- God has a plan for every human
- abortion is viewed as murder and the Bible tells us 'Thou shalt not kill' in the Ten Commandments.

Arguments For abortion (pro-choice arguments)

Some Christians may feel that, while abortion is not good, it may be the 'lesser of two evils'. They may argue that:

- Jesus taught compassion towards others
- we cannot be sure life begins at conception
- in cases of rape or incest, abortion may be the kindest action
- medical technology allows us to identify any problems with the foetus so children do not need to be born who would perhaps have suffered painful lives or died shortly after birth
- abortion is best if the mother's life is at risk.

Non-religious arguments

There is no 'one' Atheist or Humanist view on abortion. **Atheists** may argue that:

- it is the woman's right to choose
- the rights of the mother outweigh those of the child, as it is not considered a person until born
- abortion is wrong, but not for religious reasons.

Humanists do not believe the foetus becomes a 'person' until well after conception, so they may believe that:

- the woman should make the right choice for her
- life is special, but that abortion needs to be there as an option.

Christian responses to non-religious arguments

Christians may use some of the above arguments in their reasoning about the issue of abortion. Yet all Christians would maintain that life is special, as God created it. Although some Christians consider abortion necessary in some circumstances, many argue against it.

Some people may follow **situation ethics** principles, which argue that each situation should be considered individually and the right action may be different in each case.

Now try this

Explain **two** reasons why some Christians believe abortion is always wrong. **(4 marks)**

Abortion is a controversial topic for Christians, as there is disagreement on when life begins. Your answer should show awareness of this.

Life after death (1)

Christians believe in the afterlife, accepting the existence of heaven and hell. They will use various teachings, such as the proof of the resurrection of Jesus, to support their view.

Christian beliefs about life after death

1 The Bible and the Gospels talk of the death and resurrection of Jesus.

2 Jesus taught Christians that there is an afterlife: 'My Father's house has many rooms; if that were not so, would I have told you that I am going there to prepare a place for you?' (John 14:2)

3 Jesus taught that God sent Him to Earth so that humanity may have eternal life in heaven.

> And God raised us up with Christ and seated us with him in the heavenly realms in Christ Jesus. (Ephesians 2:6)
>
> For God so loved the world, that he gave his one and only Son, that whoever believes in him shall not perish but have eternal life. (John 3:16)
>
> I am the resurrection and the life. The one who believes in me will live, even though they die. (John 11:25)

Christians believe that Jesus' resurrection (that he rose again from death) shows there is life after death.

Non-religious arguments For life after death

Some non-religious people have reasons for believing in life after death.

Reason	Belief	Christian response
Remembered lives	People may believe they have flashback memories of previous lives, suggesting that death is not the end.	Christians believe that life after death is in heaven (or hell), so memories of previous lives are mistaken.
Paranormal events	Paranormal events are unexplained events with a spiritual cause, e.g. ghosts which some people consider to be evidence of life after death.	Christians do not accept these as evidence of life after death as nothing in the Bible supports ideas of souls coming back to Earth after death.
Logic	Some may think it is logical there is an afterlife, to give life meaning.	Christians might respond that it is more than logic, as evidence is given in the Bible.
Reward	It makes sense to many people that there should be reward after death for living a good life on Earth – but this would not be with God.	Christians agree that good deeds may be rewarded in heaven, but that it is only through having faith in Jesus that we are reconciled with God. See page 5 on salvation.
Comfort	The idea of life after death can give people hope and make them less afraid of death.	Christians agree, but also believe they will be reunited with God in heaven.
Meeting loved ones who have passed on.	Meeting loved ones who have died is a key reason people believe in the afterlife.	Views of heaven differ, but most Christians believe that we will be reunited with loved ones in heaven.

Significance of belief in life after death for Christians

- Christians will try to live their life well and please God, so that they achieve eternal life in heaven.
- Christians are comforted that their loved ones live on after death.
- Christians have a purpose in life – to live as God intended so that they can be rewarded after death.
- It helps them cope with death, as following Christian teachings shows them that death is not the end.

Now try this

Explain **two** reasons why Christians support a belief in life after death.

(4 marks)

Consider including references to Christian teachings within your answers to show you understand the importance of belief in the afterlife.

Life after death (2)

Many people who are not religious will argue that there is nothing after a person dies. They may suggest that a person is born, lives and then simply dies.

 Comfort

Some people may believe that holding beliefs about an afterlife provides a false sense of comfort, and they consider that is the reason that it is a popular, though misguided, belief.

 Humanist beliefs

Humanists believe that when a person dies their body decays and there is nothing else. Life after death is seen as an impossibility.

Non-religious arguments against life after death

 Social control

Some people think that believing in an afterlife gives people a false sense of control over what they fear the most (i.e. death). They see belief in an afterlife as a coping mechanism that offers false hope. Also, the Church may in the past have been seen to 'control' people's behaviour through making them afraid of going to hell.

 Lack of evidence

There is no evidence of an afterlife – no one has ever returned to prove it exists. Many would argue that science disproves religious ideas of an afterlife and suggests there is nothing after death.

 Fraudulent accounts

Some people have tricked others into believing they can contact people who have died, and some vulnerable people have been taken advantage of in this way. This kind of behaviour has caused some people to reject the idea of an afterlife completely.

Christian responses to non-religious arguments against life after death

Christians may reject the above arguments because:

1. they believe that there is evidence of life after death, found in the resurrection of Jesus and the teachings of the Bible (see opposite and page 31)

2. they believe that having faith is about accepting things without question, and belief in life after death is part of this

3. they hold beliefs about God creating the world and loving his creation, and they don't think he would just allow it all to end

4. their belief in an afterlife gives their life meaning and purpose.

Evidence for an afterlife in the Bible

It saves you by the resurrection of Jesus Christ, who has gone into heaven and is at God's right hand – with angels, authorities and powers in submission to him. (1 Peter 3:21–22)

Very truly I tell you, whoever hears my word and believes him who sent me has eternal life and will not be judged but has crossed over from death to life. (John 5:24)

Christians maintain that the Bible teaches there is life after death, which, if they follow Jesus, they too can achieve.

Now try this

Explain **two** reasons why Christians reject arguments against life after death. **(4 marks)**

 Make sure you provide **two different** reasons in your answer.

Euthanasia

Euthanasia is the painless killing of someone who is dying – it is also referred to as 'assisted dying'. It is a controversial issue because some see it as murder, while others see it as a compassionate act.

The nature of euthanasia

There are three different types of euthanasia:

1. **Voluntary euthanasia** – where a person's life is ended deliberately and painlessly at their request.

2. **Assisted suicide** – where a person is given the means to end their own life.

3. **Non-voluntary euthanasia** – ending a person's life when they are unable to ask, but there is good reason for thinking it is what they would want. For example, if a person is on life support and there is no medical chance of recovery.

Christian teachings on euthanasia

There are important messages in the Bible that show life is special.

> So God created mankind in his own image. (Genesis 1:27)
>
> Your bodies are temples of the Holy Spirit... (1 Corinthians 6:19)
>
> You shall not murder. (Exodus 20:13)

Arguments Against euthanasia

Many Christians are against euthanasia because:

- the sanctity of life argument says all life is sacred
- the slippery slope argument shows that if euthanasia were legalised, it could lead to, for example, infanticide being allowed
- hospices provide palliative care – relieving the symptoms of a condition a person is dying from – meaning euthanasia is not needed
- it is murder and against the Ten Commandments: 'You shall not murder' (Exodus 20:13)
- examples in the Bible such as that of Job show that although faith may be tested, suffering may have a purpose and euthanasia is wrong: 'Shall we accept good from God, and not trouble?' (Job 2:10)

Arguments For euthanasia

Although most Christians would see euthanasia as wrong, some may say it is the kinder action in some circumstances because:

- it allows a person to die a gentle, pain-free death
- the patient dies with dignity
- euthanasia can save medical costs
- it relieves the burden on the family and society generally
- if it is what a person has asked for, it is abiding by their wishes.

Non-religious arguments about euthanasia

Some **atheists** and **humanists** would argue that the kindest thing might be to let a person end their life, if it is what they want and they are in pain.

Some may argue using principles of **situation ethics** – each situation should be judged individually.

Christian responses to non-religious arguments

Most Christians would say that euthanasia is always wrong, due to teachings from the Bible and belief in the sanctity of life. They may also argue that suffering has a purpose even though we don't know what it is.

Now try this

Put each belief in a separate sentence.

Outline **three** beliefs about euthanasia for Christians.

(3 marks)

Had a look ☐ Nearly there ☐ Nailed it! ☐

Issues in the natural world

Today's natural world faces many threats, often from humans.

Threats in the world

The world today is being damaged by pollution, global warming and humanity's excessive use of natural resources. Many animal species are threatened with extinction, while the world's fast-growing human population is becoming unsustainable.

Issues in the natural world put our world at risk of global environmental catastrophe.

Christian responses

Christians believe they should care for the world and not waste its resources because:

1. the Bible teaches that we should care for the world

2. Christians see the world as a sacred gift from God

3. Christianity teaches that humans will be judged after death on how they treated the Earth

4. God gave humans the responsibility of stewardship of the Earth – caring for it for future generations.

God blessed them and said to them, 'Be fruitful and increase in number; fill the earth and subdue it. Rule over the fish in the sea and the birds in the sky and over every other living creature that moves on the ground.' (Genesis 1:28)

The Lord God took the man and put him in the Garden of Eden to work it and take care of it. (Genesis 2:15)

The Christian Declaration on Nature, Assisi 1986

At a meeting in Assisi, Italy, religious leaders of Buddhism, Christianity, Hinduism, Islam and Judaism met to discuss how their faiths could combine to save the natural world. The outcome was a shared commitment to working to help the environment. Beliefs such as that of stewardship – where individuals believe they have a responsibility to care for the world – were crucial here.

Use of animals for food

Christians tend to agree that it is acceptable for animals to be used for food, as God gave them to humans for this purpose. The Bible also states that God gave humans dominion over animals.

Christians also believe that only humans were given souls and were 'made in the image of God', which suggests animals are not as important as people.

Some Christians may choose to be vegetarian, as they believe that since God created animals, they are important and should not suffer and that, in Genesis, He only gave the plants and trees as food, not animals.

The ethical theory of **utilitarianism** could be applied, which states that the 'right' action is that which gives the greatest happiness to the greatest number. In this case, the use of animals for food may be acceptable if large numbers of humans benefit.

Worked example

Explain **two** ways in which Christians respond to the use of animals in experimentation. **(4 marks)**

Some Christians may argue that animal experimentation is acceptable if it benefits human life, e.g. if it leads to new drugs being developed and cures for diseases.

Other Christians may argue that all animal experimentation is wrong, and that humanity has a duty of stewardship to look after animals as God created them.

Now try this

Explain **two** reasons why Christians feel it is important to care for the natural world.
(4 marks)

Justice

The nature of justice

Christians believe that the treatment of offenders should take into consideration the reasons for the crime. Justice is fair treatment or behaviour. For example, a person who steals because of hunger may be treated differently from a person who steals for greed.

> I am filled with power, with the Spirit of the Lord, and with justice and might. (Micah 3: 8)

Importance of justice for the victim

1. To make them feel safe.

2. To make it seem fair that a person has been punished for their crime.

3. To make a victim feel that the criminal has 'paid' for their crime, especially if the punishment involves giving back to society.

Importance of justice for Christians

1. God is seen to be just and people should act in the same way.

2. Jesus taught that everyone should be treated fairly and also aim to treat people as they would like to be treated: 'Do to others as you would have them do to you'. (Luke 6:31)

3. Christian churches teach the importance of justice.

4. God will judge people after death and will forgive those who are truly sorry for their crimes.

5. The Bible teaches that God wants people to act justly: 'And what does the Lord require of you? To act justly and to love mercy and to walk humbly with your God.' (Micah 6:8)

Worked example

'Justice is important today for Christians.'
Evaluate this statement considering arguments for and against. In your response you should:
* refer to Christian teachings
* refer to non-religious attitudes
* reach a justified conclusion.   **(12 marks)**

Most Christians agree that justice is important. They follow Jesus' teachings in the Bible, which say to treat others as you would like to be treated and love your neighbour. Christians understand from this that they should care for and treat others in a just way. Rules such as the Ten Commandments also show justice is important by providing guidelines on how to behave. Most Christians believe people deserve to be punished when they do something wrong, and rewarded when they do something right. God is seen to be fair.

Non-religious attitudes to justice

Non-religious people such as **atheists** and **humanists** agree that justice is important. It seems fair to them that those who do wrong are punished.

Christians share these views of the importance of justice but would add that a key reason is that this is what God intended.

This is the start of a student's answer. The student has suggested why most Christians would agree with the statement and made reference to Christian teachings to support this view. They would go on to develop the idea of reward and punishment and maybe link it to the afterlife. They also need to describe non-religious views and Christian responses to them and then draw their answer to a conclusion.

Now try this

Explain **two** reasons why justice is importance for Christians. In your answer you must refer to a source of wisdom or authority.   **(5 marks)**

One of these reasons needs to be linked to a quote from a source of wisdom, such as the Bible.

Crime

A crime is an action someone commits against the laws of the state, for example murder, theft, physical assault or drink-driving. A crime is a type of sin – an action against God's will.

Crime and sin

Christianity teaches us that sin is part of human nature – the very first people, Adam and Eve, disobeyed God in the Garden of Eden and ate fruit from the forbidden tree.

> ... for all have sinned and fall short of the glory of God ... (Romans 3:23)
>
> ... but each person is tempted when they are dragged away by their own evil desire and enticed. (James 1:14)
>
> Anyone who does not do what is right is not God's child. (1 John 3:10)

Crimes are sins that are not only disobeying God's wishes, but are also illegal, i.e. against the law of the land.

The causes and problem of crime

Crime is a problem in the world today as laws are established to protect society – breaking laws hurts people. Christians feel that victims of crime need to be cared for and that everyone has the responsibility to make the world a fair place.

Causes of crime may vary – including poverty, upbringing, racism, politics and drugs.

Christian beliefs and teachings about crime

- Christians believe that the Bible teaches the difference between right and wrong and ignoring God's will leads to disaster.
- Examples of rules in the Bible include the Ten Commandments, which teach that actions such as killing and stealing are wrong.
- Christians believe they should forgive the sins of others in the same way that God forgives them for their sins – key ideas contained in the Lord's Prayer. Christians

look to the example of Jesus, who taught about the importance of forgiveness.

- The Bible teaches that no one is free from sin and we should not judge others but offer forgiveness and help. In John 8:3–7, a woman accused of adultery is brought to Jesus and he is asked if she should be stoned. He replies, 'Let any one of you who is without sin be the first to throw a stone at her.'

Action taken to end crime

Some Christian individuals and organisations work to reduce crime. Examples include:

 Prison Fellowship

- Works to support criminals while in prison.
- Includes volunteers from local churches.
- Donates money to provide support.
- Organises prayer groups and victim-awareness programmes (so prisoners understand how their crimes hurt others).
- Supports families of prisoners so that festivals such as Christmas can be shared.
- Includes letter-writing programmes to prisoners so they don't feel so alone.

 Street Pastors

- Are groups of trained volunteers who work on the streets.
- Often seen on Friday and Saturday nights providing support and guidance to those in crisis or needing help, to build community relationships and work for safer streets.
- Work in local schools and educational establishments to support young people.
- Attend and provide support and care where a crisis has occurred (response pastors).

Now try this

> Remember that teachings come from sources of authority, so you need to focus on what, for instance, the Bible says or what Jesus did to answer this question.

1 Outline **three** Christian teachings about crime. **(3 marks)**

2 Explain **two** reasons why Christian individuals or groups work to end the causes of crime. **(4 marks)**

Good, evil and suffering

Christians have clear teachings on ideas about good, evil and suffering. They believe that those who are good will be rewarded and those who are bad will be punished.

Good actions

Christians believe that if a person lives their life according to the rules of God and performs good deeds, God will reward them in the afterlife by sending them to heaven.

> Do not be overcome by evil, but overcome evil with good. (Romans 12:21)

Evil actions

Christians believe that if a person is evil within their life and does wrong and hurts others, God will punish them in the afterlife by sending them to hell.

> To those who by persistence in doing good seek for glory, honor and immortality, he will give eternal life. But for those who are self-seeking and who reject the truth and follow evil, there will be wrath and anger. (Romans 2:6–8)

The Parable of the Sheep and the Goats

Jesus used parables to teach people about how they should behave and treat others. One of his most important teachings is the Parable of the Sheep and the Goats, which explains how God will judge people on whether they helped those in need. Those who help others will be rewarded, while those who do not will be punished.

To those who helped other people, Jesus said, '"Truly I tell you, whatever you did for one of the least of these brothers and sisters of mine, you did for me."' (Matthew 25:40)

Divergent Christian teachings about why people suffer

Christianity teaches that God gave humans free will – the choice of whether to do good or evil. Therefore, humans are responsible for their own actions and some people therefore suffer due to the actions of others.

Some Christians believe that suffering is a test of faith, while others believe that suffering has a purpose in life, even if humans do not understand it.

Non-religious attitudes towards evil and suffering

Atheists hold no religious beliefs and use the existence of evil and suffering as an argument against God, arguing that an all-loving, powerful God would not let his creations suffer.

Humanists don't accept that evil and suffering is a test or punishment or part of a divine plan. They believe humans have a degree of choice in their lives and must, therefore, take some responsibility for 'evils' such as war, famine and poverty. They also believe that some people may suffer through no fault of their own, due to natural causes such as illness or floods.

Christian responses to non-religious attitudes

- Suffering has a purpose – even if we don't understand it.

- God gave humans free will – the ability to choose whether to do good or evil. We therefore are responsible for the consequences of those actions.

- We need to look to Jesus' teachings in the Bible, such as the Parable of the Sheep and Goats, to understand why people suffer.

Now try this

Make sure you give **three different** beliefs to answer this question.

Outline **three** Christian beliefs about good, evil and suffering.

(3 marks)

Punishment

Punishment is intended as a means to achieve justice – to ensure that someone has paid for their sins. Punishments, in the UK, can range from a fine or community service to imprisonment.

Christianity and punishment

1	**Importance of punishment** 	Christians believe that when a crime has been committed (when a law has been broken) an appropriate punishment is required. This helps people to learn that their behaviour is wrong and gives them the chance to reform. Christians believe God commands people to follow the laws of the country where they live, so they should abide by these laws. However, in cases where laws are wrong (for example, they are racist or suppress minority groups) many Christians believe they should be challenged.
2	**Biblical teachings** 	In the Bible, God is presented as a God of justice. From this, Christians believe punishments should be applied when crimes are committed to achieve justice. However, Jesus also taught about the importance of forgiveness, allowing people to change their behaviour for the better. Do others what you would have them do to you. (Matthew 7:12) Be merciful, just as your Father is merciful… Do not judge and you will not be judged. Do not condemn, and you will not be condemned. Forgive and you will be forgiven. (Luke 6:36–37) The servant who knows the master's will and does not get ready or does not do what the master wants will be beaten with many blows. (Luke 12:47)
3	**Punishment is justice** 	For Christians, punishment should be fair to achieve justice. An appropriate punishment means the victim gains retribution while the criminal is given the opportunity to realise their actions are wrong and to change. There are many stories in the Bible of prophets speaking out against injustice, including Amos, Isaiah, Micah and even Jesus. When Amos saw that people were worshipping God but exploiting those who were poor, he wrote: 'But let justice roll on like a river, righteousness like a never-failing stream'. (Isaiah 5:24) Isaiah called on people to behave justly towards others and Jesus was angry at the way the Temple courtyard had been turned into a trader's marketplace.
4	**Necessity of punishment** 	Christians realise that punishment is needed in society to maintain order. They also accept that punishment helps members of society to feel safe and protected, and that it encourages them to follow society's rules. The Bible gives examples of punishment. For we must all appear before the judgment seat of Christ, so that each of us may receive what is due for the things done while in the body, whether good or bad. (2 Corinthians 5:10)

Remember to show awareness that, for Christians, punishment is important and has a purpose. However, Christians also believe that forgiveness is important, so there may be some divergent views within the religion regarding this statement.

Now try this

1 Explain **two** reasons why, for Christians, punishment might be needed in society.   **(4 marks)**

2 'It is more important to punish criminals than it is to forgive them.'
Evaluate this statement considering arguments for and against. In your response you should:
- refer to Christian teachings
- refer to different Christian points of view
- reach a justified conclusion.   **(12 marks)**

Aims of punishment

Punishment has a number of key aims, which Christians would support.

Aims of punishment

Aim of punishment	Christian attitude
Protection	A key purpose of punishment is to protect society from violent or dangerous criminals by keeping them away from society so they can't hurt others. Christians agree that protecting society is important. Human life is sacred as God created it.
② Retribution	Punishment should make criminals pay for what they have done wrong. • In Christianity, God is a God of justice, so making criminals pay for what they have done wrong seems just. • The Old Testament has a teaching that says, 'eye for eye, tooth for tooth' (Exodus 21:24). This seems to suggest ideas of retribution. • Some Christians, however, believe retribution is important in making a criminal 'pay' but this is not the same thing as revenge. They argue that a criminal should be punished through the legal system in a fair way.
③ Deterrence  **MUGGER GETS FIVE YEARS** A serial mugger was sentenced yesterday at Newtown county court to	The purpose of a deterrent is to discourage someone from breaking the law. Christians agree that punishment is good if it helps stop someone from reoffending or committing a crime in the first place.
④ Reformation 	Punishment shows the criminal what they have done wrong and gives them the opportunity to change. This could mean educating them or providing skills/a job so they don't need to turn to crime. This is a key idea within Christianity. • Jesus taught about the importance of agape love (selfless and unconditional love) and Christians believe this is needed in order for a person to have a new start and seek forgiveness. • Even when Jesus was on the cross and dying, he forgave the criminals crucified alongside him as well as those who carried out his crucifixion. This demonstrates the importance of giving criminals the chance to ask for forgiveness and to reform.

Biblical teaching about punishment

Christianity teaches that punishment is necessary when a person has done wrong.

> For in the same way you judge others, you will be judged, and with the measure you use, it will be measured to you. (Matthew 7:2)

> Anyone who does wrong will be repaid for their wrongs, and there is no favoritism. (Colossians 3:25)

Christians also believe that a person will face God after death and have to account for their actions. This is believed to determine their afterlife.

> Then they will go away to eternal punishment, but the righteous to eternal life. (Matthew 25:46)

This teaches Christians to help others who have committed sins, but warns about being careful not to commit sins themselves. This shows the importance of ideas of forgiveness and helping others, while recognising that all humans have the ability to sin and can be led astray.

> Brothers and sisters, if someone is caught in a sin, you who live by the Spirit should restore that person gently. But watch yourselves, or you also may be tempted. (Galatians 6:1)

Now try this

Explain **two** reasons why Christians support the aims of punishment. **(4 marks)**

Forgiveness

The nature of forgiveness

Forgiveness is to stop blaming someone for what they have done, accept that they are sorry and work towards **reconciliation** (bringing people back together after conflict). Ideas of forgiveness are important to Christians: Jesus taught about forgiveness through the Lord's Prayer and through his actions towards others. He forgave those who crucified him before he died on the cross.

> For if you forgive other people when they sin against you, your heavenly Father will also forgive you. But if you do not forgive others their sins, your Father will not forgive your sins. (Matthew 6:14–15)
>
> Do not judge, and you will not be judged. Do not condemn, and you will not be condemned. Forgive, and you will be forgiven. (Luke 6:37)
>
> Father, forgive them, for they do not know what they are doing. (Luke 23:34)

Restorative justice

Restorative justice brings together the offender and the victim of a crime to try to restore peace. Prison Fellowship, a Christian organisation, runs a victim awareness programme called Sycamore Tree. This explores the effect of crime on victims and their families. Victims of crime come and talk to offenders as part of the programme.

Worked example

Outline **three** beliefs about why restorative justice is important for Christians. **(3 marks)**

The Bible teaches that we should try to forgive those who hurt us, even if it is difficult. Christians believe reconciliation and making up with others is the best way of solving conflict. They also believe it gives offenders the opportunity to reform and change their behaviour.

Now try this

Explain **two** Christian teachings about forgiveness. In your answer you must refer to a source of wisdom and authority. **(5 marks)**

Forgiveness for offenders

Offenders can be reintegrated within their local community, sometimes through Christian organisations such as Street Pastors or the Prison Fellowship, by providing them with an education and the opportunity to learn vocational skills. They may also be asked to pay back into their community, for example by helping to improve their local area.

It is important to Christians that offenders realise the wrongness of their actions and make retribution to those whom they have wronged. Forgiveness and reformation are seen as central to this because they help to unite people as a community.

See page 39 for more on retribution and reformation.

These prisoners are carrying out community service, to help make amends for their crimes.

Importance of restorative justice and forgiveness

1. Jesus died on the cross to bring forgiveness and reconciliation between God and humanity.

2. Christians should try to forgive others, even when it is difficult – God helps them to do this.

3. Seeing the effects of crime on victims may help change offenders' behaviour

4. The Bible teaches that it is important to settle conflicts, forgive and reconcile wherever possible.

> If you hold anything against anyone, forgive him. (Mark 11:25)
>
> Be kind and compassionate to one another, forgiving each other, just as in Christ God forgave you. (Ephesians 4:32)

Treatment of criminals

Although Christians recognise the importance of the aims of punishment, forgiveness, and fairness, Christians may disagree about the treatment of criminals.

Christian teachings about the treatment of criminals

Christians believe that those in society who cannot stand up for themselves need to be protected. This could include victims of crime, as well as those who commit crimes.

Speak up for those who cannot speak for themselves, for the rights of all who are destitute. Speak up and judge fairly; defend the rights of the poor and needy. (Proverbs 31:8–9)

Christians are taught not to judge others – because they could have bigger faults than the person they are judging. Therefore Christians believe that criminals need to be treated fairly and justly and not just judged by others.

Why do you look at the speck of sawdust in your brother's eye and pay no attention to the plank in your own eye? (Matthew 7:3)

Divergent Christian attitudes towards the treatment of criminals

Use of torture	The Bible appears to acknowledge the use of torture, which could lead some Christians to consider its use: … handed him over to the jailers to be tortured. (Matthew 18:34) Most Christians today would not support the use of torture. Arguments against it include that all humans were created by God and deserve fair and respectful treatment. Some Christians may consider that if the outcome of torturing a person is positive (e.g. it could save many other lives) it may be justified as a last resort. This view could be supported by **situation ethics**, whereby each individual situation is considered separately.
Human rights	Christians recognise that all humans deserve to have human rights because God created all humans equal: … you are all one in Christ Jesus. (Galatians 3:28) Christians accept that criminals deserve to be punished for their crimes and this may involve the removal of some human rights (e.g. their freedom), but this is seen as justice and fair treatment for their crime. They believe basic human rights should be upheld, such as the right to food and water.
Fair trial	This is where the person accused of the crime has both the evidence against them and a defence for them put forward. Christians believe justice is important and support the idea of a fair trial. When justice is done, it brings joy to the righteous but terror to evildoers. (Proverbs 21:15) Does our law condemn a man without first hearing him to find out what he has been doing? (John 7:51)
Trial by jury	This is a where a group of people make the decision as to whether a person is guilty based on evidence. Christians support trial by jury, as a group of objective peers can make an informed decision based on the evidence presented. The Bible teaches the importance of being fair: Do not pervert justice or show partiality. Do not accept a bribe, for a bribe blinds the eyes of the wise and twists the words of the innocent. (Deuteronomy 16:19)

Now try this

There are many arguments you can refer to in this question. Make sure you refer to the diverse Christian views on issues such as torture and why situation ethics could be used to make a decision.

'Criminals should always be treated in a respectful and just way.'
Evaluate this statement considering arguments for and against. In your response you should:
- refer to Christian teachings
- refer to relevant ethical arguments
- reach a justified conclusion.

(12 marks)

The death penalty

Capital punishment is also known as the death penalty. There are many arguments, both religious and non-religious, which support or are against capital punishment.

Capital punishment

Capital punishment is execution, where the life of a condemned prisoner is taken away. It has been abolished completely in the UK, although still exists in some countries, including some states in the USA.

Purpose of the death penalty

1 To provide punishment for the most severe crimes committed.

2 To act as a deterrent to other criminals.

3 To make victims feel as though punishment has been given.

4 To make sure that the offender cannot commit the same crime again.

Arguments for the death penalty

- The Old Testament teaches that the death penalty should be sought for some crimes.

- Jesus never taught the death penalty was wrong.

- The Christian Church used the death penalty in the Middle Ages for those who challenged the authority of the Church.

- St Paul teaches in the New Testament that Christians should accept and obey the laws of their country – this could include the death penalty.

Whoever sheds human blood, by humans shall their blood be shed; for in the image of God has God made mankind. (Genesis 9:6)

For in the same way you judge others, you will be judged, and with the measure you use, it will be measured to you. (Matthew 7:2)

Arguments against the death penalty

- The overall message from Christianity is to love and forgive others, and capital punishment goes against this.

- Jesus taught that revenge was wrong.

- It goes against the sanctity of life argument – human life is special as God created it.

- Most Christian Churches have spoken out against capital punishment.

You shall not murder. (Exodus 20:13)

You have heard that it was said, 'Eye for eye, and tooth for tooth.' But I tell you, do not resist an evil person. If anyone slaps you on the right cheek, turn to them the other cheek also. (Matthew 5:38–39)

You have heard that it was said, 'Love your neighbor and hate your enemy.' But I tell you, love your enemies and pray for those who persecute you. (Matthew 5:43–44)

Non-religious attitudes and Christian responses

Humanists generally oppose the use of the death penalty, as they believe premeditated killing is wrong – even when carried out by the state. There is also the possibility of error.

Atheists may support or oppose the death penalty – some will think the most severe crimes justify this punishment, while others may think the use of the death penalty means the criminal escapes rather than is given justice (a long prison sentence). They may adopt situation ethics, where you need to look at each situation and individual case to decide the best course of action.

Christians will recognise that there is some agreement between their views and those held by atheists and humanists, although their reasoning differs. Many Christians maintain that taking life under any circumstances is wrong and, therefore, suggest that the death penalty should not be used.

Now try this

The use of capital punishment is controversial – some Christians support its use, while others do not. Read the question carefully, so you are certain you know which arguments you need to focus on.

1 Outline **three** Christian beliefs about the death penalty. **(3 marks)**
2 Explain **two** reasons why Christians might not support the use of the death penalty. **(4 marks)**

Peace

Peace is the absence of war or conflict. It is an important idea in Christianity, as Christians believe this is what God intended for the world when he created it. To achieve peace, Christians believe people need to work together and support each other.

Why peace is important for Christians

- A central belief of Christianity is the idea of seeking peace and justice within the world.
- Christians believe all members of the Church are part of a community – shaking hands during Sunday services is seen as a 'sign of peace'.
- There are many examples of peace being promoted within the Bible.
- Jesus represents and taught many ideas of peace and Christians want to follow his example.

Christians use the image of a dove and an olive branch as a symbol of peace.

I have told you these things, so that in me you may have peace. (John 16:33)

Divergent Church teachings on peace

- The Church teaches that peace is important. Jesus taught his disciples to 'Love your enemies and pray for those who persecute you' (Matthew 5:44).
- The Christian Church uses Jesus' teachings to show that Christians should strive for peace within the world.
- However, some Christians point to teachings that appear to justify the use of violence. These include: 'But if there is serious injury, you are to take life for life, eye for eye, tooth for tooth, hand for hand, foot for foot' (Exodus 21:23–24). This quote seems to suggest that violence may sometimes be appropriate, but conflicts with Jesus' later teachings.
- Although the church actively promotes ideas of peace, there have been times when violence has been considered necessary in order to bring about peace.

Jesus as peacemaker

1. Jesus taught that people should love one another and treat others as they would like to be treated: 'Do to others as you would have them do to you' (Luke 6:31).

2. Jesus embraced the worst sinners, cared for the sick and dying, performed miracles to help others and showed that all people were equal and should be at peace.

3. Jesus taught in the Sermon on the Mount: 'Blessed are the peacemakers' (Matthew 5:9) and encouraged achieving peace through love: 'Love your neighbour as yourself'. (Mark 12:31)

4. When Jesus was arrested in the Garden of Gethsemane the disciples turned to violence, but Jesus stopped them: 'When Jesus' followers saw what was going to happen, they said:

   "Lord, should we strike with our swords?" And one of them struck the servant of the high priest, cutting off his right ear. But Jesus answered, "No more of this!" And he touched the man's ear and healed him' (Luke 22:49–51).

5. Jesus died on the cross to bring forgiveness and reconciliation between God and humanity, forgiving his enemies even as he was dying.

Now try this

Explain **two** beliefs about peace for Christians.   **(4 marks)**

Remember that, when answering questions such as this, you need to state a belief and then explain what Christians understand by it.

Peacemaking

Peace is important to Christians. There are many examples of Christian organisations and individuals working towards peace.

Importance of justice, forgiveness and reconciliation

1 **Justice** is the idea of fairness being achieved. Christians believe there is a direct link between the ideas of justice and peace. A lack of peace is often seen in places around the world where injustices occur. If justice can be attained, peace will naturally follow.

'Do to others as you would have them do to you.' (Luke 6:31)

2 **Forgiveness** is to be able to move on from what has happened and attain peace through working together. Christians believe that they should follow the example of Jesus, who taught about the importance of forgiveness.

'... if you hold anything against anyone, forgive them...' (Mark 11:25)

3 **Reconciliation** is the idea of making up after conflict. According to Christianity, when people talk through their issues and reconcile, peace can be achieved.

'Be kind and compassionate to one another, forgiving each other, just as in Christ God forgave you.' (Ephesians 4:32)

Christian organisations working for peace

World Council of Churches

- ✓ Ecumenical organisation founded in 1948.
- ✓ A fellowship of Churches that encourages Christians from all denominations to heal divisions and work together for the common good in the world.
- ✓ Involved in struggles in South Africa, South Sudan, the Korean Peninsula and Latin America.

Pax Christi (the Peace of Christ)

- ✓ International Catholic Organisation constituted in 1920.
- ✓ The organisation is opposed to war and violence and works to create a peaceful world.
- ✓ Encourages people and governments to solve their conflicts through discussion, peace and reconciliation.

Hold interfaith conferences to demonstrate unity and pray for those without peace.

Go into schools and youth groups to promote peace.

What they do

Take part in public demonstrations, e.g. against war or injustices within the world, to raise awareness and campaign against oppressive governments.

Encourage peace talks between groups to end conflict and support reconciliation.

Educate others about the injustices across the world and teach forgiveness.

Help victims of injustice.

Why do Christian organisations work for peace?

- They believe God intended peace in the world and they have a duty to work to achieve this.
- They believe unity is important and Christianity teaches that working together in harmony with others will help lead to peace.
- They believe that sources of authority, such as the Bible, teach that peace is important.
- Teachings from Jesus such as the Beatitudes suggest that peace is important.

Blessed are the peacemakers, for they will be called children of God. Blessed are those who are persecuted because of righteousness, for theirs is the kingdom of heaven. (Matthew 5:9–10)

Now try this

Outline **three** ways a Christian group has worked for peace today.   **(3 marks)**

Conflict

Conflict, where an argument or disagreement has led to a breakdown in a relationship, can cause serious problems within society, such as the inability to work together.

Christian responses to the nature and causes of conflict

Christians believe that they have a duty to work to end the causes of conflict, such as differences over politics, money, resources, culture and religion.

Christians feel that the Bible promotes striving for peace and unity within the world, so that people can live in harmony.

Christian teachings on conflict

1 The Bible provides guidelines on how Christians can work for peace, reconciliation and justice, which they should follow.

2 Christians believe it is their duty to work for peace, as this is what God intended.

3 Christians follow the example of Jesus, who gave many teachings about peace and set an example.

Christian responses to the problems conflict causes

1 Christians may try to reconcile groups and help them to resolve and achieve peace.

2 They may take a position of pacifism and non-violence and be totally against any form of conflict or fighting.

3 They may refer to the example of Jesus' arrest, where his disciples tried to defend him using violence. Jesus responded by healing the guard who was injured and teaching the disciples that violence was not the answer.

4 They may refer to **situation ethics**, which states that each and every situation needs to be dealt with separately rather than applying one absolute rule to each situation.

'Put your sword back in its place,' Jesus said to him, 'for all who draw the sword will die by the sword.' (Matthew 26:52)

Here, Jesus teaches that violence only helps to cause more violence, rather than solving conflict.

Non-religious attitudes about the role of religion in the causes of conflict

- Many non-religious people such as atheists and Humanists may claim that religion itself is at the root of many conflicts in the world.

- They may believe that differences in beliefs causes conflict and religion cannot offer a satisfactory solution to bringing peace to the world.

- They might argue that without religion, there would be less conflict.

- Non-religious people may not agree with conflict but may advocate that sometimes violence is required in order to bring peace to the world.

Christian responses to non-religious attitudes

Christians emphasise that although there is division both between and within religions, many conflicts are not caused directly by religion. They would suggest that rather than identifying the differences between people, they should work on finding the things held in common to unite people and bring peace. Christians would give examples of many Christians who work for peace and believe that their religion provides teachings on how to do this.

Now try this

1 Explain **two** reasons why Christians believe it is important to work to end the causes of conflict.　**(4 marks)**

2 'All people should work to end the causes of conflict in the world.'
   Evaluate this statement considering arguments for and against. In your response you should:
   - refer to Christian teachings　• refer to non-religious points of view　• reach a justified conclusion.

   (12 marks)

Pacifism

Pacifism is the belief that war and cannot be justified under any circumstances.

Christian views

- Some Christians refuse to take part in war and may join peace rallies.

- Some Christians may not accept pacifism, believing that sometimes fighting is the only way to bring about peace.

For more on Christian belief on when war is justified, see page 47.

History of pacifism

1. Many Christians see Jesus as a pacifist; many of his teachings were about peace: 'Blessed are the peacemakers' (Matthew 5:9).

2. Some British pacifists (conscientious objectors) refused to fight in the two world wars.

3. Martin Luther King Jr was a pacifist who, refused to use violence in his fights to overcome injustices.

Christian teachings on pacifism

You shall not murder. (Exodus 20:13)

You have heard that it was said, "Love your neighbour and hate your enemy." But I tell you, love your enemies and pray for those who persecute you. (Matthew 43:44)

"Put your sword back in its place," Jesus said to him, "for all who draw the sword will die by the sword. (Matthew 26:52)

But I tell you, do not resist an evil person. If anyone slaps you on the right cheek, turn to them the other cheek also.' (Matthew 5:39)

So God created mankind in his own image. (Genesis 1:27)

The Ten Commandments forbid killing, supporting the idea of pacifism.

Jesus taught that people should love their enemies.

This recognises the need for peace and not using violence in the world.

Passive resistance

Passive resistance is non-violent opposition to authority, especially a refusal to co-operate with legal requirements to fight. Some Christians agree with this.

Peace I leave with you; my peace I give you. (John 14:27)

Reverend Martin Luther King Jr led peaceful protests against racist laws in the USA in the 1950s and 1960s.

The Quakers

The **Quakers** (Religious Society of Friends) are a Christian denomination opposed to violence.

- They believe that God is in every person, and oppose anything that harms people.

- They believe they should act in the world against injustice – peacefully. Many Quakers may be conscientious objectors.

- In the past, some Quakers refused to defend themselves from attack.

Now try this

'All Christians should be pacifists.'

Evaluate this statement considering arguments for and against. In your response you should:

- refer to Christian teachings • refer to different Christian points of view • reach a justified conclusion.

(12 marks)

The Just War theory

A 'just war' is one that Christians think is fought for the right reasons, in the right way and is therefore seen as being justified.

Criteria for a just war

Some religious believers think war is permitted when:

- ✓ there is reasonable chance of success
- ✓ its aim is to bring peace
- ✓ it is used only after other non-violent methods have failed
- ✓ no innocent civilians will be killed
- ✓ the cause of the war is just, e.g. resisting aggression or injustice
- ✓ the methods used are fair.

The nature, history and importance of the Just War theory

The Just War theory is a largely Christian doctrine employed by those in authority, providing guidance to help decide whether or not war is right and just. It applies to states, not individuals and provides a framework for discussions of possible wars. It does not justify wars but prevents them by showing that going to war, except in certain limited circumstances, is wrong, so encourages other ways of resolving conflict.

> The idea of a Just War was first formulated by St Augustine. Centuries later, St Thomas Aquinas formulated this into a set of criteria.

Christian teachings on just war

- The Just War Doctrine of the Catholic Church is found in the 1992 Catechism of the Catholic Church. Many Christian Churches have accepted this doctrine.
- There appears to be some Bible support for the Just War theory.
- Many Christians believe it is right to have armed forces to protect a country.
- Sometimes it can be argued that violence is necessary. For example, if a country is invaded, the people of that country should be allowed to defend themselves.

> Let everyone be subject to the governing authorities, for there is no authority except that which God has established. The authorities that exist have been established by God. (Romans 13:1)

Divergent Christian views on just war

Christians disagree on whether war is ever justified. Some accept the Just War theory, using arguments similar to those used by Catholics, while others feel that both sides in war may claim their cause is just and, instead, use teachings relating to peace.

> In the Second World War, Hitler claimed the Nazis were right in their fight. This raises the question of whether any war is just.

Situation ethics

Many people – both religious and non-religious – may take a situation ethics standpoint when deciding whether or not war is justified, judging each individual situation at the time.

> St Paul told people they had a duty to obey those who hold authority.

Now try this

1 Explain **two** reasons why the Just War theory is important to some Christians.   **(4 marks)**
2 'No war is ever just.'
   Evaluate this statement considering arguments for and against. In your response you should:
   - refer to Christian teachings
   - refer to different Christian points of view
   - reach a justified conclusion.   **(12 marks)**

Holy war

A holy war is one where religious believers think God is 'on their side' and they are therefore fighting because it is the right thing to do.

Bible teachings

Whoever does not take up their cross and follow me is not worthy of me. Whoever finds their life will lose it, and whoever loses their life for my sake will find it. (Matthew 10:38–39)

Love your enemies and pray for those who persecute you. (Matthew 5:44)

For all who draw the sword will die by the sword. (Matthew 26:52)

Nature of a holy war

In the 11th, 12th and 13th centuries, Christians went on crusades to 'free' the holy places in Palestine. These were considered to be holy wars, as they were believed to be what God wanted.

Christian responses to holy war

✓ Some passages from the Bible seem to suggest that war may sometimes be the right action. 'The Lord said to Moses, "Take vengeance on the Midianites for the Israelites."' (Numbers 31:1–2). However, as these were Old Testament teachings, Christians today would not support the view that war is justified to defend God, believing it is better to find a peaceful solution to conflict.

✓ The Bible has a general message of peace, and Jesus was given the title 'Prince of Peace'. "Blessed are the peacemakers, for they will be called children of God." (Matthew 5:9) This recognises the importance of peace and that holy war is therefore wrong.

✓ Some Christians (e.g. Quakers) may be pacifist – they do not support war at all.

Non-religious attitudes to holy war

- As non-religious people do not accept God, they would almost certainly oppose holy wars.
- Most would also oppose war in general, except in exceptional circumstances, but religion would never be a justifiable reason for war.

See pages 45–7 for attitudes on war generally.

Christians would generally agree that wars should not be fought in God's name and violence should only be used as a very last resort, if at all.

Worked example

'Holy war is justified for Christians.' Evaluate this statement considering arguments for and against. In your response you should:

- refer to Christian teachings
- refer to different Christian points of view
- explain non-religious beliefs
- reach a justified conclusion.

(12 marks)

Some Christians may agree with this statement as they accept that war, especially holy war, may sometimes be necessary. There are examples in history of Christians taking part in holy wars such as the Crusades in defence of Christianity. There are also passages in the Bible, such as Numbers 31:1–2, suggesting God has authorised war in circumstances where it is needed. Some Christians may use this evidence to argue that holy war is acceptable.

To continue this answer needs to explain why other Christians may not hold the same view and include some reference to what non-religious people may say about the statement and how Christians may respond to this.

Now try this

Outline **three** teachings about war in the Bible.   **(3 marks)**

Weapons of mass destruction Paper 2

Weapons of mass destruction (WMD) include nuclear, biological or chemical weapons that are intended and able to cause widespread devastation and loss of life. Christians are against their use.

Perceived benefits of WMD

- A stronger and quicker way to win a war.
- Minimal losses are incurred on the side of the attackers.
- A threat to deter other nations from starting a war.

Perceived problems of WMD

- Moral question of whether the devastation caused is ever justified.
- Dangers from stockpiling WMD.
- Conditions of the Just War theory would not be met using WMD.

Christian responses to WMD

1. Most Christians accept that the problems of WMD outweigh any benefits.

2. Christian teachings focus on ideas of peace found in the Bible and taught by Jesus, suggesting violence is unacceptable.

3. Christians would be concerned about the high loss of life caused by WMD.

4. Christians recognise that the nature of war has changed since biblical times, but respond to the benefits and problems of WMD by arguing that their use cannot be justified.

Bible teachings

Deuteronomy 20 may be interpreted in two ways. God tells his people to 'Completely destroy' cities in the war and 'do not leave alive anything that breathes' which might seem to imply that complete destruction is acceptable in some cases. However, in other sections He tells them not to destroy women, children, livestock and trees, which would suggest that mass destruction is against God's wishes.

Christian attitudes to WMD

Worked example

Explain **two** reasons why Christians are generally against the use of weapons of mass destruction. **(4 marks)**

Weapons of mass destruction are intended to inflict as much damage as possible and Christians believe 'God created man in his image', so all human life is sacred and should not be destroyed.

WMD also damage the environment, which is God's creation. Christians believe they will be judged after death on how they have treated the world.

Non-Christian attitudes to WMD

- **Atheists** who have seen the results where WMD have been used are not likely to support their use.
- **Humanists** believe life is special, but for non-religious reasons. They are unlikely to support the use of WMD because they cause so much damage and threaten life to such a great extent.
- Some people might refer to ethical theories such as **utilitarianism**, where the right action is that which brings about the greatest happiness for the greatest number. In this case, WMD should not be used as they would cause too much destruction and suffering.

Christians would respond by lending their support to these non-religious views, agreeing that WMD should not be used. They would, however, offer religious reasons, such as the sanctity of life argument or the teaching that peace is more important than war.

Now try this

Outline **three** problems of weapons of mass destruction for Christians. **(3 marks)**

Paper 2

Issues surrounding conflict

Many Christians are concerned that people are increasingly turning to violence in the modern world. The use of modern weaponry means conflict has taken on a new meaning.

Christian attitudes to issues surrounding conflict

1 Violence

Christians do not believe that fighting is the way to solve conflict, as the Bible and Jesus' teachings support ideas of peace.

Conflict in the world

2 War

Some Christians believe the Bible suggests war is acceptable in some circumstances, and if all peaceful methods have first been tried. Many Christians, however, believe that war is never the answer, especially today when weapons are more destructive than ever before.

3 Terrorism

Christians recognise the changing nature of the world and the growth of terrorism. Christians can never justify the use of this extreme method, as it targets innocent lives.

This teaching from Jesus shows that Christians believe fighting is not the answer and peace should be used to try to resolve issues of conflict.

Love your enemies, do good to those who hate you, bless those who curse you, pray for those who mistreat you. If someone slaps you on one cheek, turn to them the other also. (Luke 6:27–29)

Worked example

Explain **two** Christian teachings on issues surrounding conflict in the world. **(4 marks)**

Jesus taught his followers to 'Love your enemies', so that peace rather than fighting should be used to bring an end to conflict.

Ephesians 4:32 teaches that forgiveness and reconciliation are important and Christians should try to apply this teaching to conflict in the world.

Non-religious views and Christian responses

- **Humanists** do not believe in the afterlife, so consider life on Earth very valuable. Violence costs lives, so they would always seek to find non-violent solutions. They might point out that conflict can be caused by religious differences, which they believe to be pointless.

- **Atheists** also value human life, although also not for religious reasons. They believe that conflict in the world is wrong and that it is often caused by religious differences.

- **Christians** agree that human life is important because it is sacred, and so non-violent means should be tried to resolve conflict – violence is a last resort, e.g. against injustice. They would say that Christians today seek peace, rather than fighting wars in the name of God.

How Christians have worked to overcome conflict in the world

After conflict has happened, Christians believe it is important to come together and form a sense of community. Sometimes they hold candlelit vigils and pray; at other times they offer practical help to those affected by conflict. Christian charities offer support to those affected.

Now try this

'All Christians have a duty to work to overcome conflict in the world.' Evaluate this statement considering arguments for and against. In your response you should:
- refer to Christian teachings
- refer to non-religious arguments
- reach a justified conclusion.
(12 marks)

Revelation

Many people claim to have experienced God and believe that these experiences are evidence of the existence of God.

What is revelation?

Revelation is when the truth of something is revealed. In Christianity, it is believed to be the way in which God reveals his presence to humanity.

For Christians, God is revealed through:

- the Bible
- visions
- miracles
- prayer
- the natural world
- Church teachings and the example set by great Christians.

Revelation as shown through Noah

Christians believe God spoke to Noah and made a covenant (promise) to him never to send a worldwide flood to destroy the Earth again. The rainbow is the sign of this covenant today and, when seen, Christians believe it is a reminder of the message of God's faithfulness.

I establish my covenant with you: Never again will all life be destroyed by the waters of a flood; never again will there be a flood to destroy the earth … I have set my rainbow in the clouds, and it will be the sign of the covenant between me and the earth. (Genesis 9:11–13)

This covenant is important to Christians, as it involves all living things.

Revelation as shown through Abraham

God made a covenant to Abraham that he would give him a son if he and his descendants worshipped God. Abraham's faith was then tested when God asked Abraham to sacrifice his son. Abraham was willing to do this but God stopped him at the last minute, explaining that it was a test of faith. Jews see the covenant as evidence that they are 'God's chosen people', and since this time male Jewish babies have been circumcised as a sign of the covenant.

Walk before me faithfully and be blameless. Then I will make my covenant between me and you and will greatly increase your numbers. (Genesis 17:1–2)

Christians identify Abraham as an important prophet.

Revelation as shown through Jesus

Christians see Jesus as a form of **revelation**, as they accept that he is the Incarnation of God, (God in human form).

In the past God spoke to our ancestors through the prophets at many times and in various ways, but in these last days he has spoken to us by his Son. (Hebrews 1:1–2)

Now try this

Explain **two** ideas about the nature of God shown through revelation.

(4 marks)

Divergent understandings about God

Revelation helps Christians to understand the characteristics of God:

- **omnipotence** (all-powerful)
- **omniscience** (all-knowing)
- **benevolence** (loving and caring).

Christians believe that the fact that God communicates with humanity shows that he is close **(immanent)**, yet at the same time he is **transcendent** and remains beyond full human understanding.

Most Christians place great emphasis on revelation, believing it is God communicating with humanity. Some Christians choose some forms of revelation over others, e.g. placing greater importance on the Bible.

Visions (1)

A vision is something that a Christian sees, possibly in a dream, which may connect to God. Often, a revelation is made where truth is revealed. Christians believe visions are evidence for the existence of God, as he is communicating with humanity.

Nature of visions

Christian visions may involve the appearance of angels, saints or messengers, although some people believe they have seen God. Visions generally pass on a message from God, helping people to understand him.

Importance of visions

Visions are an important form of religious experience. People often only believe things that they can see, so experiencing a vision may be considered to be more reliable than other types of religious experiences.

Biblical and non-biblical examples of visions

Saul/St Paul Saul, a persecutor of Christians, was on the road to Damascus when he saw a bright light and he heard the voice of Jesus. Saul was struck blind and could not see for three days. This experience convinced him of the truth of God and Christianity. When his vision returned, he became a Christian and changed his name to Paul.	 Saul discovered God after he was struck blind on the road to Damascus.
Joseph Joseph, the earthly father of Jesus, received a dream from God where an angel appeared to him after he found out Mary was pregnant. The angel convinced him that Mary would give birth to the Son of God. After Jesus was born, Joseph received two more visions in dreams; the first telling him to take his family to Egypt so Herod could not kill Jesus; and the second telling him that Herod was dead and he could return home with his family.	 Joseph's visions occurred in dreams, when an angel appeared to him.
St Bernadette Bernadette was a child living in Lourdes, France, who, in 1858, was believed to have seen numerous visions of the Virgin Mary. During one of these, Mary asked her to drink from a spring, but as there was no spring visible, Bernadette dug in the mud to look for one. Many people thought she had gone mad, but soon afterwards a spring appeared on the spot. The spring is still there today and many Catholics believe it has healing properties.	 St Bernadette had a vision of the Virgin Mary.

Now try this

State **three** examples of visions in Christianity that are believed to illustrate the existence of God. **(3 marks)**

To answer this question successfully, remember to use the examples above (or others that you have studied).

Visions (2)

Why might visions lead to belief in God?

1 People may believe that God is contacting them and passing on a message.

2 People may think that it connects them to God and helps them to get closer to him.

3 The visions will help Christians to understand God better and develop a relationship with him.

Non-religious arguments about visions

Non-religious people may suggest that visions are not 'proof' of God's existence because they may:

1 believe that visions are not 'real'

2 offer alternative explanations for visions, such as people experiencing hallucinations or having dreams

3 only believe things that can be verified (confirmed) scientifically.

Worked example

Explain **two** reasons why visions may lead to belief in God. **(4 marks)**

Christians believe that God may be contacting them through a vision and perhaps passing on a message. This is seen, for example, in the vision of Saul, who received the message to become a Christian.

Visions will also help Christians to get closer to God and understand him better. This was seen in the visions of Joseph, where he understood God's purpose for him in protecting Jesus.

Christian responses to non-religious arguments

Christians believe visions provide real evidence of God. Examples such as the healing miracles at Lourdes, which have resulted from the vision received by Bernadette, provide this. They claim that religious believers would not be under the influence of stimulants and even though they may face persecution because of visions, they maintain them, claiming they have nothing to gain through lying. It is through visions that Christians claim they can 'know' God.

Visions as evidence of the nature of God

Christians believe that visions help to reveal what God is like and help them to understand him better. Christians believe that some of God's characteristics can be demonstrated through visions.

omniscience
Visions demonstrate the knowledge of God and show that he is able to communicate in ways that humanity will understand.

omnipotence
The fact that God can cause visions shows he is powerful and can do what he wants.

Visions are evidence of God's…

benevolence
The fact that God communicates with his creation shows that he cares for it and loves what he has made, including humans.

immanence
God, through visions, is trying to get close to humanity so they can develop a relationship with him.

Now try this

Explain **two** reasons why visions are important proof of God for Christians. **(4 marks)**

Try to include some examples of reasons in your answer, to show how important visions are as proof of God. You also need to make reference to what visions reveal about God.

Miracles

Miracles are amazing events that the laws of nature and science can't explain. There are many examples of miraculous events in the world – both in the past and today.

Importance of miracles to Christians

Christians believe that miracles:

- prove the existence of God as a greater being who is involved with and acting in the world
- show God cares for his creation
- show he wants to be involved in the world
- provide people with the comfort that God is close.

'Unless you people see signs and wonders,' Jesus told him, 'you will never believe'. (John 4:48)

Here, Jesus gives a reason why he performed miracles – to help people believe in God. Christians believe that, although they have faith in God, signs in the world that confirm his presence help to strengthen their faith.

Biblical examples of miracles

1. **Healing miracles** – There are reports of healing miracles happening in religious places, such as holy cities in Israel.

2. **The miracles of Jesus** – in the Bible, Jesus performs many miracles, such as walking on water, turning water into wine, feeding a large crowd of people, as well as healing people and bringing people back from the dead. These are often called 'nature miracles'.

3. **Resurrection of Jesus** – it is considered a miracle that Jesus was crucified on the cross and then three days later came back to life.

One of the miracles that Jesus performed was walking on water.

Why miracles might lead people to believe in God

- ✓ People are amazed by what has happened and cannot explain it any other way (e.g. by science).
- ✓ Miracles can be seen as evidence of a personal God acting within the world.
- ✓ Miracles are proof of God's existence and his love for the world. The power of God is show through laws of nature being broken.

Non-religious arguments

Non-religious people might suggest miracles are not 'proof' of God's existence because:

- ✓ there could be other scientific explanations that require no mention of God
- ✓ two people could experience a miracle and yet interpret it differently, meaning there is lots of uncertainty about what happened or whether it was even real
- ✓ they may not believe that miracles actually happen or, if they do, that it is not God causing them.

Christians might respond by pointing to the evidence of miracles, e.g. healing at Lourdes. They might point out that science does not have the answers to everything, and that we cannot fully understand God.

Now try this

1. Outline **three** examples of biblical miracles.   **(3 marks)**
2. Explain **two** reasons why miracles may not lead to belief in God.   **(4 marks)**

Religious experiences

Although many religious believers claim to have had a religious experience that confirms their beliefs about God, many people do not accept religious experiences as real.

What is a religious experience?

A religious experience is where a person undergoes revelation of God in some form. Through this experience they believe they have got to 'know' God better. Religious experiences could take the form of visions, voices, miracles or some other event.

> There the angel of the Lord appeared to him in flames of fire from within a bush. Moses saw that though the bush was on fire it did not burn up. (Exodus 3:2)

Why religious experience might be seen as revelation

Revelation is communication from God – a message, or something about His nature. Christians believe revelations can appear through scripture or through religious experience, e.g. Moses and the burning bush: God gave Moses a task. Revelation gives the religious experience meaning; it would be pointless for God to create miracles for no reason, so they must have a purpose.

Because many Christians have experienced personal revelation of God over time, this is seen by some Christians as providing evidence of God's existence – how can so many different people be wrong?

Non-religious arguments

Some people, including atheists and humanists, may argue that religious experiences aren't real at all; they are simply natural experiences that have been misinterpreted in a religious way.

1 Lack of evidence

- There is not enough evidence to suggest religious experiences actually happen and 'prove' that God exists.
- Individual experiences are always subjective, giving opportunity for criticism and challenge of how it is interpreted.
- Any experience could be claimed to be 'religious'.

2 Use of stimulants

Those who undergo a religious experience may be under the influence of drugs or alcohol, so their experiences cannot be trusted. Stimulants change how a person interprets things around them.

3 Wish fulfilment

Some people may be so desperate for a message from God that they interpret normal events as religious experiences.

> **Arguments why religious experiences are not proof that God exists**

4 Hallucinations

Mental health issues or illness may cause a person to hallucinate and interpret normal events as religious experiences.

Christians might respond to non-religious arguments by saying:
- religious experiences are real and believers have no reason to lie or make them up
- many religions including Christianity are based on religious experiences, making them significant
- religious believers would not take stimulants so this does not explain experiences that have happened

Now try this

Explain **two** Christian responses to arguments that suggest religious experiences do not prove God's existence.　**(4 marks)**

Remember that this question asks for Christian responses to non-religious arguments. You are not required to explain the non-religious arguments themselves.

Prayers

Prayer is a way in which Christians communicate with God. Many Christians feel that their prayers being answered is evidence that God exists. Prayer can be used to thank and praise God or to apologise or ask God for help.

The nature of prayer

Prayer can take many forms, such as:

- an internal conversation with God, or a traditional set Christian prayer
- spoken aloud or said silently. For example, the Lord's Prayer can be said in these ways
- alone at home or together in a group with others in a more formal church service
- in a church community on a Sunday.

The importance of prayer

Prayer is a central part of being a Christian. Prayer is important because:

- it allows Christians to develop a personal relationship with God
- Christians can understand God better and get closer to him
- Jesus taught the importance of prayer
- knowing God is listening comforts Christians.

What does the Bible teach about prayer?

Therefore I tell you, whatever you ask for in prayer, believe that you have received it, and it will be yours. (Mark 11:24)

Prayer is important and should be used to communicate with God in the belief that he will answer.

This is the confidence we have in approaching God: that if we ask anything according to his will, he hears us. And if we know that he hears us – whatever we ask – we know that we have what we asked of him. (1 John 5:14–15)

God hears all prayers and Christians should not be afraid to look to God in prayer. Although Christians believe that answering prayers may not always come in the manner expected, they accept that God hears and listens, answering what people ask of him.

But when you pray, go into your room, close the door and pray to your Father, who is unseen. Then your Father, who sees what is done in secret, will reward you. (Matthew 6:6)

Prayer is important and Christians should put their trust in it. Here, it is a private conversation between an individual and God.

Belief in God

Answered prayers might lead to belief in God because:

1. people ask for something and receive an answer, showing God is real
2. this shows God cares about his Creation and wants to help humanity
3. people feel closer to God and develop a personal relationship with him.

Why prayers may not be answered in the way people expect

Christians believe that God has a mysterious nature. One element of this is that prayers may not be answered in the way they expect, or would like, because, although God listens, He knows more about what is best for us or for the world than we ourselves do.

Now try this

When answering this first question, aim to use the word 'because' in your answer, to show you are explaining why prayer is important to Christians.

1 Explain **two** reasons why prayer is important to Christians.   **(4 marks)**

2 'Prayers are proof that God exists.'
Evaluate this statement considering arguments for and against. In your response you should:
- refer to Christian teachings
- reach a justified conclusion.   **(12 marks)**

The design argument

The design argument tries to prove the existence of God by arguing that the universe was designed. This leads some people to believe in an all-powerful, all-knowing eternal creator God who designed the universe.

Overview of the design argument

| Design is the result of intelligent thought. | → | The universe shows evidence of being designed (e.g. gravity, ozone layer). | → | This suggests that a being with intelligence designed the universe. | → | The universe is too complex to have happened by chance or be designed by any being other than God. | → | Therefore, God exists. |

The classical design argument suggests that God cared about his creation and planned it. It also shows he is benevolent and omnipotent.

Divergent understandings about what the design argument may show about God

Many Christians use the design argument to confirm their belief and faith in God and His nature, as:

- **omnipotent** – all-powerful, as he designed the world to suit human life

- **omnipresent** – all-present, as he is found throughout his creation

- **benevolent** – as he cared for his creation and took time to plan it

> For since the creation of the world God's invisible qualities – his eternal power and divine nature – have been clearly seen, being understood from what has been made, so that people are without excuse. (Romans 1: 20)

This Bible passage suggests that humans can never fully understand God or grasp what he is like, as he is too great – supporting the design argument.

- **unknowable** in some ways, as God is transcendent and too great for humans to understand.

Non-religious arguments against the design argument

Some non-religious people (including atheists and humanists) offer criticisms of the design argument for the existence of God. These include:

1. Design might actually be the result of evolution, not God.
   See page 29 for more on evolution.

2. It is impossible to prove that God is the designer.

3. The universe may not be planned and designed – the argument that the it happened by chance is equally strong.

4. Science today offers more explanation of the universe and arguments such as 'God designed it' are out of date.

5. There is evidence of 'bad' design in the world, e.g. volcanoes and earthquakes. Therefore, if God does exist, why did he design evil and suffering to harm people?

Christian responses to non-religious arguments

Christians may argue that science and religion can work together to explain how the world was made and designed and that evolution was simply part of God's plan.

Although there may appear to be evidence of 'bad design' in the world (e.g. volcanoes) we cannot understand everything about God's plan for the world, so we have to trust him and respond to the events with compassion.

Now try this

1 Outline **three** beliefs about the design argument. **(3 marks)**

2 Explain **two** reasons why the design argument is important to Christians. **(4 marks)**

The cosmological argument

The cosmological argument tries to prove the existence of God by showing that everything happens for a reason. It is based on the ideas of cause and effect (e.g. a sculptor causes a sculpture to exist). Christians believe that it reinforces their belief that God created the universe.

Overview of the cosmological argument

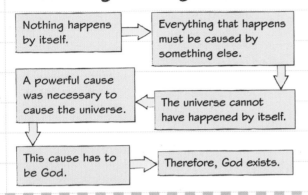

Nothing happens by itself. → Everything that happens must be caused by something else.

A powerful cause was necessary to cause the universe. ← The universe cannot have happened by itself.

This cause has to be God. → Therefore, God exists.

Christian understandings

Christians believe the cosmological argument demonstrates the nature of God as:

- omnipotent – all-powerful as he created the universe
- benevolent – as he created the universe with love and care
- unknowable in some ways – as he is transcendent and too great for humanity to fully understand.

St Thomas Aquinas' First Three Ways

The Catholic priest Thomas Aquinas (1225–74) put forward a version of the cosmological argument, summarised in the first three of The Five Ways:

1 Motion

- Everything that moves is put in motion by something else.
- Chain of movers cannot be infinite.
- There must be a **first mover**, which is God.

2 Cause

- Every effect has a cause.
- Chain of causes cannot be infinite.
- There must be a **first cause**, which is God.

3 Contingency

- Everything that is contingent relies on something else to exist.
- All things must have been brought into existence by a **necessary being**.
- This necessary being doesn't rely on anything else for its existence, so must be God.

Non-religious arguments against the cosmological argument

1. We cannot 'prove' that God caused the universe – an alternative, scientific explanation for the creation of the universe is the Big Bang.

2. Even if we accept that everything within the universe has a cause, this doesn't mean that the universe itself has a cause.

3. If everything has a cause, what caused God?

4. If God created the universe, why did he create bad things such as earthquakes?

Christian responses to non-religious arguments

Some Christians may respond by arguing that science and religion can work together to explain how the universe was made. They do not see conflict between science and religion, claiming that God created the Big Bang, which in turn created the universe.

> To answer this question successfully, you need to consider why Christians use the argument and feel it is successful and why non-religious people may feel it is a weak argument.

Now try this

'The cosmological argument is proof that God exists.'
Evaluate this statement considering arguments for and against. In your response you should:
- refer to Christian teachings
- refer to non-religious viewpoints
- reach a justified conclusion.

(12 marks)

Religious upbringing

Many people believe in God because they have been raised within Christianity.

Christian teachings about raising children

- Christian parents believe it is important to raise their children within Christianity, to introduce them to the faith.
- They may take them to church services and activities, such as Sunday School, marriages, christenings and funerals.
- Children of Christians can learn more about their faith by reading the Bible and attending church services and activities.

What the Bible teaches

Fathers, do not exasperate your children; instead, bring them up in the training and instruction of the Lord. (Ephesians 6:4)

Start children off on the way they should go, and even when they are old they will not turn from it. (Proverbs 22:6)

These passages teach parents to raise their children as Christians, to introduce them to the faith and support them in following the path of God.

Baptism

A child is **welcomed** into the Church with family, friends and the worshipping congregation promising to support them within the Christian faith.

School

Christian parents may choose a Church school that helps to **educate** children in the Christian faith.

Following parents' examples

Parents will set an example to their children. By seeing their parents praying, hearing about God through Bible stories and attending church, children will be more likely to believe in God.

How do Christian families encourage their children to believe in God?

Community

Young Christians can meet and share in activities such as Bible study groups, youth clubs, prayer meetings or other events. This offers a sense of **belonging** and community. Young adults may also meet partners in the Church community.

Confirmation

A child will be encouraged to **confirm** and renew the vows made for them in baptism when they are old enough to make this decision for themselves.

Worship

Children attend church and Sunday School to **learn** about Jesus, God and the Church.

Non-religious ideas

Some non-religious people, such as atheists and humanists, argue that being brought up in a religious family may lead children to reject religion. Some may feel that children should be given more choice about which path they want to follow. Children today may have more faith in science than in religion.

Christians could respond that even children raised as non-religious may eventually turn to religion because they need hope or purpose, or feel there is more to life than just the physical. They also want their children to go with them to heaven when they die, which is only possible through belief in Jesus. Christians believe that everyone, including those without a religious upbringing, should have the opportunity to find out about Christianity.

Now try this

1 Outline **three** features of a Christian upbringing. **(3 marks)**
2 Explain **two** reasons why Christians believe they should raise their children within the Christian faith. In your answer you should refer to a source of wisdom or authority. **(5 marks)**

Remember that you need to state a reason explaining why Christians believe they have a duty to raise their children within the Christian faith, and you then need to add new information or an example to expand and develop each point. You also need to link one of your reasons to a source of authority.

Human rights

Human rights are the basic rights and freedoms to which all human beings are entitled.

The nature, history and purpose of human rights

In the UK today, human rights are protected by law. The Universal Declaration of Human Rights says all humans are born free and equal in dignity and rights.

The Human Rights Act 1998 states that public organisations (police, government, etc.) must treat everyone equally, with fairness, dignity and respect. All citizens of the UK are entitled to life, food, liberty, free speech, racial, sexual and religious equality, education, healthcare and privacy.

The importance of human rights for Christians

Christians believe:

- ✓ the teachings of the Bible support human rights
- ✓ all humans are created by God in his image and so all are sacred
- ✓ God loves everyone equally, therefore, all people should be treated equally.

Why might Christians support human rights?

As Christians believe that God created everyone with equal rights, they support work to maintain fairness in the world.

Do to others what you would have them do to you. (Matthew 7:12) … whoever is kind to the needy honours God (Proverbs 14:31) … Whatever you did for one of the least of these brothers and sisters of mine, you did for me (Matthew 25:40)

These biblical quotes teach that we should help people in need.

Divergent Christian responses

Some Christians, such as Desmond Tutu and Martin Luther King Jr, feel that when the law is in conflict with their conscience over human rights, it is right to challenge the law.

Other Christians support **situation ethics**, and think that each individual situation should be considered separately.

Problems for Christians

Sometimes there is a conflict between Christian principles and human rights. For example, some Christians are opposed to homosexuality and female priests. Other Christians may argue that such behaviour goes against human rights and fails to value equality.

Non-religious responses

Humanists are fully committed to upholding human rights as equality and dignity are key – so it is key to fight against injustice.

Christian responses to non-religious views

Christians may share certain beliefs with atheists and humanists, such as the idea that people are entitled to certain rights. They would, however, use different reasons based on religious teachings.

Now try this

1 Explain **two** reasons why Christians believe human rights are important. In your answer you must refer to a source of wisdom and authority. **(5 marks)**
2 'Christians should always stand up when human rights are denied.' Evaluate this statement considering arguments for and against. In your response you should:
- refer to Christian teachings
- reach a justified conclusion. **(12 marks)**

You will need to consider a range of arguments for and against. Make sure you include reference to what, for example, the Bible says to support your views, and give examples such as Desmond Tutu and Martin Luther King Jr. Remember also to end with a conclusion.

Equality

Equality – the equal and fair treatment of everyone – is a key idea promoted within Christianity.

Experiences

Sometimes people don't treat others the same because of prior experiences.

Poverty

People are born into different situations, which leads to inequality.

Selfishness

Some people feel that they are more important than others and, therefore, treat others differently.

Causes of inequality

Ignorance

Some people do not care about inequality.

Global influences

What is happening in different parts of the world can lead to inequality.

These factors can cause problems in the world.

Christian teachings on equality

Christians believe humans are equal because:

1. All humans were made in the image of God.

2. God loves everyone equally and does not show favouritism.

3. The parable of the Good Samaritan teaches Christians to care for and love everyone equally.

5. Jesus treated everyone the same – even people who at the time were treated as outcasts, such as the poor, lepers, Gentiles and criminals.

'As for those who were held in high esteem – whatever they were makes no difference to me; God does not show favouritism – they added nothing to my message.' (Galatians 2:6).

There is neither Jew nor Gentile, neither slave nor free, nor is there male and female, for you are all one in Christ Jesus. (Galatians 3:28)

Possible solutions to inequality

Christians believe they can work to solve inequality through:

- **charity work** – organisations such as CAFOD, Christian Aid or Oxfam work to try to tackle the causes of inequality in the world. They try to improve people's lives by providing emergency aid and relief after disasters, addressing difficulties that people face in their daily lives and raising awareness of issues, e.g. gender inequality.

- **individuals** – people such as Martin Luther King Jr, Desmond Tutu or Mother Teresa have worked to try to challenge the inequalities in society. Individuals have worked with the government and may be involved with pressure groups and signing petitions.

This passage implies that those who have accepted Jesus in their lives are children of God, suggesting that all people are equal.

Now try this

1 Outline **three** reasons why Christians work to overcome inequality in the world. **(3 marks)**

2 Explain **two** ways in which Christians have worked to reduce inequality in the world. **(4 marks)**

Make sure that you state the reason and then develop it. To do this, you need to give an example or quote, or explain the idea more fully in your second sentence.

Religious freedom

Religious freedom is when a person is free to choose what religion they belong to, to change their religion or to have no religion at all.

Christian responses to religious freedom

- Christians believe human rights are important and religious freedom is part of this.

- Jesus taught, 'treat others as you would want to be treated' – showing that people shouldn't be treated differently, even for religious reasons.

- Jesus did not judge anyone – he simply moved on from people who rejected his religious message (Luke 9:52–6) and spoke to a Samaritan woman even though Jews would not associate with Samaritans (John 4:7–27). This supports the idea in the Bible that 'There is neither Jew nor Gentile... for you are all one in Christ Jesus'. (Galatians 3:28)

- Some Christians are afraid that religious freedom threatens Christianity. They believe that new laws and changes in attitudes, which includes acceptance of all religions and religious freedom, have threatened Christianity.

- Some Christians believe that their religion is the correct religion and may be less accepting of other faiths.

The Catechism of the Catholic Church

The Catechism of the Catholic Church 1738 and 1747 state that religious freedom is an 'inalienable right'.

1738 The *right to the exercise of freedom*, especially in moral and religious matters, is an inalienable requirement of the dignity of the human person.

Church responses to a multifaith society

Many Churches accept ideas of inclusivism, meaning they recognise there may be truth in all religions and they value the benefits of a multifaith society.

Other Christian Churches hold views of exclusivism. This means they believe that Christianity is the one true religion and that acceptance of other faiths is threatening it.

The benefits and challenges of living in a multifaith society

Benefits	Challenges
Greater tolerance and understanding of the beliefs of others.	Difficulty in understanding others' views.
Varied and rich cultural life from the religions and traditions of others.	There have been examples of religious persecution.
Better understanding of different viewpoints.	Religious tension between different faith groups.
	Beliefs and values of some groups may be ignored.

Non-religious arguments

Some non-religious people believe that religious views should be private, as people should be free to make their own choices about religion. Many recognise there are positives and negatives to a multifaith society. Christians respond by agreeing that religion is an individual's choice. Some Christians believe they have a duty to share their faith.

Now try this

'Only Christians benefit from living in a multifaith society.'
Evaluate this statement considering arguments for and against. In your response you should:
- refer to Christian teachings
- refer to non-religious points of view
- each a justified conclusion.   **(12 marks)**

Prejudice and discrimination

Christians believe that prejudice and discrimination are wrong, as all humans are equal.

- **Prejudice** is making a judgement about someone before you actually know them.
- **Discrimination** is an action – when a person is actually treated differently as a result of a prejudice.

Effects of prejudice and discrimination

- Prejudice and discrimination can cause people to be in conflict with one another and this could lead to physical violence.
- Prejudice is often seen as natural but, while it can be hard not to judge others, serious problems arise when prejudice becomes discrimination.
- Discimination is seen in events such as the Holocaust or acts of terrorism, when people target others and treat them differently because of their religion.

What the Bible says

Jesus often welcomed people whom others discriminated against. Indeed, his own situation (born in poverty to parents who were not married at the time of his conception, rejected by his home town, ridiculed for his claims) made him a subject of discrimination himself.

In Luke 15, he welcomed tax collectors and sinners, although the Pharisees disapproved.

You judge by human standards; I pass judgment on no one. (John 8:15)

The Lord does not look at the things people look at. People look at the outward appearance, but the Lord looks at the heart. (1 Samuel 16:7)

To show partiality in judging is not good. (Proverbs 24:23)

God does not show favoritism – they added nothing to my message. (Galatians 2:6)

Christian teachings on prejudice and discrimination

1. Christians believe that all humans are of equal value, as they were 'made in the image of God'. No one, therefore, should face unfair prejudice and discrimination.

2. Christians teach agape love, which supports the idea of treating all people in the same way and not discriminating.

3. Christians follow the example of Jesus, who did not discriminate.

4. The Golden Rule teaches 'treat others the way you would like to be treated'. This shows that prejudice and discrimination towards others because of their religion (or for any other reason) is wrong.

5. The Parable of the Good Samaritan demonstrates ideas of helping others and not treating them differently because of racial and religious discrimination.

Worked example

Explain **two** reasons why Christians believe prejudice and discrimination against religions are wrong. In your response you must refer to a source of wisdom or authority. **(5 marks)**

Christians follow the Bible, which says in Galatians 3:28 'There is neither Jew nor Gentile, neither slave nor free, nor is there male and female, for you are all one in Christ Jesus.' This shows that all humans are equal and should be treated the same.

Christians also believe that lives they should follow the example of Jesus, who never discriminated against anybody because of their race.

This answer offers two reasons and both are developed. They have also quoted from the Bible, as a source of authority.

Now try this

Outline **three** reasons why Christians believe prejudice and discrimination against religions are wrong. **(3 marks)**

This question doesn't require as much depth or explanation as the Worked example question. You are just required to give 3 sentences, each giving a reason.

Racial harmony

All Christians believe racism is wrong, as the Bible teaches that no one race is superior to another.

Christian teachings

- Through the Parable of the Good Samaritan, Jesus taught people to follow God's command and love one another.

- The Golden Rule states 'Treat others the way you would like to be treated.'

- Christians believe they should promote racial harmony because through doing this they are putting these teachings into practice.

> So God created mankind in his own image. (Genesis 1:27)
>
> Love your neighbour as yourself. (Luke 10:27)

Racial harmony is when all races live together happily. The Bible teaches that all Christians are 'one people'.

Christian teachings and responses to racial harmony

> A new command I give you: Love one another. As I have loved you, so you must love one another. (John 13:34)

Christians interpret this quote from the Bible in different ways. However, the generally held view is that Jesus is commanding people to care and show agape (unconditional) love towards each other.

Some Christians may link this quotation to **situation ethics**. This ethical theory is not based on universal rules, but instead states that each situation should be considered separately. The guiding principle is to do 'whatever is the most loving thing'.

Christians working for racial harmony: Desmond Tutu

- South African social rights activist.
- First black Anglican archbishop of Cape Town.
- Opposed apartheid (treating black and white people differently).
- Campaigns for racial harmony.
- Teaches that all people are equal regardless of the colour of their skin.
- Has used his profile to challenge human rights injustices.
- Works with the UN to campaign for gay rights, poverty, for Church reform and improved health care.

Archbishop Desmond Tutu (b. 1931)

Benefits of a multi-ethnic society

- Encourages racial harmony – helps people of different cultures, races and religions to understand each other.

- Helps to reduce discrimination through encouraging people to respect each other and their different backgrounds.

- Gives wider variety of music, food, clothes and culture to help people identify more with people from different backgrounds.

- Brings together people with fresh new ideas – people can learn from those who have different faiths and ethnic backgrounds as well as sharing their own faith and individual ethnic backgrounds.

Use the content on this page to think of reasons why living in a multi-ethnic society is good. Develop each reason using examples, quotes or by explaining your reason further giving new information.

Now try this

1 Explain **two** reasons why Christians have worked for racial harmony. **(4 marks)**

2 Explain **two** benefits of a Christian living in a multi-ethnic society. **(4 marks)**

Racial discrimination

Racial discrimination can lead to problems in society, such as people feeling they are not being treated with respect or fairly. Racial discrimination is such an important issue that laws have been created to protect people from it happening.

Christian teachings

Christians believe:

- everyone is made equal in the eyes of God
- biblical teachings such as 'love your neighbour as yourself' (Matthew 22:39)
- that not treating people fairly and equally causes problems in society
- God loves everyone – it doesn't matter what colour your skin is. 'There is neither Jew nor Gentile, neither slave nor free, nor is there male and female, for you are all one in Christ Jesus' (Galatians 3:28)
- God does not prefer any one person to another. 'As for those who were held in high esteem – whatever they were makes no difference to me; God does not show favoritism' (Galatians 2:6)
- the story of the Good Samaritan teaches Christians to care and love everyone equally
- Jesus taught that everyone is equal.

COLORED MUST SIT IN BALCONY

The USA and South Africa had laws enforcing segregation.

What the Bible says

From one man he made all the nations, that they should inhabit the whole earth; and he marked out their appointed times in history and the boundaries of their lands. (Acts 17:26)

This quote demonstrates the idea that, although humans were made to be different, they all share the common element of being created by God from Adam. Although this can cause problems in society, Christianity emphasises that this quote mentions 'all nations', showing that people of all races should work together.

Why racial discrimination causes problems in society

Racial discrimination has led to problems in society.

- People may feel that they are not being treated with respect – this can cause negative feeling between some racial groups of people, where some unfairly blame other groups for society's problems. Those being discriminated against resent the unfair treatment.
- Bad feeling between different racial groups can lead to a lack of trust in communities and an absence of working together. This creates social tension that could lead to rioting and violence.
- Some minority racial groups can feel isolated, causing individuals in those groups to withdraw from society. This only serves to reinforce social divisions between different racial groups.

- Being on the receiving end of racial discrimination can impact on an individual's well-being and feelings of self-worth. This could cause some people to feel limited as to what they can achieve and to live in fear of attack, which in turn could lead to other problems such as poor mental health and depression, resulting in reduced life chances and raising the risk of poverty and disease.
- Racial discrimination can lead to a lack of access to facilities and resources, such as education, health care facilities and leisure activities. This, in turn, negatively affects the life chances of those who have been excluded.

Now try this

Explain **two** reasons why most Christians feel racial discrimination is wrong. **(4 marks)**

Social justice

Social justice means ensuring there is equal distribution of wealth, opportunities and privileges in society.

Wealth and opportunity in the UK and world

Wealth and money are not distributed equally in the UK or the world. Smaller numbers of people hold larger amounts of wealth, meaning that many people live in poverty. It is also fair to suggest that people living in poverty face fewer opportunities in life as a result.

Christian teachings on social justice

- Christians have a duty to work for social justice, as this reflects Bible teachings and the example set by Jesus, which Christians believe they should follow.

- 'Love your neighbour as yourself' (Mark 12:31) – meaning Christians should help others.

- All humans are equal, as they were made in the image of God.

- Christians believe they should stand up for the rights of others.

- The Bible teaches that we have a responsibility to help those less fortunate. 'Whoever is generous to the poor lends to the Lord, and he will repay him for his deed' (Proverbs 19:17).

> The Synod [believes] that, as a matter of common humanity and of our mutual interest in survival, the world requires a new and more equitable system of economic relationships between nations. (General Synod of the Church of England, 1981)
>
> *Rich nations* have a grave moral responsibility toward those (less fortunate). (Catholic Church 2439)

Statements of belief relating to social justice.

> The King will reply, 'Truly I tell you, whatever you did for one of the least of these brothers and sisters of mine, you did for me.' (Matthew 25:40)

Jesus compared helping another person to helping him directly.

The Church and social justice

1. Many Christians promote ideas of social justice in their local communities.

2. Many Christians try to educate others about the unfairness of social injustice and how to tackle it.

3. Churches try to address issues of social injustice by providing food banks and help for those who need it.

4. Many Christians and churches are involved in charity work, to raise awareness of social justice issues and money to support them. Christian Aid, Christians Against Poverty (CAP) and CAFOD are examples of Christian charities. Turn to pages 61 and 67 to remind yourself of some of the work done by Christian charities.

Christians may favour the use of situation ethics, such as 'doing the most loving thing', an idea promoted through the example of Jesus.

The importance of the Church working for social justice

Jesus said 'the poor you will always have with you'. This suggests there will always be those who are considered poor, and that Christians should aim to help them whenever they can. Helping others will lead to reward in heaven – which many Christians see as the ultimate goal. This also reflects Jesus' example and Christian teachings such as 'treat others as you would like to be treated'.

Now try this

You need to consider what a Christian would say. You could refer to situation ethicsr. Remember a conclusion which could include your own opinion (although it doesn't have to).

'We should all work for social justice.'

Evaluate this statement considering arguments for and against. In your response you should:

- refer to Christian teachings
- refer to relevant ethical arguments
- reach a justified conclusion.

(12 marks)

Wealth and poverty

Poverty causes great suffering in the world. The cause and effects of poverty are of great concern for Christians, and many Christians work to try to reduce poverty and introduce greater financial equality between people.

The nature of poverty

Poverty is the state of being extremely poor or lacking in basics.

- **Absolute poverty** was defined by the United Nations in 1995 as severe deprivation of basic human needs including food, safe drinking water, sanitation facilities, health, shelter, education and information.

- **Relative poverty** is the standard of poverty defined in terms of the country it is within, so may vary from one country to another.

Causes of poverty in the UK and world

Poverty is caused by a combination of factors. Some of the common causes of poverty are:

1. low-paid work
2. unemployment
3. family breakdowns or illnesses
4. inadequate social benefits
5. rapid population growth leading to overpopulation
6. war and political instability
7. high national debt
8. lack of education and opportunity
9. discrimination and social inequality
10. environmental problems or natural disasters.

Christian teachings on and responses to poverty

Christians believe they should follow the example of Jesus, who showed care and compassion for others.

Many Christians choose to tithe and give 10% of their earnings to the Church for charity purposes.

Christians do not believe it is wrong to be wealthy, but it is important to gain wealth honestly and you should use it to help others.

Christians support charities, such as Christian Aid, which work to try to eradicate poverty.

The Parable of the Sheep and the Goats (Matthew 25:31–46) talks of God separating out people for reward and punishment based on whether they helped others in their lives.

Anyone who has two shirts should share with the one who has none, and anyone who has food should do the same'. (Luke 3:11)

'Go, sell everything you have and give to the poor, and you will have treasure in heaven'. (Mark 10:21)

'For I was hungry and you gave me something to eat, I was thirsty and you gave me something to drink, I was a stranger and you invited me in, I needed clothes and you clothed me, I was sick and you looked after me, I was in prison and you came to visit me'. (Matthew 25:35–36)

Virtue ethics

Virtue ethics is an ethical theory that focuses on the person doing the action rather than the act itself. It argues that a 'right act' is the action a virtuous person (someone with high moral standards) would take.

In matters of social justice, virtue ethics views helping others as the right thing to do, because it gives those helping the opportunity to develop positive characteristics such as being generous. Also, sharing wealth is how a virtuous person should act towards others.

Now try this

1 Outline **three** causes of poverty in the UK.   **(3 marks)**

2 Explain **two** reasons why Christians think wealth should be used to help others. **(4 marks)**

The Six Beliefs of Islam

There are many schools of Islam. These schools agree on most beliefs and practices within the Islamic faith, although there are differences. One of the main schools is Sunni. The **Six Beliefs of Islam** are accepted by **Sunni Muslims**. **Shi'a Muslims** accept many of the ideas of the Six Beliefs but refer to them differently – some are part of the Five Roots of 'Usul ad-Din.

For more on 'Usul ad-Din', see page 69.

 1 Tawhid – the belief in the oneness of Allah

Islam is monotheistic, meaning Muslims accept there is only one God (Allah).

 2 Malaikah – the belief in angels

Muslims accept the existence of angels who are obedient to Allah's commands. It is through them that messages are given to prophets.

 The Six Beliefs of Islam

 6 Akhirah – teachings about life after death

Muslims believe that there is an afterlife after death. They accept a Day of Judgement when every human will be judged by Allah on their actions on Earth.
For more on 'Akhirah', see page 75

3 Authority of kutub (holy books)

The main holy book for Muslims is the Qur'an, but they also recognise Sahifah (the scrolls of Abraham and the scrolls of Moses), the Tawrat (Torah), Zabur (Psalms) and Injil (the Gospel).

 5 Belief in al-Qadr

Muslims believe that Allah knows everything and, although humans have freewill, Allah knows what will happen.
For more on 'al-Qadr', see page 74

 4 Nubuwwah (prophethood) – following the prophets of Allah

Muslims recognise prophets or messengers of Allah. These include: Adam; Ibrahim (Abraham); Isma'il; Musa (Moses); Dawud (David); Isa (Jesus); and Muhammad. The nature and importance of prophethood for Muslims is called Risalah.

Purpose and importance of the Six Beliefs of Islam

- ✓ To unite all Sunni Muslims.
- ✓ To help Sunni Muslims understand their religion better.
- ✓ To support Sunni Muslims in how they should live their lives.
- ✓ To support what beliefs they should have.

The Six Beliefs of Islam are contained in the Kitab al-Iman or 'Book of Faith'. They are important for Sunni Muslims as they are the fundamental beliefs of the faith that they hold to be true.

How the Six Beliefs of Islam are expressed today

Muslims will recite the belief in the oneness of **Allah** in their prayers each day. They will also look to the Qur'an for advice to help them understand their faith better and follow Allah. They will live their lives always aware of Allah and the fact that Islam teaches that he will **judge** them on their actions after death. This will make them more aware of their behaviour.

Person praying in a mosque

Remember that this question asks you to state **three** different ways. Try to write three sentences with a different idea in each one.

Now try this

Outline **three** ways in which Sunni Muslims will express the Six Beliefs of Islam in their lives today. **(3 marks)**

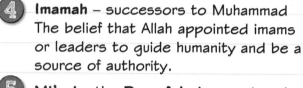
The five roots of 'Usul ad-Din in Shi'a Islam

Another major branch of Islam is **Shi'a**. Shi'a Muslims believe in the Six Beliefs of Islam, but also accept the **Five Roots of 'Usul ad-Din** based on the Qur'an.

The Five Roots of 'Usul ad-Din (foundations of faith)

1 **Tawhid** – the oneness of Allah
The idea of one God called Allah.

2 **Adl** – divine justice
Allah is understood to be fair and just in the way he treats everything.

3 **Nubuwwah** – **prophethood**
The belief that Allah appointed prophets or messengers to pass his message on to humanity.

4 **Imamah** – successors to Muhammad
The belief that Allah appointed imams or leaders to guide humanity and be a source of authority.

5 **Mi'ad** – the **Day of Judgement** and the **Resurrection**
The belief that all humans will be judged by Allah on their actions after death.

Most Shi'a believe there were 12 imams after the death of Muhammad, known as **Twelvers**. Some believe there were seven, known as **Seveners**.

Worked example

Explain **two** reasons why the Five Roots of 'Usul ad-Din are important in Shi'a Islam. **(4 marks)**

They are important to Shi'a Muslims because they unite them as Muslims. They are the key beliefs all Muslims hold to be true. For example, all Shi'a Muslims believe in Allah as the only God – Tawhid.

A second reason is that by holding these beliefs, Shi'a Muslims can understand their faith better. They help to identify the beliefs such as Mi'ad or the Day of Judgement.

This student has stated two different reasons and developed them. Your answer could also explain how the teachings come from the Qur'an 'Allah, is One' Surah 112 and that they are beliefs Muslims must hold if their practices and teachings are to be correct.

Now try this

'Tawhid is the most important Muslim belief.' Evaluate this statement considering arguments for and against. In your response you should:
- refer to Muslim teachings
- reach a justified conclusion. **(15 marks)**

You must make sure you refer to teachings within Islam, as well as explain why other beliefs may be just as important. Remember that there are also 3 extra SPaG marks available on this question.

The basis of the Five Roots of 'Usul ad-Din

Say: He is Allah, [who is] One, Allah, the Eternal Refuge. He neither begets nor is born, Nor is there to Him any equivalent (Surah 112:1–4)

The Five Roots are all based around the central idea – Tawhid, the oneness of Allah. This is explained in the Qur'an.

The nature of Allah

Islam is a **monotheistic religion**, which means Muslims believe in one God, Allah. Beliefs about what he is like are described in many places including the Muslim holy book, the Qur'an.

The eight characteristics of Allah shown in the Qur'an

 Immanence
The idea that Allah is close and involved within the world.

 Transcendence
The idea that Allah is above and beyond human understanding. It can be difficult for Muslims to fully understand Allah.

 Tawhid
The Islamic word used to describe the idea that Muslims only accept one God. This is the most fundamental belief of the religion of Islam as all other principles relate to it.

And We certainly sent into every nation a messenger, [saying], 'Worship Allah and avoid Taghut.' (Surah 16:36)

 Omnipotence
The idea that Allah is more powerful than anything in existence. He is seen to have created the world and is in control of everything.

 Beneficence
The idea that Allah is caring and loves his creation.

 Adalat
Allah is equitable and just. He created the world in a fair way and will judge humans in this way too.

Fairness and justice
The idea that Allah is fair and just and will judge humans after death in this way. Muslims believe Allah judges people in a fair and unbiased way.

Mercy
The idea that Allah forgives people for the wrong things they do.

This is only in Shi'a Islam.

Muslims believe Allah is the designer and creator of the world. He is given 99 names to help Muslims understand what he is like because they believe he is transcendent (above human experience). These include names such as Al-Rahman (the Compassionate) and Al-Hakam (the Judge).

The most beautiful names belong to Allah: so call on him by them. (Surah 7:180)

Importance of the characteristics

Muslims believe that by knowing what Allah is like they can:

✓ understand him better

✓ follow the way he wants them to live their lives

✓ strengthen their relationship with Allah

✓ encourage Muslims to strive to be better as this is what they believe Allah wants.

Now try this

You need to give **two different** ways and explain each one fully.

1 Explain **two** ways in which Allah is described by Muslims.   **(4 marks)**

2 Explain **two** reasons why the characteristics of Allah are important for Muslims. In your answer you must refer to a source of wisdom or authority.   **(5 marks)**

This style of question requires you to mention a quote from a source of authority (for example the Qur'an) to explain the point you have presented.

Risalah

Risalah is the Islamic word for prophethood or **messengers** of Allah. These messengers are the channel of communication that links Allah to humanity.

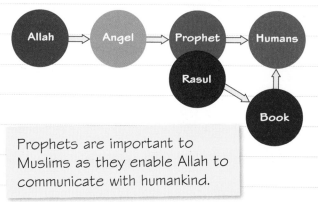

Prophets are important to Muslims as they enable Allah to communicate with humankind.

Prophets

Islam teaches that there have been many **prophets** who have acted as messengers of Allah, such as Isma'il, Muhammad and Adam. It is thought there have been as many as 124,000 but only 25 are named in the Qur'an. Prophets whose message has been written down are called **rasuls**.

Rasuls	Where their message has been written
Ibrahim	Sahifah
Musa	Tawrat
Dawud	Zabur
Isa	Injil

Adam

He was the first prophet (and human) to be created. His task was to look after the world (to be a **khalifah**), which teaches Muslims today that they, too, should look after and care for Allah's creation.

Muhammad

Muhammad is called by Muslims 'the Seal of the Prophets' as he was the last prophet and received the final message from Allah – the Qur'an. Muslims are taught from a young age that they should follow the example set by Muhammad. He is very important as Muslims believe he brought the final and perfect message in the form of the Qur'an.

Ibrahim

Ibrahim is mentioned many times in the Qur'an. It is believed that he tried to encourage the worship of Allah. The story of Ibrahim having his faith tested by Allah by being willing to sacrifice his son teaches Muslims to submit to Allah in their lives.

Prophets in the Qur'an

Isma'il

Isma'il is the son of Ibrahim and was associated with the construction of the Ka'bah in Makkah. He is praised for characteristics such as patience and kindness, showing Muslims that they too should develop these sorts of characteristics.

Musa

The Qur'an states that Musa was sent by Allah to the Pharaoh of Egypt and the Israelites for guidance and warning. His presence is also seen to confirm the message and authority of the prophets before him.

Isa

Isa is more often associated with Christianity (Jesus), but is recognised in Islam as the messenger of Allah and who received the Injil (Gospel). Muslims do not accept his resurrection or that he was the Son of God.

Dawud

Dawud is recognised by Muslims as being a lawgiver of Allah and the King of Israel, as well as a prophet. He is best known for defeating Goliath.

Say (O Muslims): 'We believe in Allah and that which is revealed unto us and that which was revealed unto Abraham, and Ismael, and Isaac and Jacob, and the tribes and that which Moses and Jesus received and that which the Prophets received from their Lord.' (Surah 2:136)

Now try this

1 Outline **three** beliefs about the role of prophets in Islam. **(3 marks)**
2 'Risalah is the most important belief in Islam.'
   Evaluate this statement considering arguments for and against.
   In your response you should:
   • refer to Muslim teachings
   • reach a justified conclusion. **(15 marks)**

Make sure you consider the statement carefully. You need to think about how important prophets are in Islam, and also consider other beliefs which may be equally or even more important.

Muslim holy books

Muslims accept five holy books (**kutub**), although the **Qur'an** is given the most importance. Muslims are commanded in the Qur'an to believe in the books also revealed to Christians and Jews, which is why Muslims are often called 'People of the Book'.

The Qur'an

The most important holy book for Muslims is the Qur'an, which was revealed to Muhammad by Allah.

1 Muslims believe that the Qur'an was revealed to Muhammad over a period of 23 years.

2 The Qur'an is written in **Arabic**.

3 The word 'Qur'an' means 'recitation' because when it was revealed to Muhammad it was spoken, as Muhammad was illiterate.

4 The Qur'an is divided into Surah (chapters) and Ayats (verses).

5 Muslims believe the holy Qur'an came from Allah.

6 Muslims use the Qur'an in prayer and to help them when they need guidance in their lives.

It is not but a revelation revealed, Taught to him by one intense in strength. (Surah 53:4–5)

---

1 The Qur'an mentions other holy books. Muslims believe these were also revealed by Allah, but that their meaning changed or became corrupted over time.

5 **Tawrat (Torah)**
Muslims believe this holy book was given by Allah to Musa (Moses). Tawrat means 'instruction' and Muslims recognise there are important laws contained within it.

We sent down the Torah, in which was guidance and light. (Surah 5:44)

4 **Zabur (Psalms)**
The holy book of Dawud (David), which some Muslims today believe is still relevant.

Kutub

2 **Sahifah (Scrolls)**
An early scripture believed to have been revealed to Ibrahim and used by his sons Ishma'il and Ishac. The scrolls are believed to be lost, having perished over time.

... and to David We gave the book [of Psalms]. (Surah 4:163)

3 **Injil (Gospel)**
The Gospel of Isa (Jesus), believed to have been revealed by Allah, contained in the books Matthew, Mark, Luke and John.

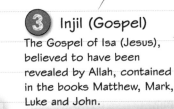

We sent, following in their footsteps, Jesus, the son of Mary...; and We gave him the Gospel....

Or has he not been informed of what was in the scriptures of Moses. (Surah 53:36)

Now try this

1 Outline **three** reasons why the Qur'an is important in Islam. **(3 marks)**

2 Explain **two** reasons why Muslims recognise a number of holy books as sources of authority in Islam. **(4 marks)**

Make sure you explain each reason fully before you move on to the next. Try to give examples where possible.

Malaikah

Malaikah are beings that are believed to be **angels** or messengers of Allah.

There can be no images of Allah or Muhammad in Islam.

Muslims believe angels act as messengers between Allah and humans. They are not thought to have **free will** or physical bodies, but can take on human shape when needed. Belief in angels is contained in the Six Beliefs of Islam for Sunni Muslims.

Importance of the angels

Angel	Why are the angels important?	What do they teach Muslims today?
Jibril, or Gabriel as he is known in Christianity and Judaism, is an important angel as it was through him that Allah revealed the Qur'an to Muhammad over 23 years. It is believed that Jibril also taught Muhammad how to pray. ... then We sent her our angel, and he appeared before her as a man in all respects. (Surah 19 (Maryam):17)	Without Jibril the message of the Qur'an would not have been received.	To live around the teachings of the holy book, often reading it every day to understand how they should live their lives.
Izra'il is the Angel of Death and is responsible for signalling the coming of the Day of Judgement (when all Muslims will be judged by Allah) by blowing a trumpet. It is believed that he will return human souls to Allah. The angel of death will take you who has been entrusted with you. Then to your Lord you will be returned. (Surah 32:11)	Izra'il is important in helping Muslims to understand that they need to live their lives how Allah wants them to, following his rules, so that they may be rewarded and not punished in the afterlife.	To live their lives in the knowledge that they will one day be judged by Allah on their actions on Earth.
Mika'il is often understood to be the Angel of Mercy or Sustenance, given the role of rewarding those who have led good lives. He is believed to bring rain and thunder to Earth. Whoever is an enemy to Gabriel – for he brings down the (revelation) to thy heart by Allah's will, a confirmation of what went before, and guidance and glad tidings for those who believe, – Whoever is an enemy to Allah and His angels and messengers, to Gabriel and Michael, – Lo! Allah is an enemy to those who reject Faith. (Surah 2:97–98)	Muslims wish to be rewarded in the afterlife and not punished so the teaching of Mika'il reassures them that it is possible.	Reassurance that it is possible to be rewarded in the afterlife.

Make sure you link one of your reasons to a source of wisdom and authority. For example, give a quote from the Qur'an that links to the point you have made.

Now try this

1　Outline **three** beliefs about angels in Islam. **(3 marks)**

2　Explain **two** reasons why angels are important in Islam. In your answer you must refer to a source of wisdom or authority. **(5 marks)**

Al-Qadr

Muslims believe in **al-Qadr** or **predestination**. This is the concept of fate or destiny – the idea that Allah is able to know and control everything that happens. Sunni Muslims recognise this as one of the Six Beliefs, although Shi'a Muslims do not fully accept al-Qadr.

Day of Judgement

Muslims believe that on the Day of Judgement Allah will judge them on how they lived their life and behaved. There is a direct link between al-Qadr and the Day of Judgement as Muslims believe that once this day comes, it is too late to beg forgiveness for wrongdoing. Al-Qadr teaches Muslims that everything is the will of Allah and, although Muslims may not understand it, the important thing is how they react to it. Reacting the right way will mean a reward on the Day of Judgement. Sahih al-Bukhari 78:685 describes how people are responsible for their own sins, as they have decided what action to take and will be judged on this.

Implications of al-Qadr

1. Muslims will want to live their lives according to the beliefs of the Day of Judgement and al-Qadr to ensure they gain reward in the afterlife

2. they will constantly be aware of their thoughts, beliefs and actions in order to ensure they behave how Allah wants them to – they will try to follow the duties given to them by Allah (e.g. the Five Pillars)

3. they will try to help others, as they believe this is what the Qur'an and Muhammad teaches them.

Worked example

This answer offers reasons that both agree and disagree with the statement. The student also correctly gives an overall conclusion to bring their argument to a close.

'Predestination is not important to Muslims.'
Evaluate this statement considering arguments for and against.
In your response you should: • refer to Muslim teachings • reach a justified conclusion. **(15 marks)**

Some Muslims, especially Sunni Muslims, would disagree with this statement as predestination, or al-Qadr, is important to them. They believe that Allah controls and knows everything, which affects their beliefs about the afterlife for Muslims. Allah is believed to judge them after death on their actions in life. However, Sunni Muslims also accept the idea that Allah gave humans free will, therefore they are free to make their own decisions. This does not detract from the importance of predestination as Sunni Muslims believe that these ideas are not in conflict, but that Allah knows when a human will use their free will to turn away from him. Predestination is shown as being important to Sunni Muslims as it is contained in the Six Beliefs of Islam.

Another reason why Sunni Muslims might disagree is because the concept of predestination demonstrates the power that Allah is seen to have in being able to control and decide what happens in the world. He is able to know everything that a person will choose to do.

In contrast, Shi'a Muslims would agree with the statement as they do not fully accept the idea of predestination. It is further supported by their acceptance of the idea of Bada', which suggests Allah has not predetermined a set course for each Muslim and they are free to make their own choices and decisions.

In conclusion, I would argue that the strongest side of the argument is put forward by the Sunni Muslims. Their recognition of predestination as one of their key beliefs and application to their lives demonstrates it is important. They are also the larger group of Muslims in the world, showing that more would probably disagree with the statement than support it.

Now try this

Explain **two** ways in which the belief of al-Qadr impacts on Muslims today. **(4 marks)**

Akhirah

Muslims believe in **akhirah** (life after death). It is considered to be one of the most important beliefs in Islam and will affect the way a Muslim lives their life.

Muslim beliefs about akhirah

After death, the angel of death will take a person's soul to barzakh (the stage between when a person dies and when they face judgement). → Allah will judge each individual on the way they lived their life. → On the Day of Judgement the body will be resurrected. → Two angels will open the book that contains the record of what a person has done in their lifetime. → If their name is recorded on the right-hand side of the book, they will be sent to al-Jannah (paradise).

If their name is recorded on the left-hand side of the book, they will be sent to Jahannam (hell).

[Mention, O Muhammad], the Day We will call forth every people with their record [of deeds]. Then whoever is given his record in his right hand – those will read their records, and injustice will not be done to them, [even] as much as a thread [inside the date seed]. (Surah 17:71)

Paradise in the Qur'an

Hell in the Qur'an

This Qur'anic quote describes **Jahannam** or hell as a place where unbelievers are punished and face dreadful torments such as fires of hell.

And fear the Fire which has been prepared for the disbelievers. (Surah 3:131)

The Qur'an describes **al-Jannah** (paradise) as a reward for believers. It is described as a garden full of flowers and birds.

Divergent ways that life after death affects Muslims today

1 Makes them more aware that Allah is always watching.

2 Makes them realise the importance of asking for forgiveness.

3 They view every action they perform as a way of worshipping Allah.

4 They try to live life as good Muslims: read the Qur'an; perform the Five Pillars; go to the mosque; help others, etc.

For more about the Five Pillars, see pages 85–89.

Similarities and differences between Christianity and Islam about life after death

Similarities	Differences
• Life is a test • Places of eternal reward and eternal punishment • Resurrection	• Christians accept sacrifice of Jesus to atone for sins of the world – Muslims believe only sinner can ask for forgiveness • Purgatory in Christian Catholicism is not the same as barzakh in Islam • Christians don't have angels recording deeds of a person like Muslims do

Now try this

Outline **three** beliefs about life after death for Muslims.   **(3 marks)**

75

Marriage

Marriage is very important in Islam. It is believed to bring stability to society.

Purpose of marriage

1 To bring a man and woman together to have children.

2 To share love, companionship and sex, which is Allah's intention for humans.

3 To create a family and strengthen society.

> Marry those among you who are single. (Surah 24:32)

> Muslims believe that marriage is important so they can have children and pass on the Islamic faith to them.

Muslim beliefs about marriage

1 Marriage in Islam is intended to be for life.

2 Many Muslims will help their children to find the right partner – **arranged marriages**.

3 Muslim women are expected to marry within the Islamic faith so children will be raised as Muslim.

4 Muslim men can marry, for example, a Christian, as children will follow the faith of the father.

5 Marriage is seen as a legal contract.

6 Muslim men may have up to four wives but Muslim women can only have one husband.

7 Islam encourages people to marry, following the example of Muhammad.

8 Allah is believed to have created man and woman for each other.

Worked example

Explain **two** reasons why marriage is important to Muslims.   **(4 marks)**

One reason why marriage is important to Muslims is because it is seen as the joining of a couple who want to make a commitment to each other. The Qur'an instructs those who are single that it is their duty to marry.

A second reason why marriage is important is because Muslims believe marriage and the family provide stability for children and society. It is believed to provide a secure basis for children to be raised, as they can be taught about Islam, raised within the Islamic faith and be shown how to be good citizens in society.

> This answer gives two good reasons and developed explanations.

Cohabitation

Cohabitation is where a couple live together without being married. Muslims do not believe this is acceptable and would not cohabit. Muslims have very traditional views about members of the opposite sex meeting up prior to marriage and, generally, the woman would be **chaperoned** by a member of her family.

Non-religious attitudes to marriage

> Being an **atheist**, I would have a **secular** marriage ceremony – I still believe that marriage is the best environment to raise children. I would happily cohabit though, too.

> Being a **humanist**, I too would have a secular marriage ceremony to show my commitment to my partner. I also would happily cohabit.

> **Muslim response:** As a Muslim, I recognise society is changing but I still value marriage in the traditional Islamic sense.

Now try this

Outline **three** beliefs about the purpose of marriage in Islam.   **(3 marks)**

Sexual relationships

Attitudes towards different types of sexual relationships have changed as society has changed. Muslims have teachings about sexual relationships outside of marriage and homosexuality.

Sexual relationships and marriage

Muslims believe that sexual relationships should only take place within the correct context of marriage. They believe that sex is an important part of a married relationship as it is a bond between the couple and is the opportunity to start a family.

> When a husband and wife share intimacy it is rewarded, and a blessing from Allah; just as they would be punished if they had engaged in illicit sex. (Hadith)
>
> Nor come nigh to adultery: for it is a shameful (deed) and an evil, opening the road (to other evils). (Surah 17:32)

Islamic teachings

Muslims teach that:

1. sex is an act of worship – Muslims believe it has the purpose of **procreation**, which is what Allah intended, and they will be rewarded for it

2. sex fulfils physical, emotional and spiritual needs

3. sex is a gift from Allah intended so that a couple can procreate

4. sex should only take place within marriage and both partners have a duty to fulfil each other's sexual needs

5. **adultery** is not acceptable – there are strict rules for married men and women, and there are strict punishments for adulterers

6. homosexuality is forbidden in Islam and in some countries it is punishable by death – sex is intended for a husband and wife.

Worked example

Explain **two** reasons why Muslims believe sexual relationships fulfil physical, emotional and spiritual needs.   **(4 marks)**

One reason why Muslims believe sexual relationships fulfil physical, emotional and spiritual needs is that Muslims believe sex is natural and a marriage is the correct context for a sexual relationship to take place. It is important for a couple to satisfy each other's needs and sex is seen to allow this.

A second reason is that sex is seen in Islam as an act of worship. Muslims believe it is what Allah intended for them to do and they will be rewarded in the afterlife, therefore fulfilling their spiritual needs.

This answer has provided two different reasons, both of which are developed and explained.

Sex before marriage, homosexuality and adultery

The Muslim response to these issues is generally different from that of humanists and atheists.

Belief	Sex before marriage	Homosexuality	Adultery
Humanists	✓	✓	✗
Atheists	✓	✓	✗
Muslims	✗	✗	✗

Now try this

'Sex is a gift from Allah.'

Evaluate this statement considering arguments for and against. In your response you should:

- refer to Muslim teachings
- refer to non-religious points of view
- reach a justified conclusion.

Make sure you include both Muslim teachings and contrasting non-religious views about this statement.

(12 marks)

Families

The family is very important in Islam. Muslims believe it is the creation of Allah and provides security and stability within society.

Muslim teachings about family

The mother and father have a **responsibility** to raise their children as Muslims.

The family is the **foundation** of the Muslim community.

The family is where many religious activities take place, e.g. prayer and festivals.

Muslims believe it is important to marry and have a sexual relationship so they can procreate.

Muslim families

Children are taught to show love, kindness, mercy and compassion to one another in the family.

Family life is the first level of community in Islam.

The family provides a healthy and loving environment for children.

The worldwide Muslim family is the ummah that all Muslims are part of.

Teachings in the Qur'an

The Qur'an contains teachings about the purpose of family:

And We have enjoined upon man, to his parents, good treatment. His mother carried him with hardship and gave birth to him with hardship, and his gestation and weaning [period] is thirty months. [He grows] until, when he reaches maturity. (Surah 46:15)

Quotes such as these demonstrate the importance of family encouraging each person to respect their parents and treat them well, remembering all the sacrifices they have made.

Outline **three** purposes of family in Islam.   **(3 marks)**

One purpose is for Muslim parents to raise their children as Muslims. A second purpose is that the family gives stability to society. A third purpose is that the Muslim community – the ummah – is strengthened.

The student has correctly identified and listed three purposes of the family in Islam.

Different types of family

There are different types of family in society:

1. Nuclear – two parents (man and woman) with children.

2. Single parent – one parent and children.

3. Same-sex parents – two parents of the same sex and children.

4. Extended – parents, children, grandparents, aunts, uncles, cousins, etc.

5. Blended – stepfamilies who have joined together through remarriage.

Divergent Muslim responses to different types of family

Traditional Muslim families are often extended, enabling them to care for both young and old. However, today some Muslims live in nuclear families because:

- issues such as **migration** make it impossible to keep everyone together
- Muslims in Western countries become used to the nuclear family as normal.

Many Muslims recognise other types of family, but prefer more traditional family structures.

'Family is not important today.'
Evaluate this statement considering arguments for and against. In your response you should:

- refer to Muslim teachings
- reach a justified conclusion.

    (12 marks)

The family in the ummah

Muslims believe that family has such an important role that, when conflict arises, they believe it is their duty to do all they can to help. The **ummah** is the worldwide family of Muslims showing the unity there is between all Muslims.

Support for families

② Rites of passage
Muslims will celebrate events such as Bismillah, weddings and funerals as a family together with Muslims from their local community.

③ Classes for parents
Parenting classes provide an opportunity for parents to prepare before the birth of a child or share their issues while raising children. They can gain help, advice and support.

① Worship
Muslim families will attend prayer at the mosque together as a family or they will pray together at home.

How the ummah supports family life

④ Groups for children
The local Muslim community runs the **madrassah** – mosque school. Children attend to learn more about the faith, as well as their role within their family.

⑥ Supporting each other

> And hold fast, all of you together, to the cable of Allah, and do not separate. (Surah 3:103)

⑤ Counselling
Muslims will provide support such as counselling if families are struggling. They will also turn to their extended families for support, as often the parents of a couple were involved in the arranging of the marriage.

This demonstrates the importance of supporting each other through the ummah as it is seen to strengthen it.

Muslims believe that family is important as it is where good Muslim children can be raised or support can be given when they may face personal problems. Family is what Allah intended, so providing support is the community's way of following this.

Divergent understandings of the ummah

Most Muslims believe that the support offered by the ummah to the family unit is of vital importance. It helps them to unite and brings them together, strengthening their bond within the ummah. Some Muslims, however, may feel that in today's world this support can also be gained in other ways, including through social systems in place in society. They may feel that in the Western world this support must be balanced with the idea of 'fitting into society'. Some Muslims may also feel that they do not need support from the ummah as their individual family unit or local community is sufficient.

Now try this

Make sure you give two different reasons. Each one needs to be developed by using examples.

1 Outline **three** ways the Muslim community tries to support family. **(3 marks)**
2 Explain **two** reasons why it is important for the Muslim community to support families. **(4 marks)**

Contraception

Contraception is the intentional prevention of pregnancy. There are many different types of contraception and different Muslims hold differing views about whether or not they are acceptable.

Guidance from the Hadith Sahih al-Bukhari

Sahih al-Bukhari is a collection of books (**Hadith**) compiled by Imam Muhammad al-Bukhari and gives some guidance on contraception.

> 'What is your opinion about coitus interruptus?' The Prophet said, 'Do you really do that? It is better for you not to do it. No soul that which Allah has destined to exist, but will surely come into existence. (Sahih al-Bukhari 34:432)

> We used to practice coitus interruptus during the lifetime of Allah's Apostle while the Quran was being Revealed. (Sahih al-Bukhari 62:136)

Muslims may hold different views about the use of contraception as there is no single approach to this issue. The first quote suggests Prophet Muhammad did not support the use of natural forms of contraception such as the withdrawal method. The second quote, however, appears to contradict this, saying that it was a common practice during the time of Muhammad. Many Muslims believe that in matters such as contraception, if Allah wills for a new life to be created, it should be his decision.

Differing opinions on contraception

Some Muslim authorities may accept the use of contraception to:

- preserve the life of the mother if her life would be under threat through having another pregnancy
- protect the well-being of the current family unit if having another child would put too much strain on the family in terms of money or support
- plan when to have their family using non-permanent methods because this still allows for procreation in the future.

Some may not accept contraception because:

- only natural methods are allowed – this is what many Muslims feel sources of authority promote
- there is no possibility of procreation, which is the purpose of a sexual relationship, if permanent methods are used
- some methods could be considered an early abortion and, therefore, infanticide
- having children is what Allah intended for humans and using contraception prevents this.

Muslim response to non-religious views

Why couples might use contraception in non-religious communities	The Muslim response
They can plan when to have a family	Some agree this is OK, others do not
Pregnancy could be harmful to the mother	OK if to preserve the life of the mother
Lifestyle not compatible with having children	OK if having another child would put a strain on the current family unit
Safe from sexual transmitted infections (STIs)	Shouldn't be an issue as Muslims do not believe in sex outside of marriage
Avoid genetic disorders being passed on	Most agree that it is OK in this case

Make sure you read the question carefully to ensure you present the correct arguments for what the question is asking. State each reason and then develop it by using examples or quotes to support the reason you have given.

Now try this

Explain **two** reasons why Muslims will accept the use of contraception.   **(4 marks)**

Divorce

Divorce is the legal termination of a marriage and it has become more acceptable in today's society. In Islam, divorce is allowed but should only be a last resort because marriage is a contract.

Muslim teachings on divorce

Islam teaches that divorce should be a last resort. First, the husband will announce his intention to divorce his wife (which may be stated up to three times).

→

Then there is a three-month waiting period (**iddah**), where the couple live together but do not have sex.

↓

The couple must wait to ensure the woman is not pregnant.

←

Muslims hope it is possible to reconcile and Allah will forgive them.

↓

After four months, the couple can divorce if they wish.

Some Sunni Muslims believe the iddah needs to take place after each declaration of the intention of divorce.

Those who take an oath not to have sexual relations with their wives must wait four months:

... if they return (change their idea in this period), verily, Allah is Oft-Forgiving, Most Merciful. (Surah 2:226)

... it is not lawful for them to conceal what Allah has created in their wombs (Surah 2:228)

And if they decide on divorce – then indeed, Allah is Hearing and Knowing. (Surah 2:227)

Sunni Muslims do not require witnesses to the husband declaring his intention for divorce, whereas Shi'a Muslims do.

Muslim beliefs and attitudes

Although divorce is allowed by Allah, Muslims believe it is detestable – it is hated by Allah as it is disrespectful to him and the gift of marriage. Although Islam does not encourage divorce, it is recognised as being available as guidelines are given in sources of authority. Most Muslims would maintain that marriage is intended to be for life and is a contract, but if the marriage has broken down and reconciliation is not possible, then divorce may be the only answer. When a couple experience problems in their marriage they are expected to attempt to reconcile. The extended family, as well as the local community, may be involved in trying to resolve their issues.

Marriage is a contract in Islam so can be dissolved

The Qur'an allows divorce and gives guidelines

May be better for children to avoid anger and bitterness

Shari'ah law permits divorce

⟷ Accept divorce as a last resort   No divorce under any circumstances

Muhammad didn't divorce and Muslims want to follow his example

Damages family unit and stability of society

Marriage contract (nikah) should not be broken

Although a Muslim woman may, perhaps, have more reasons to seek a divorce – including desertion, cruelty and a lack of maintenance – it is far easier for Muslim men to obtain divorces. If a woman wishes to divorce, she usually needs the consent of her husband.

Use any relevant quotes from Muslim teachings, such as the Qur'an or Hadith to support the points you make.

Now try this

Explain **two** reasons why some Muslims may dislike divorce. In your answer you must refer to a source of wisdom and authority.

(5 marks)

Men and women in the family

Muslims believe that Allah created all humans as equal but not the same. Therefore, men and women are identified as having different roles and responsibilities within the family.

The role of men and women in the family

Women are expected to help raise children as good Muslims

Women are free to work and have a career, if they wish

Women are required to have children

Women are expected to look after the home

Men are seen to be the 'protectors of women'

Men provide for their family, helping to raise children as good Muslims

Abu Huraira narrated The Prophet (saw) said, 'The righteous among the women of Quraish are those who are kind to their young ones and who look after their husband's property.' (Sahih al-Bukhari 64:278)

Divergent Muslim beliefs

O mankind! Be careful of your duty to your Lord Who created you from a single soul and from it created its mate and from them twain hath spread abroad a multitude of men and women. (Surah 4:1)

All people are equal … as the teeth of a comb. (Hadith)

These quotes from Islamic sources of authority seem to suggest ideas of equality between the roles of men and women. The first quote suggests men and women were created equally from one soul, while the second suggests they were created to be together and support each other, meaning their roles complement each other.

Men are in charge of women by [right of] what Allah has given one over the other and what they spend [for maintenance] from their wealth. So righteous women are devoutly obedient … But those [wives] from whom you fear arrogance – [first] advise them; [then if they persist], forsake them in bed; and [finally], strike them. But if they obey you [once more], seek no means against them. Indeed, Allah is ever Exalted and Grand. (Surah 4:34)

The Qur'an, however, also contains quotes that suggest inequality. This gives the impression that men have power over women within the family and women have a role of obedience towards their husband within the family.

In the time of Muhammad

Muhammad witnessed many examples of poor treatment of women. He brought about improvement in the conditions for women:

👍 the ability for women to own property

👍 the right for women to be able to divorce their husbands

👍 improvements in the provision of education for women.

These changes, which are attributed to the vision of Muhammad in seeing more equality between the genders, helped to shape the future of Islam.

Now try this

1 Explain **two** ways in which the roles of men and women are understood in Islam. **(4 marks)**

2 'Men and women should be treated the same.'
Evaluate this statement considering arguments for and against. In your response you should:
• refer to Muslim teachings
• reach a justified conclusion. **(12 marks)**

Gender prejudice and discrimination

Many people believe men and women should be treated equally, although this is not always practised. When a person is treated unfairly and unequally, it is known as **discrimination**.

Prejudice and discrimination

Gender prejudice (or **sexism**) is when a person is judged on their gender to be superior or inferior. It is an opinion or judgement being made, not an action.

Gender discrimination is when a person is treated differently from another as a direct result of their gender. It is an action rather than just an opinion.

Muslim attitudes

Muslims believe gender prejudice and discrimination are wrong because:

1. Islam teaches everyone was created by Allah and is therefore equal

2. Muslims believe men and women will be treated equally and judged in the same way by Allah after death

3. men and women are both expected to marry and they have the same rights in terms of religion and education.

However, although Muslims hold the above beliefs and accept men and women are equal before Allah, they accept that men and women are physically and psychologically different and suited to different roles and responsibilities.

Teachings about gender prejudice and discrimination

For Muslim men and women – for believing men and women, for devout men and women, for true men and women, for men and women who are patient and constant, for men and women who humble themselves, for men and women who give in Charity, for men and women who fast (and deny themselves), for men and women who guard their chastity, and for men and women who engage much in Allah's praise – for them has Allah prepared forgiveness and great reward. (Surah 33:35)

This quote teaches Muslims that there should be equality between men and women in Islam. It supports the idea of gender prejudice and discrimination being wrong because regardless of who a person is – male or female – they will be judged equally by Allah and have the same opportunities and abilities to be rewarded.

Inspirational Muslims, such as Nadiya Hussain, who won 'The Great British Bake Off' competition, have raised the importance of gender equality in promoting that all people can achieve.

Malala Yousafzai stood up to the Taliban to achieve equality in education.

Sisters in Islam work to empower women with a voice to challenge mistreatment and gender discrimination through challenging laws that appear to make women inferior, including: polygamy; child marriage; dress in Islam; and violence against women.

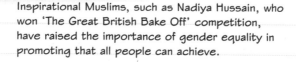
Gender equality in action

The Inclusive Mosque Initiative campaigns for more equality when praying in mosques.

Make sure you read each question carefully to understand what it requires. The trigger words in these questions ('Outline' or 'Explain') instruct you on what you are required to do.

Now try this

1 Outline **three** beliefs in Islam about gender prejudice and discrimination.   **(3 marks)**

2 Explain **two** ways in which Muslims respond to gender discrimination.   **(4 marks)**

The Ten Obligatory Acts of Shi'a Islam

The **Ten Obligatory Acts of Shi'a Islam** are important for Shi'a Muslims. Sunni Muslims believe in the **Five Pillars of Islam**. Four of the Five Pillars of Islam are also included in the Ten Obligatory Acts, so are important beliefs for all Muslims.

Nature and purpose of the Acts

The Ten Obligatory Acts are duties that all Shi'a Muslims must perform. Their purpose is to:

- ✓ guide them in how they should live their lives
- ✓ allow them to get closer to Allah in performing the actions he wants
- ✓ help them achieve the reward of paradise after death by following the rules of Allah
- ✓ help them continually focus actions in their lives towards Allah
- ✓ unite all Shi'a Muslims and give meaning to their lives.

History of the Acts

The Ten Obligatory Acts were given by the 'Twelvers', who Shi'a Muslims believe were chosen by Allah to lead after the death of Muhammad – they are also known as 'the Twelve Imams'.

⬇

After the death of Muhammad, Shi'a Muslims believe it was Ali Talib, Muhammad's cousin and son-in-law, who was the successor to Muhammad.

⬇

The Ten Obligatory Acts were established as the foundational practices in Islam for Shi'a Muslims.

The Ten Obligatory Acts

1. **Salah** – compulsory prayer five times a day. Shi'a Muslims combine some of the prayers and pray three times.

2. **Sawm** – fasting during daylight hours in the ninth Islamic month (Ramadan).

3. **Zakah** – donating 2.5 per cent of wealth to help the needy.

4. **Hajj** – pilgrimage to Makkah made by every Muslim once in their lifetime.

5. **Khums** – annual taxation was the historical obligation of Muslims in the army to pay one-fifth of the spoils of war. Today, this money is given to the descendants of Muhammad and Shi'a Muslims, but is also used to help the needy and Shi'a Islamic leaders.

6. **Jihad** – striving to overcome evil, e.g. defending an individual, holy war and personal struggles to resist daily temptations.

7. **Amr-bil-Maroof** – commandment from the Qur'an that instructs Shi'a Muslims on how they should act and behave.

8. **Nahi Anil Munkar** – forbidding what is evil – the need to resist temptation and not sin against Allah.

9. **Tawalla** – expressing love towards what is good, following the examples of the prophets.

10. **Tabarra** – moving away from evil, such as staying away from those who choose to turn away from Allah.

You can find out about the Five Pillars of Islam on pages 85–89.

The Qur'an and the Acts

The believing men and believing women are allies of one another. They enjoin what is right and forbid what is wrong and establish prayer and give zakah and obey Allah and His Messenger. Those – Allah will have mercy upon them. Indeed, Allah is Exalted in Might and Wise. (Surah 9:71)

Now try this

Explain **two** reasons why the Ten Obligatory Acts are important to Shi'a Muslims.

(4 marks)

The Shahadah

The **Shahadah** is the first Pillar of Islam – the statement of belief or declaration of faith that is accepted by all Muslims, both Sunni and Shi'a. It is believed to uphold all other beliefs of Islam and shows acceptance of both Allah and Muhammad.

There is no God but Allah and Muhammad is his Messenger.

The Shahadah contains the basic beliefs of Islam that every Muslim holds to be true – namely that they believe in Allah (God) and that Muhammad is the prophet of Allah. Muslims will recite this daily to remind them of the importance of these beliefs.

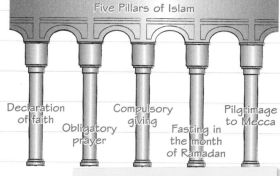

Five Pillars of Islam

Declaration of faith   Obligatory prayer   Compulsory giving   Fasting in the month of Ramadan   Pilgrimage to Mecca

A visual representation of the Five Pillars of Islam.

The Shahadah in the Qur'an

The patient, the true, the obedient, those who spend [in the way of Allah], and those who seek forgiveness before dawn. Allah witnesses that there is no deity except Him, and [so do] the angels and those of knowledge – [that He is] maintaining [creation] in justice. There is no deity except Him, the Exalted in Might, the Wise. (Surah 3:17–18)

The key belief in Allah of the Shahadah is mentioned in the Qur'an. This demonstrates its importance for Muslims and is considered to be at the centre of the Islamic faith.

Another point is that it recognises the importance of Muhammad in bringing the unaltered word to humanity from Allah.

Nature of the Shahadah

The Shahadah is the basic statement of Islamic faith and Muslims consider that anyone who cannot recite this is not a Muslim. Muslims believe it demonstrates their loyalty to Allah, the Prophet Muhammad and the religion of Islam.

Worked example

Explain **two** reasons why the Shahadah is important to Muslims. **(3 marks)**

The Shahadah is important to Muslims because it contains the basic beliefs central to Islam and being a Muslim, which are acceptance of the oneness of Allah and Muhammad being the messenger of Islam. Everything else in the religion is seen to centre around these key beliefs.

Shahadah is also important to Muslims because all other pillars and practices in Islam are based around the key concept of belief in Allah.

Role of the Shahadah today

Recited out loud in front of witnesses to profess the Muslim faith.

Whispered into the ears of newborn babies so it is the first thing they hear.

Shahadah

Said before death to demonstrate a commitment to the religion of Islam.

Recited throughout the day to remind Muslims of the basic beliefs of Islam. It forms part of Salah as it is contained in the **adhan**, call to prayer.

Now try this

'The Shahadah is the most important pillar for Muslims.'
Evaluate this statement considering arguments for and against. In your response you should:
• refer to Muslim teachings   • reach a justified conclusion.   **(12 marks)**

See pages 86–89 to find out about the other pillars.

Salah

Salah is the second of the Five Pillars of Islam and it is the compulsory prayer that takes place five times a day.

Nature, history and purpose of Salah

Nature	History	Purpose
Demonstrates unity	Prophets of Allah performed daily prayers and it was commanded by Muhammad	Brings Muslims closer to Allah

Dawn	Midday	Afternoon	Sunset	Night
Fajr	Dhuhr	Asr	Maghrib	Isha'a

Ablutions (wudu)

Before prayer, Muslims perform wudu, which is a ritual cleansing. This is done to ensure they are spiritually and physically clean for Allah. It also gives them time to be in the correct frame of mind to be able to pray to Allah.

The Qur'an and Salah

So exalt [Allah] with praise of your Lord and be of those who prostrate [to Him]. And worship your Lord until there comes to you the certainty (death). (Surah 15:98–99)

This quote highlights the importance of worshipping Allah and mentions the idea of prostrating, which is when a Muslim submits to Allah. This can be seen within Salah in the rakahs – prayer positions.

Recite, [O Muhammad], what has been revealed to you of the Book and establish prayer. Indeed, prayer prohibits immorality and wrongdoing, and the remembrance of Allah is greater. And Allah knows that which you do. (Surah 29:45)

Divergent understandings

Shi'a	Sunni
Combine five daily prayers into three	Five daily prayers
Raise hands three times at end of prayers	Move head from right to left
Touch foreheads directly to the floor when prostrating	May rest their head while prostrating on a piece of wood

Other differences are the wording of prayers and Sunni believe that anyone who doesn't pray five times a day is an unbeliever.

This quote demonstrates the importance of prayer as regular communication with Allah and the significant role it has in the life of every Muslim.

How prayer is performed

Muslim men are expected to attend the mosque to pray, women are not. Prayer can happen anywhere that is clean and if wudu has been performed. On a Friday, all Muslim men are expected to attend the **Jummah** service as part of Salah. Women may also attend.

bowing

standing   prostrating

When praying, Muslims face the direction of **Makkah** and recite verses and prayers. They follow a set pattern of movements.

Now try this

Outline **three** reasons why Muslims pray.

(3 marks)

Sawm

Sawm (fasting) is the fourth Pillar of Islam. The main period of fasting is during **Ramadan** – the ninth month of the Islamic calendar when all Muslims are required to not eat or drink during daylight hours, as well as avoid evil thoughts and deeds. There are other times when Muslims fast, but these times are not compulsory. There are also times when it is forbidden to fast.

Nature, role and purpose of Sawm

> : O ye who believe! Fasting is prescribed for you … (Surah 2:183)

Muslims believe the Qur'an was first revealed to Muhammad during the month of Ramadan, which gives Sawm importance. Fasting is an act of worship of Allah and has a long history. It is completed because it is a duty in Islam, but it also helps Muslims to develop discipline and understand the problems others may face.

Significance of Sawm

Sawm is important to Muslims because:

- ✓ It is one of the Five Pillars and is compulsory for most healthy adult Muslims – it shows a Muslim is obeying God
- ✓ It helps Muslims to learn self-discipline
- ✓ It helps Muslims to appreciate what Allah has provided, develop sympathy with the poor and realise the importance of charity
- ✓ It helps Muslims to remember the importance of the Qur'an, which was first revealed during Ramadan
- ✓ It brings the Muslim community (ummah) together and strengthens their unity.

What is forbidden in daylight hours during Sawm?

No food   No smoking   No sexual activity   No bad thoughts or deeds

Who is exempt from Sawm?

The elderly, young children, pregnant women, those travelling and Muslims who are physically or mentally unwell do not have to take part, as it could be considered harmful if they did.

> If a Muslim adult does not fast, they should carry out the fast at another time or make a donation to the poor.

Nature and history of Laylat al-Qadr

Sawm is performed to commemorate the moment when Muhammad received a religious experience while meditating in a cave on Mount Nur during Ramadan. The Angel Jibril appeared to him and revealed the Qur'an from Allah. This event is known as the Night of Power or Laylat al-Qadr.

Cave on Mount Nur

Purpose of Laylat al-Qadr

- To remember the gift of the Qur'an being given to humanity.
- To give Muslims the opportunity to ask for forgiveness for the things they have done wrong and worship Allah.
- To commemorate Muhammad receiving revelation from Allah.

> Worshipping Allah in that night is better than worshipping Him a thousand months. (Surah 97:3)

Muslims believe that they will be rewarded for marking this important occasion.

Now try this

Explain **two** reasons why some Muslims do not have to fast.   **(4 marks)**

Zakah and khums

Zakah is the third Pillar of Islam and involves the obligatory giving of money to charity.
Khums is a religious tax.

Zakah

Nature: Zakah is a type of worship or self-purification involving obligatory almsgiving.

Role: It involves giving 2.5 per cent of one's wealth each year to benefit the poor.

Significance: This duty is contained in the Qur'an and has a long history within Islam.

Purpose: Benefits of Zakah are to obey Allah, to show that everything a Muslim owns comes from Allah, and to support the idea of sharing and charitable actions.

Khums

Nature: In Shi'a Islam, khums is one of the Ten Obligatory Acts.

Role: Khums is paying 20 per cent of one's surplus income – half to the ummah and the to the poor.

Significance: This form of giving is mentioned in the Qur'an.

Purpose: Traditionally, the recipients of khums have been the descendants of Muhammad and those within the Shi'a Islamic faith.

The Qur'an and Zakah and khums

> Zakah expenditures are only for the poor and for the needy and for those employed to collect [zakah] and for bringing hearts together [for Islam] and for freeing captives [or slaves] and for those in debt and for the cause of Allah and for the [stranded] traveler – an obligation [imposed] by Allah. And Allah is Knowing and Wise. (Surah 9:60)

> And know that anything you obtain of war booty – then indeed, for Allah is one fifth of it and for the Messenger and for [his] near relatives and the orphans, the needy, and the [stranded] traveler, if you have believed in Allah and in that which We sent down to Our Servant on the day of criterion – the day when the two armies met. And Allah, over all things, is competent. (Surah 8:41)

This talks about the uses and purpose of Zakah in helping others. It recognises that it is commanded by Allah.

This demonstrates the use of khums and who it is intended to benefit.

Importance of khums for Shi'a Muslims

- It gives special recognition to Muhammad, his descendants and leaders within Shi'a Islam.
- It is used to help build Islamic schools or Islamic projects.
- It is used to help the poor or those who may be suffering.
- It is used to promote the religion of Islam through education.
- It is one of the Ten Obligatory Acts.

Sunni Muslims also recognise the historical importance of khums, but do not attribute it the same significance

Importance of Zakah for Sunni Muslims

- It is one of the Five Pillars, so is a duty.
- Wealth is believed to be a gift from Allah that should be shared.
- Muslims believe it is what Allah wants them to do and they will be judged on their actions and the way they helped others after death.
- It is a sign of unity and supports the ummah.
- It helps a Muslim to grow spiritually and frees them from greed and selfishness.
- It helps those who need it most – some Zakah money is used by Islamic charities such as Islamic Relief or Muslim Aid to respond to disasters around the world.

Shi'a Muslims also perform Zakah

Now try this

Explain **two** benefits for Muslims of receiving Zakah.   **(4 marks)**

Hajj

Hajj, the fifth Pillar of Islam, is the annual Muslim pilgrimage that takes place in and around Makkah. All Muslims are obligated to make this journey once in their lifetime if they are physically fit and can afford to do so.

Nature

Hajj is a holy journey that Muslims are expected to make to Makkah, Saudi Arabia. It is held annually in the month of Dhul-Hajjah, lasts five days and over two million Muslims attend. Makkah is the holy city for Muslims as it is where Muhammad was born and lived, and where Muslims face when they pray.

Role

Hajj is intended to allow Muslims to get closer to Allah, as well as follow the example of Muhammad, who began the ritual.

Origins

Hajj is built around many events and people who hold importance in Islam. The rituals completed during Hajj were established by the Prophet Muhammad, who demonstrated the actions to his followers shortly before his death.

Significance

Hajj is important to Muslims as it is one of the Five Pillars. It reminds them of the importance of recognising that all Muslims are equal and equally part of the ummah. It is a struggle to complete Hajj, but Muslims believe it teaches them to be patient and gives them time to reflect on Allah and their faith.

The Qur'an

Surah 2:124–127 talks about the story of Ibrahim, who, it is believed, built the first **Ka'bah** (House of Allah) – the sacred shrine in Makkah. Surah 22:27–29 also talks of proclaiming the Hajj to followers.

How Hajj is performed

- Put on ihram (white, seamless robes).
- Perform Tawaf – circling of the Ka'bah seven times.
- Complete the sa'y – running between the hills of Safa and Marwa in remembrance of Hagar searching for water in the desert.
- Stand on Mount Arafat and pray and read from the Qur'an.
- Throw stones at pillars to symbolise rejecting the devil.
- Celebrate the festival of Id-ul-Adha on the last day to remember the sacrifice Ibrahim was willing to make of his son, Ishma'el.
- Perform Tawaf – circling of the Ka'bah seven times again.

Benefits of Hajj

👍 Shows commitment to Allah – Muslims believe they will be rewarded in al-Jannah.

👍 Strengthens the ummah and the faith of individual Muslims.

👍 Gives an opportunity to focus on Allah, ask for forgiveness and get closer to him.

Challenges of Hajj

👎 Muslims have to be physically fit and financially stable.

👎 Over two million Muslims attend Hajj every year, making it difficult to have a personal experience due to large numbers.

👎 There have been incidences due to the large volume of people.

Now try this

Develop each benefit by adding extra information that links to the reason.

1 Outline **three** actions completed on Hajj.   **(3 marks)**
2 Explain **two** benefits of attending Hajj for Muslims.   **(4 marks)**

Jihad

Jihad means 'struggle' and has its origins in the Qur'an. It is used to describe the personal struggle of every Muslim to follow the teachings of Islam. There are two types of jihad (greater and lesser).

Greater and lesser jihad

Greater jihad	Lesser jihad
Inner struggle to be a better Muslim and closer to Allah by: • studying the Qur'an • doing good deeds • attending mosque regularly • resisting temptation, greed and envy.	**Outer struggle** to defend Islam: • Can be non-violent and in some cases violent • Fought for a just cause • Fought as a last resort • Authorised and accepted by Muslim authority • The minimum amount of suffering should be caused • Ends when enemy surrenders • Innocent civilians not attacked • Aims to restore peace and freedom.

Worked example

Explain **two** reasons why greater jihad is important to Muslims. **(4 marks)**

Greater jihad is important to Muslims as it is viewed as an act of sacrifice for Allah. It involves Muslims giving up time, money, skill or even their life in order to resist any temptations they may face and overcome them through moral actions.

Greater jihad is also important to Muslims because it shows how Muslims should live life as Allah intended. Muslims believe struggling against evil and temptation in the world helps them to develop characteristics such as self-discipline, compassion and honesty.

Lesser jihad and the Qur'an

Fight in the cause of Allah those who fight you, but do not transgress limits; for Allah loveth not transgressors. (Surah 2:190)

Permission [to fight] has been given to those who are being fought, because they were wronged. And indeed, Allah is competent to give them victory. (Surah 22:39)

The Qur'an makes it clear that there are strict conditions when lesser jihad can be declared and therefore justified.

This answer gives two reasons, which are both developed successfully. The explanation given is accurate and shows the knowledge of the student about this topic.

Divergent understandings of jihad

• Most Muslims agree that greater jihad is the most important as this is stressed in the Qur'an.

• Greater jihad is a personal battle, which many Muslims understand to be the true meaning of the term.

• Even though Muhammad was involved in military battles, he supported greater jihad as being more important.

• There may be occasions when the religion of Islam or the name of Allah is threatened and it would be appropriate to defend Islam, but Islam does have set conditions for this.

Make sure you state the reason and then develop it by adding an example or indicating more knowledge about your reason.

Now try this

1 Outline **three** conditions needed for the declaration of lesser jihad. **(3 marks)**

2 Explain **two** reasons why greater jihad is seen as more important to some Muslims than lesser jihad. **(4 marks)**

Celebrations and commemorations

Muslims celebrate or commemorate special days and events throughout the year. For example, **Id-ul-Fitr** celebrates the end of Ramadan. A commemoration, like **Id-ul-Adha**, is a reminder of an important event that has happened in the past.

Why Muslims have celebrations and commemorations

1 To remember past events and important people within Islam.

2 To strengthen the ummah and unite Muslims together.

3 To share beliefs that they have in common.

4 To have a cycle of special days and events that are marked throughout the year.

> This day I have perfected for you your religion and completed My favor upon you and have approved for you Islam as religion. (Surah 5:3)

Quote from the Qur'an citing Id-ul-Ghadeer.

> Whomsoever to him I am master (Maula), Ali is also his/her master (Maula). O God, love those who love him, and be hostile to those who are hostile to him. (Hadith)

Quote from the Hadith citing Id-ul-Ghadeer.

Festival	Sunni	Shi'a
Id-ul-Adha End of Hajj ID-UL-ADHA	• Known as the 'Festival of Sacrifice'. • Remembers Ibrahim's willingness to sacrifice his son when God asked him to. This story is found in the Qur'an 37:100–111 and reminds Muslims of the test of faith faced by Ibrahim and how they should apply this to their own lives, as well as the mercy shown by Allah. • Signifies the end of Hajj. • Muslims remember their own willingness to sacrifice anything to God's wishes. They celebrate with the sacrifice of an animal, which is shared among family, friends and the poor. • Prayers, cards and presents are given.	
Id-ul-Fitr End of Ramadan Id Mubarak	• A time to celebrate and thank Allah for his help in getting through the month of fasting. • Begins when first new moon is seen. • The first Id is believed to have been celebrated by Muhammad, so it commemorates this event in Islamic history. • Homes are decorated. There will be special services and a celebratory meal is shared.	
Ashura Tenth day of Muharran, the first month of the Islamic calendar	• A day of fasting and mourning to remember how Nuh (Noah) left the Ark and how Musa (Moses) and the Israelites were saved from the Egyptians. • People wear black and no music is allowed.	• As Sunni, but the event is also one of mourning to remember the martyrdom at Karbala in 680CE of Hussain, who was a grandson of Prophet Muhammad.
Id-ul-Ghadeer Occurs eight days after Id-ul-Adha	• Sunnis do not celebrate this festival as they do not recognise Iman Ali as the successor to Muhammad.	• To celebrate the appointment of Imam Ali as successor to Muhammad.

Now try this

Outline **three** ways Id-ul-Adha is celebrated.

(3 marks)

Origins of the universe

The main scientific explanation for the origin of the universe is the **Big Bang theory**. There are also other theories.

The Big Bang theory

The Big Bang theory is the belief that the universe started around 14 billion years ago when matter was concentrated into a great mass and began to expand. This expansion continues today, but at a slower rate, with everything moving away from everything else.

The stars and planets are thought to have formed by the cooling of matter and more diverse kinds of atoms forming and eventually condensing.

Muslim beliefs about the origin of the universe

- ✓ Everything was created by Allah.
- ✓ He created balance in the universe – e.g. night and day, sea and land.
- ✓ It took periods of time to create the universe.
- ✓ Creation was intended, planned and designed by Allah.
- ✓ After creating the Earth, Allah created all living things, including humans.

Muslim responses to scientific explanations

Most Muslims believe science does not affect their beliefs in Allah's creation of the universe because:

- the explanation of the Big Bang helps to fill in gaps of what is not explained in the Qur'an
- they believe scientific explanations give them a better understanding of Allah and his creation.

They believe the Qur'an has an account of the creation of the universe similar to that offered by science:

> And the heaven We constructed with strength, and indeed, We are [its] expander. (Surah 51:47)

However, some Muslims may view the Big Bang theory as contradicting the Islamic creation story, as it appears to question whether a loving God planned the creation of the universe.

> Blessed is He in whose hand is dominion, and He is over all things competent – [He] who created death and life to test you [as to] which of you is best in deed – and He is the Exalted in Might, the Forgiving – [And] who created seven heavens in layers. You do not see in the creation of the Most Merciful any inconsistency. So return [your] vision [to the sky]; do you see any breaks? Then return [your] vision twice again. [Your] vision will return to you humbled while it is fatigued. And We have certainly beautified the nearest heaven with stars and have made [from] them what is thrown at the devils and have prepared for them the punishment of the Blaze. (Surah 67:1–5)

The Qur'an is the source for beliefs about the universe.

The universe – gift or commodity?

Some Muslims believe humans are the most important part of Allah's creation. The universe was created for them and they can take what they need.

Some Muslims believe the universe is a gift from God and that they should carry out the task given by Allah to be kalifahs (stewards) who care for the universe. To avoid being judged in the afterlife, they must look after the universe and not take what they want.

Now try this

"The Qur'an and science are in conflict over how the world was created.'
Evaluate this statement considering arguments for and against. In your response you should:

- refer to Muslim teaching
- reach a justified conclusion. **(12 marks)**

Sanctity of life

Muslims believe that life is special and holy. This will determine how they act or behave, as well as their views and beliefs about some issues.

Sanctity of life is the belief that life is holy and special.

Muslims will have views on issues such as abortion, euthanasia and murder that agree with their view that life is special and holy.

Muslims believe:

1. life is special and holy as all life is created by Allah

2. they should respect all life and not harm any living thing

3. that, as all life is holy, every human life is worth the same value as any other

4. that, as Allah is the creator of life, only he can take it away.

See pages 95 and 98 for more information on abortion and euthanasia.

Because of that, We decreed upon the Children of Israel that whoever kills a soul unless for a soul or for corruption [done] in the land – it is as if he had slain mankind entirely. And whoever saves one – it is as if he had saved mankind entirely. And our messengers had certainly come to them with clear proofs. Then indeed many of them, [even] after that, throughout the land, were transgressors. (Surah 5:32)

This suggests that it is wrong to take a life away as it is holy. Preserving and recognising that life is special benefits the whole of mankind.

O you who have believed, do not consume one another's wealth unjustly but only [in lawful] business by mutual consent. And do not kill yourselves [or one another]. Indeed, Allah is to you ever Merciful. (Surah 4:29)

It is clear from this verse that life should not be taken and the reason for this is because it was created by Allah.

Worked example

Explain **two** divergent Muslim understandings about the importance of the sanctity of human life. You must include a source of wisdom and authority in your answer. **(5 marks)**

Some Muslims believe that life starts at conception as it was created by Allah. They believe it is holy and intended to be special and, therefore, would not accept life being taken away in cases of abortion, euthanasia or capital punishment.

Other Muslims may recognise that life is holy as it was created by Allah, but believe that some teachings in the Qur'an indicate it can be ended in some circumstances. The Qur'an teaches that, if Islam is threatened, it may be acceptable to use violence to end life in order to protect the religion even though life is sacred. The Qur'an states: whoever 'kills a soul unless for a soul or for corruption [done] in the land – it is as if he had slain mankind entirely.' (Surah 5:32)

This question requires you to give and develop two different reasons and link one of them to a source of authority, which this student has done.

You must make sure you offer two clear and different reasons in your response.

Now try this

Explain **two** reasons why Muslims believe life is holy.   **(4 marks)**

The origins of human life

Within Islam, there are different responses to scientific explanations about the origins of human life. You will need to understand the scientific **theory of evolution** to understand Muslims' responses.

The theory of evolution

The ascent of man

In his book 'On the Origin of the Species' published in 1859, Charles Darwin put forward a scientific and non-religious theory of evolution. He argued that the origin of human life was a gradual development of the species over millions of years from simple life forms to more complicated life forms. The characteristics or features that are strongest survive, while weaker ones die out and disappear. This is known as **natural selection**. Darwin also used the term 'survival of the fittest' to describe the species best suited to the environment.

Muslim responses to the theory of evolution

The majority of Muslims and other religious people, as well as non-religious people, in today's world hold that science offers more believable explanations for the world than religion. Therefore, it is important for religious believers such as Muslims to try to adapt their beliefs to be able to accept both what religion and science tell them.

Who perfected everything which He created and began the creation of man from clay. Then He made his posterity out of the extract of a liquid disdained. (Surah 32:7–8)

This is what the Qur'an says about humans being created by Allah from clay, which appears to be in conflict with ideas of evolution.

Have those who disbelieved not considered that the heavens and the earth were a joined entity, and We separated them and made from water every living thing? Then will they not believe? (Surah 21:30)

This reinforces the view that Allah is the origin of human life.

Worked example

Explain **two** ways in which Muslims respond to scientific explanations about the origins of human life.   **(4 marks)**

One way in which Muslims respond to scientific explanations about the origins of human life is that some traditional Muslims would believe that evolution is in conflict with Qur'anic teachings about the origin of humans. Evolution suggests it was through natural selection and adaptation, whereas the Qur'an teaches that Allah made humans from clay and gave life.

A second way would be for some Muslims to accept ideas from Islam being compatible with scientific ideas of evolution. They would argue that evolution was part of Allah's plan for how humans were created. Adaptation and survival of the strongest characteristics are how humans came about, but were Allah's intentions.

This answer has offered two different ways in which Muslims can respond to ideas of evolution. Further information has then been added.

Now try this

'There is no way of accepting Muslim ideas about the origins of humans along with scientific views about evolution.' Evaluate this statement considering arguments for and against. In your response you should:
• refer to Muslim teachings
• refer to different Muslim points of view
• reach a justified conclusion.   **(12 marks)**

Show awareness of different Muslim views within your answer, as some may accept evolution while others may reject it.

Muslim attitudes to abortion

Muslim teachings about the sanctity of life affect Muslim views on **abortion**. Many Muslims do not agree with abortion, using the sanctity of life argument as evidence for their views.

Nature of abortion

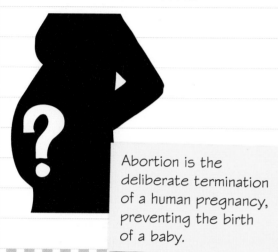

Abortion is the deliberate termination of a human pregnancy, preventing the birth of a baby.

The value and sanctity of life

Muslims are divided over the issue of abortion, so some traditional teachings may not apply. Some may view allowing abortion as 'the lesser of two evils' as both options in cases where abortion is being considered may be disliked. Some may believe that by allowing abortion, it offers a 'slippery slope' to allowing other actions (such as infanticide), which are not accepted within Islam.

Some Muslims, however, would hold to traditional teachings such as the sanctity of human life, maintaining that life is holy as it was created by Allah and should never be threatened or taken away.

Non-religious views on abortion and Muslim responses

Non-religious arguments about abortion	Muslim responses to arguments
Abortion is a personal decision and it is the woman's right to decide what is best.	Abortion is wrong as all life is created by Allah (sanctity of life) and only he can decide when life should end.
Some parents might neither be ready to have a child nor be able to afford one.	The Qur'an teaches: 'And do not kill your children for fear of poverty.' (Surah 17:32). This quote recognises the sanctity of human life.
Abortion is always wrong as the foetus is a human life.	An unplanned pregnancy, worry about providing for a child and pregnancy as a result of adultery are not acceptable reasons for abortion.
Individual circumstances should be taken into account and the best decision decided based on these (situation ethics).	Some Muslims believe abortion is acceptable if the life of the mother is at risk, or in the case of rape, because it upholds the sanctity of the mother's life.

Ensoulment

Allah's Apostle, the true and truly inspired said, '(as regards your creation), every one of you is collected in the womb of his mother for the first forty days, and then he becomes a clot for another forty days, and then a piece of flesh for forty days. Then Allah sends an angel to write four words: He writes his deeds, time of his death, means of his livelihood, and whether he will be wretched or blessed (in religion). Then the soul is breathed into his body.'
(Sahih al-Bukhari 55:549)

This passage describes the point 120 days after conception when the soul enters the body – this is called ensoulment. Sunni Muslims forbid abortion before and after this time, preserving the sanctity of life. Under certain circumstances, others might agree to an abortion taking place before ensoulment, for example if the life of the mother is affected.

Now try this

Outline **three** Muslim teachings about abortion.

(3 marks)

Death and the afterlife (1)

Muslims believe in akhirah (life after death). It is considered to be one of the most important beliefs in Islam and will affect the way a Muslim lives their life.

Muslim teachings about death and the afterlife

1. Allah has full control over life and death.

2. The world will end when Allah chooses and at this time people will face judgement.

3. Good deeds and bad deeds will be judged.

4. People will either be sent to al-Jannah as a reward for a good life or Jahannam for a bad life.

Barzakh is viewed as the barrier between the physical and spiritual worlds – it is where the soul waits after death before resurrection on Judgement Day.

The Qur'an and death and the afterlife

Then is he whom We have promised a good promise which he will obtain like he for whom We provided enjoyment of worldly life [but] then he is, on the Day of Resurrection, among those presented [for punishment in Hell]? (Surah 28:61)

This shows ideas of reward and punishment after death.

And to every soul will be paid in full (the fruit) of its Deeds; and Allah knoweth best all that they do. (Surah 39:70)

This teaches that Allah is aware of every action and thought of humans.

… those who have believed and worked righteous deeds shall be made happy … those who have rejected faith and falsely denies our Signs … shall be brought forth to Punishment. (Surah 30:15–16)

This identifies the reward for those who deserve it and recognises that those who don't will be punished after death.

Significance of life after death for Muslims

It is important to me because it affects how I live my life. I am constantly aware that Allah is watching me.

I want to go to al-Jannah after death so need to live my life as Allah wants.

The Qur'an teaches me that this life is a test and prepares me for the afterlife. Death is the gateway to life after death.

Believing in akhirah gives my life meaning and purpose.

A Muslim funeral

Muslim responses to non-religious arguments for life after death

1. **Memories of previous lives**

   Muslims recognise the afterlife, but Islam does not teach that people have had past lives.

2. **Paranormal, e.g. ghosts and spirits**

   Muslims do not accept ideas of the paranormal.

3. **Logically death cannot be the end**

   Muslims agree that having a reward and punishment after death and a belief in the afterlife gives life meaning and purpose.

4. **Reward for living a good life**

   Muslims agree that those who have lived a good life deserve to be rewarded after death.

5. **Makes people less afraid of death**

   Ideas of the afterlife give Muslims comfort.

6. **Meeting loved ones who have passed on**

   Meeting loved ones again is not of primary importance in Islam.

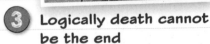

Now try this

Explain **two** reasons why Muslims support the existence of life after death.   **(4 marks)**

Death and the afterlife (2)

Many people who are not religious will argue that there is nothing after a person dies. They suggest that death is the end.

Life after death?

Non-religious arguments against life after death	Muslim responses to non-religious arguments against life after death
Holding beliefs about an afterlife offers a false sense of hope as there is no proof that it exists. The psychoanalyst Freud suggested that religion is an illusion that is used to provide comfort to those who need it.	But the teachings from the Qur'an give evidence that there is an afterlife. They offer proof.
There is no evidence of an afterlife – no one has ever returned to prove it exists.	But my faith means putting trust in the teachings. Allah teaches in the Qur'an that there is an afterlife (akhirah) and he doesn't lie, so this is sufficient evidence for me that the afterlife exists.
Some people have tricked others into believing they can contact people who have died. This takes advantage of vulnerable people.	I recognise that this can happen, but believe it should not detract from the importance of accepting belief in the afterlife.
Believing in an afterlife gives people control over what they fear the most. Look at the philosopher Karl Marx, who believed that religion is a way of controlling and managing people.	But my belief in the afterlife gives meaning and purpose to my life. It helps to guide me in how I should behave and act as I know Allah is watching me and will judge me after I die.
I am a humanist. I believe that when a person dies their body decays and there is nothing else. Life after death is impossible.	I disagree. Although the body may decay in the ground, it will be reunited with the soul on the Day of Judgement. The Qur'an teaches there is life after death and death is not the end.

Worked example

Explain **two** ways Muslims respond to non-religious arguments against life after death.
In your answer you must refer to a source of wisdom and authority. **(5 marks)**

Muslims would respond to non-religious arguments claiming that there is no proof or evidence of an afterlife by saying that the Qur'an is evidence. As it was written by Allah and states that life after death exists, Muslims believe that it is real and they will be judged by Allah for the afterlife on how they have lived their lives.

And they say, 'There is not but our worldly life; we die and live, and nothing destroys us except time.' And they have of that no knowledge; they are only assuming. And when Our verses are recited to them as clear evidences, their argument is only that they say, 'Bring [back] our forefathers, if you should be truthful.' (Surah 45:24–25)

In this reference, the Qur'an, which is a source of wisdom and authority, teaches that there is a life after death and Muslims believe this. They think that people who deny this do so because they have no faith.

This student has given one reason that has been developed by adding new information to explain it. It needs a source of wisdom and authority to be linked to it and a second reason now to be added.

Now try this

Complete the answer to the question in the Worked example.

Euthanasia

The word 'euthanasia' literally means 'good death' and is understood as the painless killing of a person – it is also referred to as 'assisted dying'. Muslims view euthanasia as always wrong and offer no reasons to support it.

Nature of euthanasia

There are different types of euthanasia:

1 Voluntary euthanasia – where a person's life is ended deliberately and painlessly at their request.

2 Assisted suicide – where a person is given the means to end their own life.

3 Non-voluntary euthanasia – ending a person's life painlessly when they are unable to ask, but you have good reason for thinking it is what they would want.

Non-religious arguments in favour of euthanasia

Many atheists would argue that the kindest thing may be to let a person end their life if it is what they want and they are in pain. Humanists would support the use of euthanasia if a person has made this decision for themselves without any persuasion. They believe a person should have the right to make decisions for themselves, especially if they are suffering from a **terminal illness**. Principles of situation ethics may be applied as many people feel the action that should be taken is whatever is most loving in the given situation – even if this means ending life early. Muslims, however, would argue that life is special and sacred and only Allah can decide when it should end.

Muslim response to euthanasia

These posters reflect the strong views Muslims have on upholding the sanctity of life in responding to the issue of euthanasia. They believe euthanasia is murder and is wrong under all circumstances.

Indeed we belong to Allah , and indeed to Him we will return. (Surah 2:156)

The Qur'an teaches the sanctity of life, which is the idea that life has value and is holy as it was created by Allah.

Muslim teachings about the nature and use of euthanasia

E

U

TEST OF FAITH: Suffering is a test and part of life – it is not a person's decision to end their life.

HOSPICES: There are alternatives to euthanasia and they include hospices. These are places where a person with a terminal illness can spend their final days and receive palliative care. Hospice care will not cure the illness but will manage its symptoms, making the end of life more bearable.

ALL LIFE IS SACRED: Therefore, it is important to care for the elderly as much as anyone.

NO SOUL: can ever die except by Allah's leave and at a term appointed (Surah 3:145).

ALLAH: Only Allah can decide how long a person's life is.

SANCTITY OF LIFE: Euthanasia is suicide and does not respect the sanctity of life.

IS ALWAYS WRONG: Because life is sacred and holy.

A

Now try this

1 Outline **three** Muslim teachings about euthanasia. **(3 marks)**

2 Explain **two** reasons why Muslims will not support the use of euthanasia. **(4 marks)**

Issues in the natural world

Today's natural world faces many threats, often from humans. Muslims believe they have a responsibility to care for the world as it was created by Allah.

The world is being damaged by humans in many ways.

Threats to the natural world

Muslims believe they should care for the world and not waste the world's resources because:

- ✓ Allah created the world and humans are its trustees
- ✓ they have been given a duty by Allah to be khalifahs – stewards who care for the world
- ✓ after death they will be called to answer for any ill-treatment of the planet
- ✓ Allah created the world with love and they should show respect by treating it in the same way.

Allah's Apostle said, 'There is none amongst the Muslims who plants a tree or sows seeds, and then a bird, or a person or an animal eats from it, but is regarded as a charitable gift for him.' (Sahih al-Bukhari 3:513)

And the earth He has laid (out) for creatures. (Surah 55:10)

The Earth is green and beautiful, and Allah has appointed you his stewards over it. (Hadith Bukhari)

These quotes from teachings are used by Muslims to either support ideas of animals having rights because they are creations of Allah, or to suggest that animals should not be seen as equal to humans.

Caring for our environment.

Use of animals for food

- Animals were created by Allah and given to humans so Muslims can eat meat.

- Animals exist for the benefit of humans, but should be treated with respect and kindness as a creation of Allah.

- The Qur'an says: 'It is Allah who made for you the grazing animals upon which you ride and some of them you eat.' (Surah 40:79)

- Some Muslims may choose to be vegetarian, believing that animals should not be eaten.

- Some Muslims may use ethical theories such as utilitarianism, which states that 'the greatest happiness for the greatest number'. This may refer to using animals to benefit humans through food or experimentation.

Worked example

Explain **two** ways in which Muslims may respond to the use of animals in experimentation. **(4 marks)**

One way in which Muslims would respond to the use of animals in experimentation is to only allow animals to be used for medical research that would benefit or hopefully save human life, as humans are at the top of Allah's creations.

A second way that Muslims may respond is to reject all animal experimentation as they have a duty to care for the creation of Allah. Muslims believe they will be judged on their actions in the afterlife.

This answer gives two developed and specific responses.

Now try this

Use specialist language where you can.

'Everyone should care for the natural world.'
Evaluate this statement considering arguments for and against. In your response you should:
- refer to Muslim teachings
- reach a justified conclusion.

(12 marks)

Justice

Muslims recognise the importance of **justice** because the Qur'an and the law of Allah teaches that Muslims should act with fairness. Many Muslims campaign for peace and justice.

The nature of justice for Muslims

Justice is fair treatment or behaviour. In terms of punishment, Muslims would understand justice to be the fair treatment of a person according to the crime they have committed.

The importance of justice for Muslims

1 Justice is a key idea promoted in the Qur'an.

2 Shari'ah law has strict rules about justice and acting fairly.

3 The Five Pillars support ideas of justice (e.g. Zakah – sharing wealth makes society fairer).

4 Muslims believe that justice is important to Allah and this is what he intended for his creation.

5 Muslims will be judged in the afterlife on how they treated others, so they should always act fairly and in a just way.

O you who have believed, be persistently standing firm in justice, witnesses for Allah. (Surah 4:135)

This quote from the Qur'an demonstrates the importance of justice in Islam by setting down the requirements of what it means to be a Muslim. This includes standing up for justice and acting in a just and fair way within their lives.

Non-religious attitudes to justice	Muslim response to non-religious attitudes to justice
• It means fairness has been applied. • Everyone involved feels the appropriate action has been taken in response to what has happened. • Ideas of equality can be upheld that are important to all people, regardless of religion.	• Muslims would agree, although they would refer to Islamic teachings or key beliefs in Islam as reasons why they are significant.

Worked example

Explain **two** reasons why justice is important for Muslims. In your answer you must refer to a source of wisdom and authority. **(5 marks)**

Justice is important to Muslims because it is what they believe Allah intended. The Qur'an teaches this and Muslims will try to stand up for justice so they can please Allah and follow his teachings. The Qur'an says: 'O you who have believed, be persistently standing firm in justice, witnesses for Allah' (Surah 4:135).

Justice is also important to Muslims because Shari'ah law (Islamic code of behaviour) supports ideas of justice. Shari'ah law is considered to be the laws of Allah and Muslims want to follow them to be rewarded in the afterlife. Therefore, they want to behave and act in a just way in their lives.

The student has correctly mentioned and explained a source of authority for the first reason, which is required by this style of question.

Now try this

Outline **three** Muslim teachings about justice. **(3 marks)**

Crime

A crime is an action someone commits against the state – for example, murder, theft or drink-driving. Crime is always considered to be a problem in society.

This quote emphasises appropriate conduct in society, such as not committing crime.

Indeed, Allah orders justice and good conduct and giving to relatives and forbids immorality and bad conduct and oppression. He admonishes you that perhaps you will be reminded. And fulfill the covenant of Allah when you have taken it, [O believers], and do not break oaths after their confirmation while you have made Allah, over you, a witness. Indeed, Allah knows what you do. (Surah 16:90–91)

This quote reinforces the view that Muslims should live by Allah's rules and avoid temptation.

O you who have believed, indeed, intoxicants, gambling, [sacrificing on] stone alters [to other than Allah, and divining arrows are but defilement from the work of Satan, so avoid it that you may be successful. (Surah 5:90)

Crime is a distraction from Allah.

Allah orders justice.

Muslim teachings about the problem of crime

The ummah is important and there is a duty to look after and help others, especially those involved in crime or affected by crime.

Islam teaches that all humans were made equal by Allah and deserve to be treated fairly and not hurt by others.

It is important to follow the example of Muhammad who taught the importance of living a good life and not committing crimes.

Some causes of crime might be due to: poverty; political dissatisfaction and difference of opinion; struggles between different racial groups; addiction to drugs and alcohol; and low self-esteem.

Muslim actions to end crime

Muslim Chaplains' Association

This organisation:

- supports Muslim chaplains working in prisons
- works towards resettling prisoners when released
- provides support and mentoring both within and outside the prison system.

Mosaic

Established in 2007, Mosaic supports people of all backgrounds growing up in deprived communities. They have a young offenders' programme linking people with role models to assist in supporting them.

Now try this

1 Outline **three** Muslim responses to crime.   **(3 marks)**
2 Explain **two** reasons why Muslims work to end crime.   **(4 marks)**

Good, evil and suffering

Muslims have clear teachings on good, evil and suffering. These ideas are seen to be related to each other through the ideas of reward for good behaviour and the infliction of suffering for evil behaviour.

Good actions and reward

Helping and caring and leading a good life

⬇

Reward is an afterlife in al-Jannah

Muslims believe that Allah is always watching them and they will be judged on their actions after death. For this reason, they will try to live their lives helping others, for example helping at a food bank.

Evil actions and punishment

Carrying out evil acts such as committing crimes

⬇

Punishment is an afterlife in Jahannam – a place where unbelievers face terrible torments

Indeed, Allah is ever Knowing and Wise. He admits whom He wills into His mercy; but the wrongdoers – He has prepared for them a painful punishment. (Surah 76:30–31)

This teaches Muslims that for those who do wrong, they will be judged by Allah and receive a suitable punishment in the afterlife.

Humans make their own choices and should take responsibility for their actions.

There is no afterlife, so I don't believe in the judgement of God.

Non-religious attitudes to suffering

Evil and suffering are not punishments.

The existence of evil and suffering is evidence that there is no God.

We have no control over some evils like natural disasters.

Divergent Muslim responses to why people suffer

1. Suffering is part of Allah's plan.
2. Suffering is a test of faith and character.
3. Suffering is a reminder of sin and the revelation of Allah.
4. Some suffering is due to human action.
5. Good can come from suffering.

Worked example

'Suffering is part of Allah's plan.'
Evaluate this statement considering arguments for and against.
In your response you should:
- refer to Muslim teachings
- refer to different Muslim points of view
- reach a justified conclusion.   **(12 marks)**

Some Muslims may agree with this statement because they believe that suffering has a purpose and is part of Allah's plan. They accept that they may not understand the reasons why they suffer, but that they need to trust and have faith in Allah that he will not make them suffer more than they can cope with. Other Muslims may also agree, but offer the view that Allah gave humans free will as the Qur'an states. This is what Allah intended so that life is a test to see if Muslims can resist temptation and earn their place in al-Jannah.

This answer starts well, stating why a Muslim might agree with the statement and giving two divergent reasons. The student makes reference to the Qur'an, but it would be better to use a quote to support the Islamic teachings they are discussing. To continue this answer, the student needs to explain why some Muslims may hold alternative views to the reasons offered. The answer also needs a well-argued conclusion.

Now try this

Explain **two** different Muslim teachings on suffering.   **(4 marks)**

Punishment

In order for the law to work properly, those who break the law should be punished.

Nature of punishment and divergent opinion

In the UK, law is made by parliament and crimes are judged in courts of law. In many Islamic countries, the law is derived from the Qur'an and the courts refer to Shari'ah law, which is based on the teachings of the Qur'an.

Shari'ah law was established when society was very different from what it is today. For example, the punishment for theft in Shari'ah law is by amputation of the hand. Western law and society would say this is totally inappropriate. This can lead to differences of opinion.

The Qur'an and punishment

O you who have believed, prescribed for you is legal retribution for those murdered – the free for the free, the slave for the slave, and the female for the female. But whoever overlooks from his brother anything, then there should be a suitable follow-up and payment to him with good conduct. This is an alleviation from your Lord and a mercy. But whoever transgresses after that will have a painful punishment. (Surah 2:178)

This quote shows the idea of punishment being justice for the crime that has been committed. It seems to suggest that it is appropriate for there to be a punishment.

Importance of punishment to Muslims

In order to:

- build a peaceful society as Allah intended
- create a stable society and prevent further crimes
- give offenders the chance to change their behaviour
- make some amends for the crime committed.

Punishment is justice

This enables the victim to gain retribution.

Islam and punishment

Some Muslims believe principles of situation ethics should be applied and the punishment should fit the crime and circumstances of the people involved. For example, the crime might have been carried out because of poverty and this should be taken into account.

Why punishment is needed in society

In order to:

- maintain law and order
- set expected behaviour for society
- give a chance for offenders to mend their ways
- make victims safe
- give a chance for offenders to reflect on the impact of their crime on others.

Now try this

When referring to the source of authority, explain what it says.

1 Explain **two** reasons why punishment is important for Muslims. **(4 marks)**

2 Explain **two** reasons why Muslims believe punishment is needed in society. In your answer you must refer to a source of wisdom and authority. **(5 marks)**

Aims of punishment

Punishment has a number of key aims: protection, retribution, deterrence, and reformation. Muslims may have divergent views about which of these aims is most important.

Type of punishment	What is it?	Muslim response
Protection	To protect society from dangerous criminals by keeping them away from society so they can't hurt others.	Strongly support this idea, believing that the protection of people in society is of paramount importance. This could be seen as justice (see Surah 4:135).
Retribution	Punishment should make criminals pay for what they have done wrong.	Muslims believe they should strive to achieve this by giving a punishment that enables justice to be achieved (see Surah 57:25).
Deterrance MUGGER GETS FIVE YEARS A serial mugger was sentenced yesterday at Newtown county court to	To discourage someone from doing something against the law. Punishment may stop someone committing the same crime or seeing someone else punished for a crime might put someone off doing that action.	Deterring others from committing the same crime again reduces crime in society and maintains order and justice. Some punishments suggested in the Qur'an may encourage others not to commit the same crime (see Surah 5:41).
Reformation ABC	Punishment should show the criminal what they have done wrong and give them time to change so they do not repeat the offence. This could mean education or providing skills or a job so they become a law-abiding citizen.	Forgiveness is important and Islam teaches that just as Allah is forgiving, his followers should also try to apply this within their lives. To give someone a chance to change their behaviour and become a better person is important (see Surah 4:26– 28).

Qur'anic teachings about punishment

- The Qur'an gives specific instructions for particular crimes. This shows the use of punishment as a means of reforming the criminal, as they will not want the punishment to happen to them again. Stricter punishments are considered to be last resorts.

- Muslims believe that punishment establishes peace and justice on Earth as Allah intended.

Allah wants to make clear to you [the lawful from the unlawful] and guide you to the [good] practices of those before you and to accept your repentance. And Allah is Knowing and Wise. Allah wants to accept your repentance, but those who follow [their] passions want you to digress [into] a great deviation. And Allah wants to lighten for you [your difficulties]; and mankind was created weak. (Surah 4:26–28)

This Qur'anic quote shows that Islam teaches that fair punishment is important, but that those who do wrong need to be given the opportunity to repent and change.

Remember to consider all the aims of punishment. Evaluate what a Muslim would say about why punishment is important. Give two views and a conclusion.

Now try this

1 Outline **three** aims of punishment for Muslims.   **(3 marks)**

2 'The most important aim of punishment is reformation.'

Evaluate this statement considering arguments for and against. In your response you should:

- refer to Muslim teachings
- refer to different Muslim points of view
- reach a justified conclusion.   **(12 marks)**

Look at Muslim attitudes to punishment on page 103 to help you.

Forgiveness

Forgiveness is accepting someone's apology for their misdeed and moving on. It is an important idea in Islamic life.

Nature and importance of forgiveness

Muslim teachings say that:

- Allah is compassionate and merciful and forgives people so Muslims should too
- if a person truly repents, then they should be forgiven
- people should try to forgive those who have wronged, as Muhammad taught
- Islam is a religion of peace
- a killer may be forgiven if they pay compensation to the family (Qur'an)
- on the Day of Judgement people will be judged on their behaviour and those who repent will be forgiven.

Being forgiven by the community is important for offenders

Gain skills and education from the punishment

Reintegrated into the community

Carry out community service to make amends for wrong

A way of protecting the ummah

Ease tensions in the community because victims can see justice has been done

> O you who have believed, indeed, among your wives and your children are enemies to you, so beware of them. But if you pardon and overlook and forgive – then indeed, Allah is Forgiving and Merciful. (Surah 64:14)

Restorative justice

Restorative justice is an attempt to bring together the offender and victim of a crime to try to restore peace and allow a community and individuals to heal.

Now try this

Explain **two** reasons why forgiveness of offenders is important for Muslims. **(4 marks)**

Worked example

Explain **two** reasons why restorative justice is important to Muslims. **(4 marks)**

1. Restorative justice is important as it brings peace. It is also important as it is following the teachings of Muhammad.

2. Restorative justice is important as it gives the offender and victim the opportunity to restore peace, which is important. Islam teaches the importance of forgiveness and Muslims should follow Allah's example of being forgiving.

A second reason why restorative justice is important is that Muhammad taught that people should forgive others when they do wrong and are sorry. Muslims believe they should follow the example of Muhammad and forgiving an offender allows everyone to move forward with their lives.

The first answer offers two reasons, but neither is developed or explained. The second answer shows how the reasons can be explained more fully.

Treatment of criminals

Muslims believe that it is important for criminals, even though they have committed crimes, to be treated in a fair way.

Muslim teachings about the treatment of criminals

> And they give food in spite of love for it to the needy, the orphan, and the captive ... (Surah 76:8)

The Qur'an teaches that even someone who has done wrong and is being kept captive deserves to be treated in the correct, humane way. Muslims believe in justice and believe that criminals should be given the chance to reform.

Some Muslims, however, may believe that if someone has done wrong, their freedoms and human rights should be limited. Shari'ah law is very clear about those who have been convicted being given punishments, and some Muslims may accept appropriate retaliation against those whose guilt has been proven.

Fair trial

Barrister addressing a jury in court. A jury assesses the case for the prosecution and defence and makes a decision on whether the person on trial is guilty or innocent. This makes for a fair trial.

Use of torture

To inflict any pain is wrong. Even though criminals have done wrong, they are still human and deserve fair and respectful treatment. As all humans were created by Allah, they should be treated respectfully.

There might be instances, however, where situation ethics could be applied and questions are asked: What is the best course of action for the greater good? Is torture justifiable for this reason?

Muslim beliefs about the treatment of criminals

Human rights

Muslims believe all humans have equal rights, although they do accept that criminals deserve punishment for their crimes. This may involve the removal of some human rights (e.g. freedom if put in prison), which would be fair treatment for the crimes committed.

Human rights are the fundamental rights of every person whatever their age, gender, colour or religious beliefs to basic necessities such as water, food and shelter and the right to a fair trial.

Trial by jury

Trials need to be conducted fairly so a jury would work to achieve this.

Fair trial

Muslims believe justice is important and criminals have the right to a fair trial where both sides of the case are considered. They believe it is important that the laws of the state are recognised and upheld and punishment is given when a person is found guilty of a crime.

Consider developing some of these ideas as reasons: Allah is just and merciful; the Quran teaches that justice is important; all humans were created by Allah.

Now try this

Explain **two** reasons why fair treatment of criminals is important to Muslims.

(4 marks)

The death penalty

Capital punishment is also known as the death penalty. There are many arguments, both religious and non-religious, that support or are against capital punishment.

The nature of capital punishment

Capital punishment is execution – where the life of a condemned prisoner is taken away. It has been abolished completely in the UK, although some countries, as well as some states in the USA, still have the death penalty.

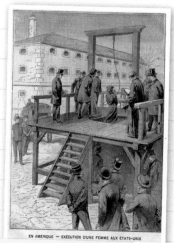
EN AMERIQUE — EXECUTION D'UNE FEMME AUX ÉTATS-UNIS

Death by hanging of a woman convicted of murder in the USA, 1906.

The purpose of capital punishment

1. To offer a punishment for the most severe crimes committed.

2. To act as a deterrent for other criminals.

3. To make victims feel as though punishment has been given and to offer closure for the victim's family.

4. To make sure that the offender cannot commit the same crime again.

5. To give a chance for the offender to repent by facing up to what they have done.

Muslim attitudes to the use of capital punishment

In support of capital punishment	Against capital punishment
• The Qur'an says the death penalty can be used for certain crimes. • Shari'ah law agrees with the Qur'an. • Muhammad made statements suggesting he agreed with the death penalty. • When Muhammad was the ruler of Medinah, he sentenced people to death for committing murder.	• The scholars of Shari'ah law do not agree when or how the death penalty should be applied, showing there are differences in opinion. • The Qur'an states that capital punishment is one option – but it is not the only option. • Strict conditions given by the Qur'an about capital punishment are often not met. • Some Muslims may use the argument that life is special and sacred and it is not the place of humans to take it away in any circumstances. • If there is no capital punishment in the country they live in, then they accept this law.

Muslim teachings on capital punishment

In Hadith (Sahih Muslim 16:4152), it suggests that the death penalty can be used for the crimes of murder and for Muslims who refuse to do their Islamic duty. The Qur'an also indicates that the death penalty can be for crimes of rape, homosexual acts and apostasy (when someone works against Islam).

Non-religious attitudes

Humanists and atheists generally oppose the use of the death penalty, as they believe premeditated killing is wrong – even when carried out by the state. There is also the possibility of error. When situation ethics are applied, some may believe that in certain circumstances capital punishment might be the better option.

Now try this

Explain **two** reasons why some Muslims might support the use of the death penalty. **(4 marks)**

Peace

'Islam' is derived from the root of the word 'salaam' which is often understood to mean 'peace'. The Qur'an teaches about peace and that peace is not easy to achieve. Muslims accept that sometimes war may be necessary in certain circumstances in order to bring about peace.

Nature of peace

For Muslims, peace is understood to be the absence of oppression, tyranny, injustice and corruption. They believe it is directly linked to the attaining of justice within the world.

Muslims at a rally in the USA promoting peace

Islam as a religion of peace

1. Islam is a religion that has been misrepresented and associated with terrorism where, in reality, it is a religion of peace.

2. Muslims believe Allah created and wants a peaceful world.

3. There are many examples of peace being shown within Islam, demonstrating its importance. For example, Muslims greet each other with the words 'As-salamu alaykum' (peace be with you).

4. The Qur'an is seen to promote messages of peace and Muslims promote peace and unity through being part of the ummah.

The Qur'an and peace

> And the servants of the Most Merciful are those who walk upon the earth easily, and when the ignorant address them [harshly], they say [words of] peace. (Surah 25:63)

The Qur'an teaches that peace is an important idea for Muslims, even when they may face criticism or hate towards them.

Muslim teachings about peace

1. Allah created the world with the intention that peace would be part of his creation.

2. Muslims believe in the personal struggle for peace or the greater jihad.

3. All Muslims belong to the ummah, which demonstrates ideas of living together peacefully.

4. Standing up for justice in the world is one way of achieving peace.

5. In some cases, it may be necessary to go to war to secure peace.

Worked example

Explain **two** ways in which peace may be understood in the life of a Muslim. In your answer you should make reference to a source of wisdom or authority. **(5 marks)**

One way is how Muslims should behave towards others in a peaceful way. The ummah unites all Muslims in peace, as they are all equal and should help and care for each other. A quote that supports this is: 'And the servants of the Most Merciful are those who walk upon the earth easily, and when the ignorant address them [harshly], they say [words of] peace' (Surah 25:63).

Another way is how Muslims may greet each other with a message of peace. They may say 'As-salamu alaykum', which means 'peace be with you'. This shows they are giving them their good wishes.

The reason given is stated and then developed. This student then gives a quote from a source of authority to support the point they have made.

Now try this

Outline **three** reasons why peace is important to Muslims.   **(3 marks)**

108

Peacemaking

Peace is important to Muslims and there are examples of organisations who promote ideas of peace, such as Islamic Relief and Muslim Peace Fellowship.

Importance of justice, forgiveness and reconciliation

Justice

Muslims believe there is a direct link between the ideas of **justice** and peace. If justice and fairness can be attained, peace will follow. The ummah demonstrates ideas of equality and justice, as all Muslims are of equal worth and value and support each other.

> And not equal are the good deed and the bad. Repel [evil] by that [deed] which is better; and thereupon the one whom between you and him is enmity [will become] as though he was a devoted friend. (Surah 41:34)

Forgiveness

Muslims believe that **forgiveness** is important in achieving peace. They recognise that everyone makes mistakes and deserves to be given a second chance. Muslims believe Allah is merciful and they should follow his example and try to forgive others when they do wrong.

Surah 41:34 reinforces the view that good deeds and evil deeds are not equal and that justice, forgiveness and reconciliation are important in overcoming conflict and bringing peace.

Reconciliation

Reconciliation is the idea of making up after conflict. According to Muslims, this is needed in order to live in an ordered and peaceful world as Allah intends.

Muslim organisations working for peace

Islamic Relief:
- Founded in 1984 to help victims of war.
- Inspired by Islam to promote ideas of caring for others and achieving peace.
- Works in countries such as Somalia, Iraq and Bosnia.
- Raises awareness of children living in extreme poverty.
- Provides teachers and school materials for children living in poverty.
- Supports refugees with medical care and food in war-torn countries.
- Provides emergency aid and relief.

Muslim Peace Fellowship:
- Founded in 1994 and works to promote world peace.
- Works against injustice – reaches out to people of all faiths.
- Develops understanding and mutual respect.
- Promotes the Islamic ideas of peace and non-violence through conferences, publications, talks and prayer.

Remember that you need to relate one of your reasons in your answer to a quote from a source of authority or wisdom.

Why do Muslims work for peace?

- ✓ To follow the teachings of Islam, which promote peace and working together rather than conflict.
- ✓ The Qur'an contains many quotes relating to ideas of peace. Muslims believe they should apply these through supporting charity and helping others.
- ✓ To live as Allah intended and to work to try to bring justice to the world.
- ✓ To help care for others in the world, which is a duty outlined by Muhammad to humans.
- ✓ To support and strengthen the ummah.

Now try this

'Peace is the most important thing in today's world for Muslims.' Evaluate this statement considering arguments for and against. In your response you should:
- refer to Muslim teachings
- reach a justified conclusion.

(12 marks)

Conflict

Conflict, where an argument or disagreement has led to a breakdown in a relationship, can cause problems within society such as a lack of communication and trust. Muslims believe everything possible should be done to try to resolve conflicts within the world.

Causes of conflict

There can be many causes of conflict, including politics, resources, history, culture and religion. Many conflicts that emerge do so because of differing beliefs or a greed for wanting something someone else may have, such as land, power and resources.

The Qur'an on conflict

Fight in the way of Allah those who fight you but do not transgress. Indeed. Allah does not like transgressors. (Surah 2:190)

Muslim teachings and responses to the nature and cause of conflict

1. Every Muslim is part of the ummah and deserves equality and respect. When conflict happens, Muslims should work to resolve it.

2. Muslims may try to reconcile groups who are in conflict in order to achieve peace.

3. Muslims believe that Allah is merciful and forgiving and they should try to follow this principle in their own lives.

4. Muslims can be seen to adopt a situation ethics standpoint on issues of conflict, and the action taken may differ from one situation to another.

5. Despite Islam being a religion that supports the idea of peace, it does recognise that war and fighting may be needed in some circumstances as a last resort when all else has been tried and failed.

6. Muslims believe that they should not forgive those who work against Islam.

Muslims believe that Allah commands that they should fight back when necessary but remain just. This is a form of situation ethics where sometimes conflict is needed to bring peace.

Worked example

Outline **three** Muslim responses to the problems conflict causes within society. **(3 marks)**

1. Muslims may respond by working to resolve conflict.

2. Muslims may respond by working to resolve conflict through getting people to talk. They could educate others about peace and reconciliation. They could also look to teachings of the Qur'an to help people understand the importance of working together to overcome conflict.

This student has given one response – to improve this answer, two more responses must be included, as in answer 2.

Muslim response to non-religious views on conflict

Religion is a cause of conflict, as different beliefs between religious groups can cause problems in society.

Non-religious view

Allah wishes for a peaceful world without conflict and all Muslims should work to achieve this.

Muslim view

Now try this

Explain **two** reasons why Muslims believe they should work to bring an end to conflict. **(4 marks)**

Pacifism

Muslims believe it is important to promote ideas of peace, forgiveness and reconciliation. Islam is not a **pacifist** religion as it is accepted that sometimes war and fighting is necessary, but it can sometimes be seen to promote ideas that are in line with pacifism.

Nature of pacifism

Pacifism is a belief held that war and violence are wrong under all circumstances. This is the logo for CND (Campaign for Nuclear Disarmament) – an organisation that campaigns non-violently to rid the world of nuclear weapons.

History of pacifism in Islam

When Muhammad was persecuted and forced to leave Makkah in an event known as the Hijrah, he was forced to use violence. Therefore, historically, pacifism has not been a part of Islam.

⬇

After the exile, Qur'anic revelations seemed to adopt a more defensive perspective.

⬇

Today, violence is not rejected completely by Islam, but ideas of peace are promoted within a minority movement.

If you should raise your hand against me to kill me – I shall not raise my hand against you to kill you. Indeed, I fear Allah, Lord of the worlds. (Surah 5:28)

This quote suggests ideas in line with pacifism or passive resistance. Namely, that a person should not face violence with violence. Some Muslims may interpret it this way, while others may argue that it is not suggesting the use of non-violence, but rather that a Muslim should not be the first person to attack another.

Muslim teachings about passive resistance

1. Islam teachings in the Qur'an and Hadith strive for justice and to resist oppression.

2. Muslims believe it is important to resist zulm cruelty and injustice).

3. Islam teaches the importance of reconciliation and working together to achieve peace using non-violent protest.

4. 'Islam' is often taken to mean 'submission to Allah' and 'peace'.

Passive resistance in Islam

Muhammad and his followers continued to preach the message of Allah and confronted non-believers even when faced with violence.

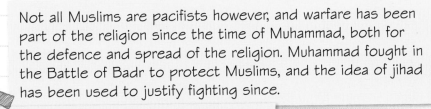

Not all Muslims are pacifists however, and warfare has been part of the religion since the time of Muhammad, both for the defence and spread of the religion. Muhammad fought in the Battle of Badr to protect Muslims, and the idea of jihad has been used to justify fighting since.

The Arab Spring was a democratic uprising that spread across much of the Arab world in 2011. It contained elements of protest using passive resistance.

Now try this

Explain **two** reasons why Muslims may accept ideas of passive resistance.

(4 marks)

The Just War theory

A just war is one that is fought for the right reasons, in the right way and is, therefore, seen as being justified. The **Just War theory** is a set of principles that is used to decide whether a war is fair and just and meets the criteria to be justified.

The nature and importance of the Just War theory

The theory suggests that:

- it is wrong to take human life
- countries may need to protect their people and war may be necessary to do this
- protecting moral values may require force.

The Just War theory is important because it:

- provides a set of rules as to the best way to act at times of conflict
- offers a framework to decide whether war is the best option
- aims to prevent war.

Just War theory in Islam

Has the support of the community and not one person

Is declared by a religious leader

Will not harm the environment

Conditions of a Just War – the lesser jihad

Is an act of defence

Does not aim to win new land or power

Will not threaten lives

Is a last resort

Is not an act to convert people to Islam

Divergent responses to the Just War theory

Some Muslims believe that war is permitted in self-defence. Other Muslims believe war is never justified and should never happen.

Tanks at war

- Some Muslims recognise that war is necessary and sometimes required as a last resort – the Just War theory permits this.
- Sunni and Shi'a Muslims may conflict over the exact interpretation of the Just War theory. Shi'a Muslims recognise jihad as one of the Ten Obligatory Acts, whereas Sunni Muslims do not place the same emphasis on it.
- Some may traditionally accept that Islam allows war in self-defence and to protect the innocent and oppressed, for example, as seen in the Hijrah when Muhammad and his followers were persecuted or the Battle of Badr.
- Other Muslims may believe that war is never the right choice, believing that peace and reconciliation are at the heart of Islam.

Is a just war possible?

Yes	No
Depending on the circumstances (situation ethics), it might be reasonable	No circumstances would necessitate war
Fighting might be the only way to achieve peace	Other ways can achieve better results
Weapons programmed to damage set targets rather than affect innocent lives	There's always the risk of causing suffering
Qur'an suggests fighting to defend Islam is acceptable	Should a religious leader declare a just war, it may be too influenced by their faith

And what is [the matter] with you that you fight not in the cause of Allah and [for] the oppressed among men, women, and children who say, 'Our Lord, take us out of this city of oppressive people and appoint for us from Yourself a protector and appoint for us from Yourself a helper?' (Surah 4:75)

This quote refers to the people of Makkah, who were persecuted for embracing Islam. This illustrates one reason why it may be justified to fight – to protect the religion of Islam.

Now try this

1　Outline **three** Muslim conditions of the Just War theory.　　　**(3 marks)**

2　Explain **two** conditions of the Just War theory.　　　**(4 marks)**

Holy war

Holy war, or Harb al-Maqadis, is the name for war fought because of religious differences.

The nature of Harb al-Maqadis in Islam

Harb al-Maqadis is only justifiable in cases where the intention is to defend the religion of Islam. This can involve:

- protecting the freedom of Muslims to practise their faith
- strengthening the religion of Islam if it is being threatened
- protecting Muslims against an attack.

Muhammad and his followers were involved in holy wars, such as the Battle of Badr and the Conquest of Makkah.

> Then when the Sacred Months (the Ist, 7th, 11th, and 12th months of the Islamic calendar) have passed, then kill the Mushrikun (see V. 2:105) wherever you find them, and capture them and besiege them, and prepare for them each and every ambush. But if they repent and perform As-Salat (Iqamat-as-Salat), and give Zakat, then leave their way free. Verily, Allah is Oft-Forgiving, Most Merciful. (Surah 9:5)

> But if the enemy incline towards peace, do thou (also) incline towards peace, and trust in Allah; for He is One that heareth and knoweth (all things). (Surah 8:61)

The first quote suggests the agreement of using violence when necessary, but gives allowance if the opposition repents. This suggests peace and forgiveness are important. The second quote supports ideas of working towards peace. These quotes may appear to be in conflict and this can also be applied to lesser jihad, with diversity over its understanding and justification for war.

Teachings about holy war

The conditions for holy war to happen must:

- be for reasons of defence
- be declared by a religious leader
- be a last resort
- avoid harming innocent civilians
- not be fought to gain land
- be fought to bring about end goal
- not harm innocent people
- not cause women to be abused or raped
- treat enemies fairly, including enemy soldiers
- be stopped as soon as enemy ask for it
- not target property

Worked example

'War is always wrong.'
Evaluate this statement considering arguments for and against. In your response you should:
- refer to Muslim teaching
- refer to different Muslim points of view
- reach a justified conclusion. **(12 marks)**

Some Muslims would agree with this statement, arguing that Islam is a religion of peace and it is always wrong to use violence. They may use arguments such as teachings from the Qur'an that show ideas of peace, or use the example of Muhammad, who appeared to sometimes use examples of passive resistance and not violence. This would help them to support the idea that life is sacred as it was created by Allah and innocent people should not be threatened through war.

This student has made a good start, offering one Muslim viewpoint. To continue, the student needs to give an alternative view and include sources of wisdom, along with a conclusion.

Now try this

Explain **two** reasons why some Muslims may support war. **(4 marks)**

Weapons of mass destruction

Weapons of mass destruction (WMD) include nuclear, biological or chemical weapons that are able to cause widespread devastation and destruction of resources and loss of life.

Why some people might think there are perceived benefits to WMD

Minimal losses are incurred by the attackers

Nuclear warheads

Weapons of mass destruction can be used as a deterrent to other nations

They provide the ability to end a war quickly, preventing further casualties

Why some people might think there are problems with WMD

Moral issues of the amount of destruction and devastation caused

The attack is indiscriminate and can kill innocent victims

Can make war unfair

The destruction caused by the dropping of a nuclear bomb on Hiroshima, Japan, in 1945 by US aircraft.

Problems of stockpiling dangerous weapons

The conditions of the Just War theory would not be met using this type of weapon

Muslim teachings and responses on WMD

The Qur'an was recorded long before WMD came into existence, but lessons from the Qur'an can still be applied.

> That if any one slew a person – unless it be for murder or for spreading mischief in the land – it would be as if he slew the whole people; and if any one saved a life, it would be as if he saved the life of the whole people …
> (Surah 5:32)

1 Use of WMD not supported because of the extensive damage they would cause.

2 Innocent life should not be threatened.

3 Impossible to regulate WMD under Islamic conditions of war because of the damage that could be caused.

Non-religious attitudes and utilitarianism

It is difficult to find any justification for the use of weapons that cause so much damage and threaten innocent life to such as great extent.

Non-religious view

WMD may be justified if peace is achieved in the long term and if they act as a deterrent.

Utilitarian view

WMD are too great a threat to life and the creation of Allah.

Muslim view

Remember that this question asks you to refer to a quote from a source of authority for Muslims. You could use the Qur'anic quote on this page in your explanation.

Now try this

Explain **two** reasons why many Muslims would not support the use of weapons of mass destruction. In your answer you must refer to a source of wisdom and authority. **(5 marks)**

Issues surrounding conflict

Conflict has always existed, but today's world contains new forms of war, violence and terrorism.

Nature of conflict

 Violence

Violent acts are constantly being reported, with people seeming to be less afraid of laws and consequences, creating a sense of fear within society. Examples: increase in knife and gun crime or attacks on religious or racial grounds.

 War

War has taken on a new role with the development of new, stronger and more damaging weapons in, for example, Afghanistan, Iraq and Syria.

A fighter

 Terrorism

This is a violent form of protest that has occurred all over the world. It often has religious links, with some religious groups claiming to commit acts of terrorism in the name of God. For example, 9/11 and the attacks in Paris, Brussels and Tunisia.

Divergent Muslim views on conflict

 Islam as a religion of peace

In support of war if defending Islam

 Speak out against those who commit atrocities

People who commit atrocities supposedly in the name of Islam

There are many examples of Muslim leaders speaking out against terrorism, including Iranian president Hassan Rouhani and Qatari foreign minister Khalid al-Attiyah, who both spoke out after the Paris attacks in November 2015.

Non-religious views on conflict

Non-religious people may be concerned about the growing number of conflicts in society, as well as the increasing use of violence. Even though they hold no religious beliefs, they would value human life and believe in principles of justice and equality.

Some non-religious people may even hold religion at fault for the conflict within the world, seeing the rise in examples of terrorism and violence as centrally connected to religion.

How Muslims have worked to overcome these issues

- The Muslim Council of Britain runs education programmes to inform and break down barriers.
- Peaceful rallies and marches are held to promote peace.
- Interfaith groups work together across religions to promote peace.
- Police and community groups work together.
- Organisations such as Mosaic work to bring people within communities together.

I advise you ten things: Do not kill women or children or an aged, infirm person. Do not cut down fruit-bearing trees. Do not destroy an inhabited place. Do not slaughter sheep or camels except for food. Do not burn bees and do not scatter them. Do not steal from the booty, and do not be cowardly. (Malik's Muwatta)

This quote states the things that Muslims should not do in terms of causing conflict, using violence or starting war.

Now try this

'The biggest threat facing Muslims in the world today is conflict.'
Evaluate this statement considering arguments for and against. In your response you must:
- refer to Muslim teachings
- refer to different Muslim points of view
- reach a justified conclusion.

(12 marks)

Revelation

Many people claim to have experienced God, either directly or indirectly. These types of experiences allow Muslims to 'know' Allah, understand better what he is like and have confirmation or proof of his existence.

Direct and indirect revelation

Revelation is the way in which God reveals his presence.

1. Direct revelation is revelation that comes directly from God.

2. Indirect revelation is through a messenger, such as a prophet.

Muslims believe Allah must exist because, if he did not, he wouldn't choose to reveal himself in these ways.

The Qur'an as revelation

If I should err, I would only err against myself. But if I am guided, it is by what my Lord reveals to me. Indeed, He is Hearing and near. (Surah 34:50)

This demonstrates that Allah chooses to reveal himself directly. The Qur'an itself is revelation – Muslims can know Allah better through reading his words as they believe he is the author. Muslims can understand what Allah is like – for example, **omnipotent** or **benevolent** – as well as his teachings about how he wants Muslims to live their lives and behave.

Revelation through messengers

Muslims believe that Allah chose to reveal himself through prophets – messengers who were specially chosen. These include Adam, Ibrahim, Isma'il, Musa, Dawud, Isa and Muhammad, who is the 'Seal of the Prophets' as the final messenger. Some of these messengers brought messages from Allah, while others, such as Muhammad, brought holy books as well. Muslims believe that the messengers reveal aspects of Allah as they share his teachings with the world. Muslims can look to sources of authority such as the Qur'an for support and understanding of what Allah is like.

Divergent understandings of what revelation shows about the nature of Allah

The Qur'an demonstrates that Allah is omnipotent, **omniscient** and benevolent and cares about his creation.

But he also takes on the role of judge, especially after death in the afterlife.

Allah communicates with us so shows he exists and is close.

But he is also transcendent and remains beyond full human understanding.

Worked example

Outline **three** ways revelation proves the existence of Allah. **(3 marks)**

Revelation proves the existence of Allah in that the Qur'an is believed to be the words of Allah showing he exists. Through messengers such as Musa, Ibrahim and Muhammad, Allah is shown to exist. Revelation helps Muslims to understand what Allah is like and also proves he exists.

In this answer the student has given three different ideas in three separate sentences.

Now try this

Explain **two** ways in which Allah reveals himself for Muslims. **(4 marks)**

Visions

A **vision** is something that a person sees, possibly in a dream, which may connect to a supernatural being or God. Often a revelation is made in the vision.

Nature of visions in Islam

Many people associated with Islam, including prophets and **imams**, have undergone religious experiences where they have received a vision. Often angels or messengers appear and pass on messages from Allah, proving to Muslims that Allah is real.

Importance of visions in Islam

Visions are an important form of religious experience. People often only believe things that they can see, so experiencing a vision may be considered to be more reliable than other types of experiences. Visions provide evidence and help to strengthen faith for believers or lead people to believe in the existence of Allah because they believe:

- ✓ Allah is contacting them
- ✓ they can get closer to Allah
- ✓ they can understand Allah better.

Examples of visions

1 Musa's vision of Allah

And when Moses arrived at Our appointed time and his Lord spoke to him, he said, 'My Lord, show me (Yourself) that I may look at You.' (God) said, 'You will not see Me, but look at the mountain; if it should remain in place, then you will see Me.' But when his Lord appeared to the mountain, He rendered it level, and Moses fell unconscious. And when he awoke, he said, 'Exalted are You! I have repented to You, and I am the first of the believers.' (Surah 7:143)

These two visions are not direct visions of Allah, but Muslims believe that Allah is transcendent and, therefore, too great to be seen directly.

2 The vision of Mary

And mention, [O Muhammad], in the Book [the story of] Mary, when she withdrew from her family to a place toward the east. And she took, in seclusion from them, a screen. Then We sent to her Our Angel, and he represented himself to her as a well-proportioned man. She said, 'Indeed, I seek refuge in the Most Merciful from you, [so leave me], if you should be fearing of Allah.' He said, 'I am only the messenger of your Lord to give you [news of] a pure boy.' She said, 'How can I have a boy while no man has touched me and I have not been unchaste?' (Surah 19:16–20)

Divergent understandings of visions

Different Muslims may place a different level of emphasis on visions as proof of the existence of Allah.

Some Sunni Muslims may accept visions and use them as proof of the existence of Allah to strengthen faith. However, other Muslims, including some Shi'a Muslims, believe that visions are not needed, as faith means to put trust in Allah and therefore proof is not required. Some Muslims, such as those in the **Sufi** tradition, are more spiritual and accept ideas of mysticism, meaning they may place more emphasis on visions within their faith.

Muslim responses to non-religious arguments

Visions are not real. They are hallucinations or dreams. I would only believe in them if they were verified scientifically.

Non-religious view

Visions do happen and they are evidence of the existence of Allah.

Muslim view

Now try this

1 Outline **three** reasons why visions do not prove the existence of Allah. (3 marks)

2 Explain **two** reasons why visions are important as evidence of Allah for some Muslims. (4 marks)

Miracles

Miracles are amazing events that can't be explained by the laws of nature or science. They are believed to show the power and presence of Allah in the world.

Importance of miracles for Muslims

Miracles are important because:

- they suggest a greater being, such as Allah, who is involved and acting within the world
- the Qur'an makes it clear Allah can perform miracles if he wishes
- people often question the existence of Allah when people seem to suffer. Therefore, when miracles happen that can be attributed to him, it gives comfort and belief in a loving Allah.

Why miracles might lead to belief in the existence of Allah

1. Amazement by what has happened – there is no other way to explain it except through Allah.

2. Evidence that Allah is active within the world – they show Allah cares for creation and wants humanity to know he is there.

3. Proof of the existence of Allah because they show his love for the world.

4. Demonstrate the power of Allah in that he can act within the world.

Examples of miracles

The miracle of Nuh surviving the floods	The Qur'an as a miracle	The miracle of Al-Mi'raj when Muhammad was taken to meet Allah in the heavens
	Say, 'If mankind and the jinn gathered in order to produce the like of this Qur'an, they could not produce the like of it, even if they were to each other assistants.' (Surah 17:88)	This event occurred in the year 621 and is explained in the Qur'an and Hadith 

This event is considered miraculous because it would seem impossible.

You will need to be familiar with the whole Qur'anic passage 17:84–89. The Qur'an itself is seen as a living miracle due to the way it was passed down to Muhammad. Many Muslims believe that the Qur'an contains information that could not have been known at the time, which adds to its miraculous nature.

Non-religious arguments against miracles

Miracles can be explained scientifically. They are everyday events interpreted as miracles.

Different interpretations of events cause doubt as to their truth. They don't provide proof that Allah exists.

Muslim arguments for miracles

Miracles are real and they prove the existence of Allah.

Miracles strengthen and confirm my faith in Allah. I trust Allah.

Some Muslims place less importance on miracles. They find reading the teachings in the Qur'an, or learning through Muhammad, a better way of getting to know Allah.

Now try this

Explain **two** reasons why miracles may lead a Muslim to believe in Allah.   **(4 marks)**

Religious experiences

A **religious experience** is an experience that people claim is caused by or related to God. This could include a miracle, vision, dream or simply a connection to God. Although many Muslims claim religious experiences confirm their beliefs about Allah, many people do not accept religious experiences are real.

Islam and religious experiences

> Those who do not know say, 'Why does Allah not speak to us or there come to us a sign?' Thus spoke those before them like their words. Their hearts resemble each other. We have shown clearly the signs to a people who are certain [in faith]. (Surah 2:118)

Muslims believe that Allah clearly reveals himself to his followers. One way of doing this is through religious experiences, as Muslims can gain a personal connection and understanding of Allah.

The varying importance of religious experiences to Sunni, Shi'a and Sufis

- All Muslims recognise religious experience to some extent, as they believe the Qur'an was revealed to Muhammad through religious experience.

- Some Muslims, however, place slightly less importance on religious experience within the religion. Sunni and Shi'a Muslims believe that sources of authority, such as the prophets and the Qur'an, are better sources of evidence.

- Sufism is a smaller branch of Islam and is often considered to be more mystical. Sufis place great importance on personal experiences of Allah and their significance to following Islam and connecting with Allah.

Muslim responses to religious experiences

There are the experiences of Muhammad and modern-day Muslims to prove that religious experience is real.

> As a Muslim, I would argue that religious experiences do happen and there is evidence in the Qur'an.

> As a Muslim, I believe Allah reveals himself to us in order to confirm belief and provide understanding of who he is.

> As a Muslim, I believe that if Allah wants to communicate with us, he is able to do so through religious experiences.

Non-religious arguments questioning religious experiences

- There is a lack of evidence

- People might have been under the influence of drink or drugs

- People may have been ill and hallucinating

- People may be looking intentionally for experiences – looking for meaning to their lives.

Now try this

Explain **two** ways in which Muslims may respond to arguments against religious experience offered by non-religious people.

(4 marks)

The design argument

The **design argument** tries to prove the existence of Allah by arguing that the universe was designed.

Overview of the design argument

| Design is the result of intelligent thought. | → | The universe shows evidence of being designed (e.g. gravity, ozone layer). | → | This suggests that a being with intelligence designed the universe. | → | The universe is too complex to have happened by chance or be designed by any being other than Allah. | → | Therefore, Allah exists. |

Existence and nature of Allah

Muslims believe that the design argument shows that Allah is omnipotent – all powerful. The fact that he was able to design the universe shows his power. Muslims also believe that Allah took time and care to plan and design the world to suit humans. This shows that he cares for his creation and is benevolent and omniscient.

Muslims believe that the Qur'an offers good **philosophical proof** to suggest that Allah exists, and evidence that he designed the world can be seen all around.

The Qur'an and the design argument

Indeed, in the creation of the heavens and earth, and the alternation of the night and the day, and the [great] ships which sail through the sea with that which benefits people, and what Allah has sent down from the heavens of rain, giving life thereby to the earth after its lifelessness and dispersing therein every [kind of] moving creature, and [His] directing of the winds and the clouds controlled between the heaven and the earth are signs for a people who use reason. (Surah 2:164)

Muslims would respond to non-religious views by arguing that there is no other explanation other than Allah for the amazing world in which we live. How much emphasis Muslims place on the design argument may vary:
- Some will believe it is true, but unnecessary in confirming their belief.
- Others will say it is essential in confirming their belief.

Non-religious views against design as proof of the existence of Allah

 Design might actually be the result of evolution (the idea that species developed gradually over millions of years) and Allah might not be needed to explain the evidence of design in the world.

 Evidence of 'design' in the universe only suggests Allah is the designer – it is impossible to 'prove' this idea.

 The universe may not be planned and show evidence of design – the argument that it happened by chance is equally strong.

 There is evidence of 'bad design' in the world (e.g. volcanoes, earthquakes), which may lead some people to question why a god would design these things. This suggests that Allah did not and, therefore, does not exist.

Now try this

1 Explain **two** reasons why Muslims believe the design argument is important. **(4 marks)**

2 'The design argument is proof of the existence of Allah.'
Evaluate this statement considering arguments for and against. In your response you should:
- refer to Muslim teachings
- refer to non-religious views
- reach a justified conclusion. **(12 marks)**

The cosmological argument

The **cosmological argument** tries to prove the existence of Allah by showing that everything happens for a reason. Islam has used this philosophical proof to support the view that Allah exists.

Overview of the cosmological argument

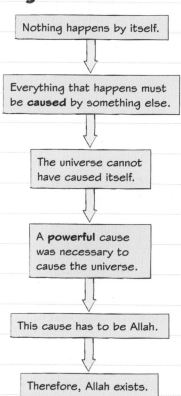

Nothing happens by itself.

↓

Everything that happens must be **caused** by something else.

↓

The universe cannot have caused itself.

↓

A **powerful** cause was necessary to cause the universe.

↓

This cause has to be Allah.

↓

Therefore, Allah exists.

The cosmological argument and its use in Islam

The cosmological argument was first put forward in the 12th century in 'the kalam', written by Al-Ghazali in his book 'Kitab al-Iqtisad fil'Itiqad'. Al-Ghazali argued:

Whatever begins to exist has a cause. → The universe began to exist. → Therefore, the universe has a cause.

The Qur'an (Surah 79:27–33) reinforces the idea that Allah created the universe.

The cosmological argument:

- ✓ Shows Allah's omnipotence in being able to create the universe.
- ✓ Shows Allah's omniscience in being able to see everything he created.
- ✓ Shows Allah caused the universe to exist.
- ✓ Shows Allah is benevolent and cares for his creation.
- ✓ Reinforces the teachings in the Qur'an about the creation of the universe.
- ✓ Supports the beliefs held about what Allah is like.

Strengths and challenges of the cosmological argument

Strengths	Challenges
Cause and effect can be seen within everything in the universe	Cannot prove that Allah caused the universe
Supports the Islamic story of creation in the Qur'an	If we accept everything within the universe has a cause, it doesn't mean that the universe itself has a cause
Compatible with scientific theories: if the Big Bang caused the universe, it could itself have been caused by Allah	If everything has a cause, what caused Allah?
There must be a first cause of the universe	

Non-religious arguments against the cosmological argument and the Muslim response

I believe the scientific explanations of how the universe came about and do not believe in the cosmological argument.

As a Muslim, I agree that science can help us to understand creation. I also accept the existence of a first cause and that cause would be Allah.

Now try this

'The cosmological argument does not prove the existence of Allah.'
Evaluate this statement considering arguments for and against. In your response you should:
- refer to Muslim teachings
- refer to non-religious points of view
- reach a justified conclusion.   **(12 marks)**

The existence of suffering

Evil and **suffering** may create problems for Muslims who believe in Allah as compassionate. It may lead some to question their faith in Allah or even reject his existence altogether.

Surah 1 and the nature of Allah as compassionate

> In the name of Allah, the Entirely Merciful, the Especially Merciful. [All] praise is [due] to Allah, Lord of the worlds – The Entirely Merciful, the Especially Merciful, Sovereign of the Day of Recompense. It is You we worship and You we ask for help. Guide us to the straight path – The path of those upon whom You have bestowed favour, not of those who have evoked [Your] anger or of those who are astray. (Surah 1:1–7)

This quote from the Qur'an suggests Allah is merciful and forgiving. It also suggests that Allah guides Muslims and helps them. Yet, this view of Allah seems to be in conflict with the fact that there is evil and suffering in the world. It can lead some to question their faith, while others may reject religion altogether.

Moral evil, for example wars that cause death, destruction and suffering

Types of evil in the world

Natural evil, for example disasters like earthquakes, which may cause multiple deaths and much suffering

Suffering and the nature of Allah

If there is suffering and evil in the world, then this raises questions for Muslims as to the compassionate nature of Allah.

If Allah is **all-good**, he would want to remove evil and suffering as he cares for his creation

omnibenevolent

If Allah is **all-knowing**, he would know how to remove evil and suffering

omniscient

Allah

If Allah is **all-powerful**, he would be able to remove evil and suffering

omnipotent

Does Allah exist at all?

Some Muslims may find that evil questions their faith in Allah existing at all.

If he exists, why doesn't he stop the evil?

If Allah existed, there would be no evil.

In your answer you must refer to a source of authority, such as the Qur'an.

Now try this

Explain **two** reasons why evil and suffering cause a problem for Muslims and their understanding of Allah as compassionate. In your answer you must refer to a source of wisdom and authority. **(5 marks)**

Solutions to the problem of suffering

The problem of evil and suffering is a challenge for Muslims. They may respond to it in different ways, perhaps by looking to sources of authority such as the Qur'an or offering practical solutions.

What the Qur'an says about coping with suffering

> O you who have believed, seek help through patience and prayer. Indeed, Allah is with the patient. (Surah 2:153)

Muslims believe that the Qur'an commands them to use prayer to cope with challenges in the world – they believe this develops characteristics such as patience.

> Surely we shall test you with something of fear and hunger, and loss of wealth and loves and crops … but give glad tidings to the steadfast who say when misfortune strikes: we are Allah's and to Him we are returning. (Surah 2:155–156)

Muslim's believe evil is a test of humanity's freewill – a test of their faith in Allah when things seem difficult. They also believe that they should accept suffering and not question it, as they are taught that Allah is compassionate and they will be reunited with him. (See also Surah 2:177.)

Life is a test

Muslims live their lives always aware that their actions will determine their afterlife. Most Muslims would recognise that there is a purpose to suffering and it is not their place to question it.

Prayer

Muslims believe regular prayer is essential and Salah is a requirement to pray five times a day. Prayer would help them to deal with the pain they may be suffering and it will offer comfort from Allah. Some may question whether more practical options have more success in helping others.

Muslim responses to the problem of evil and suffering

A person praying.

Charity

Muslims would believe that charity work is a practical way of helping those who are suffering cope with what they are going through. Many Muslims may feel this has the most impact, as it will directly benefit those who are suffering.

A Zakah box where charity money is collected.

Zakah

Think about three things that Muslims can do to help relieve suffering.

Now try this

Outline **three** ways in which Muslims may respond to suffering in the world.   **(3 marks)**

Human rights

Human rights are the basic rights and freedoms to which all human beings are entitled.

Nature and purpose of human rights

In the UK today, human rights are protected by law. The **Universal Declaration of Human Rights**, adopted by the UN General assembly in 1948, says all humans are born free and equal in dignity and rights. The purpose of human rights is to ensure equality and fairness to humans. Muslims would support human rights being upheld.

Human rights entitles every citizen of the UK to these basic rights.

Muslim teachings on human rights

1. It is our duty in life.

2. All humans were created equal by Allah – all Muslims should have the same entitlements.

3. We stand up against injustice in the world where human rights are being denied.

4. Muhammad tried to demonstrate the fair treatment of all people and we want to follow his example.

5. The Qur'an has teachings in it that support human rights.

Problems of human rights for Muslims

- When there is conflict between a human right and a law within Islam, or where individual conscience seems in conflict.

- When a Muslim sees a conflict between a human right and a law of the country they live in.

- When one human right being applied against another

- When countries have different laws and rules, resulting in inequality.

O you who have believed, be persistently standing firm for Allah, witnesses in justice, and do not let the hatred of a people prevent you from being just. Be just; that is nearer to righteousness. And fear Allah; indeed, Allah is Acquainted with what you do. (Surah 5:8)

This demonstrates that Allah wants his people to be fair and why. Muslims believe they should support human rights.

Divergent Muslim responses to human rights

☑ The majority of Muslims agree that human rights are important and need to be upheld

☑ It is fair to say that no two situations will ever be the same, yet, when rules and laws are applied, they may be dealt with in the same way, which may seem unfair to some.

☑ Some Muslims may wish for people to be treated differently depending on their circumstances – as in situation ethics.

☑ Some human rights (for example same-sex marriage) may conflict with Islamic teachings, which can cause problems.

Non-religious views about human rights

I am an atheist and I believe that every person has the right to be treated fairly.

I am a humanist and believe that human rights are at the centre of the beliefs of being a humanist – it is important that people's basic rights are recognised, established and upheld.

Muslim response: As a Muslim, I believe in human rights and equality and fairness for all, but I refer to Muslim teachings to justify why.

Now try this

1 Outline **three** Muslim teachings about human rights.   **(3 marks)**

2 Explain **two** reasons why Muslims may support human rights.   **(4 marks)**

Equality

Equality is a key idea in Islam. The religion of Islam has many followers across the world in many different countries. They believe all Muslims are part of the ummah and are equal. However, there are many causes of inequality in the world – ignorance, selfishness and greed are some of them.

Problems caused by inequality and Muslim teachings

The Hadith demonstrates that equality is needed in order for society to be fair. Sometimes the behaviour and attitudes of people can cause inequality, and problems arise as a result, impacting on people's well being. The Hadith shows that whoever commits the crime the same punishment should be given.

Breakdown in communication between people can lead to inequality

> The people of Quraish worried about the lady from Bani Makhzum who had committed theft. They asked, 'Who will intercede for her with Allah's Apostle?' Some said, 'No one dare to do so except Usama bin Zaid the beloved one to Allah's Apostle.' When Usama spoke about that to Allah's Apostle, Allah's Apostle said, (to him), 'Do you try to intercede for somebody in a case connected with Allah's Prescribed Punishments?' Then he got up and delivered a sermon saying, 'What destroyed the nations preceding you, was that if a noble amongst them stole, they would forgive him, and if a poor person amongst them stole, they would inflict Allah's Legal punishment on him. By Allah, if Fatima, the daughter of Muhammad stole, I would cut off her hand. (Sahih al-Bukhari 56:681)

Lack of respect for sources of authority and those in power as people bend the rules when they want to suit themselves leads to inequality

Refusal to follow laws as they do not see them being applied fairly can lead to inequality

Different Muslim teachings and practices that reflect equality

Islam teaches that all people were created by Allah and created equally, although not the same. This can be interpreted to mean men and women are equal but also unequal.

The Qur'an teaches: 'And among His signs is the creation of the heavens and the earth, and the difference of your languages and colours' (Surah 30:22). This shows that differences between people are not important.

Muslims are united as they are all part of the ummah, regardless of colour and nationality. They have a duty to help others and treat everyone equally.

There are many practices in Islam that show equality: completion of Hajj, all wearing white garments, praying at the same time every day, etc.

Muhammad's final sermon before his death spoke of equality and tolerance.

Islamic solutions to inequality

Zakah   Muslim Aid   Work of mosques   Prayer

Charity

Islamic Relief

Solutions to inequality

Imams speaking out against inequality

Muslims support these solutions because they believe all humans are equal as all were created by Allah; they have a duty to care for others and they should follow the example of Muhammad.

Now try this

Explain **two** ways that Muslims work to reduce inequality in the world. **(4 marks)**

Religious freedom

Muslims believe that having the freedom to be able to choose your religion is important.

Nature of religious freedom

Religious freedom is when a person is free to choose their religion, change their religion, or choose to not have any religion at all.

Symbols of different religions.

> And Allah is Hearing and Knowing. Allah is the ally of those who believe. He brings them out from darknesses into the light. And those who disbelieve – their allies are Taghut. They take them out of the light into darknesses. Those are the companions of the Fire; they will abide eternally therein. (Surah 2:256–57)

This quote shows that Muslims believe religious freedom is important.

Living in a multifaith society

Benefits

Greater tolerance and understanding of the beliefs of others	Varied and rich cultural life from experiencing the religions and traditions of others
Better understanding of different viewpoints	New ways of living and enjoying life

Challenges

It is not always easy to be open and understanding towards the views of others	There have been examples of religious persecution and hatred
Religious tension exists between different faith groups	Beliefs and values of some groups may be ignored

Most Muslims in the UK live side by side in harmony with other religious groups.

Non-religious arguments against religious freedom

Some people with non-religious views may be against religious freedom because of the impact it might have on the lives of others. For example, people might find the methods of killing animals for halal food inhumane and object to Muslims having the right to use these methods. Other examples may include the celebration of religious festivals or allowing Muslims to participate in religious holidays and prayer on a Friday.

Importance of religious freedom

Religious freedom is a fundamental human right and is part of the Universal Declaration of Human Rights. If this right is upheld, it creates the conditions for peace, and peace is an important idea within Islam. Muslims believe that community is important – demonstrated by the ummah.

Divergent responses of Muslims to a multifaith society

Limited religious freedom

Some believe that Islam is the only true faith and the only religion exclusively correct

Some hold that Islam has the whole truth but other religions have parts of the truth

Some believe they have a mission to lead non-Muslims to Allah

Some accept that all righteous people will be favoured by Allah and, therefore, it does not matter which religion a person belongs to.

Maximum religious freedom

Now try this

'It is difficult for Muslims to live in a multifaith society.'
Evaluate this statement considering arguments for and against. In your response you should:
- refer to Muslim teachings
- refer to different Muslim points of view
- reach a justified conclusion.   **(12 marks)**

Use divergent responses of Muslims to a multifaith society to help you.

Muslims would say that religious freedom as part of human rights covers all aspects of their religion.

Prejudice and discrimination

You need to know what the terms 'prejudice' and 'discrimination' mean – be careful to make sure you understand each one and don't get them confused!

Prejudice

Prejudice is pre-judging a person or making a judgement about someone before you actually know them.

Prejudice and discrimination can lead to problems in society. People may find they are in conflict with others and it could lead to physical violence.

Discrimination

Discrimination is an action – it is when a person is actually treated differently as a result of a prejudice. It can take the form of positive or negative discrimination – when a person is treated positively against others or when a person is treated negatively and unfairly.

O mankind, indeed We have created you from male and female and made you peoples and tribes that you may know one another. Indeed, the most noble of you in the sight of Allah is the most righteous of you. Indeed, Allah is Knowing and Acquainted. (Surah 49:13)

This quote shows the importance of the belief that all humans were created equally by Allah. This is a key teaching when considering why Muslims believe prejudice and discrimination is wrong.

Muslim teachings on the nature of prejudice and discrimination

1. Muslims believe Allah created all humans – they are equal although not the same – and all deserve equal respect and treatment. This includes people of different religions.

2. Muhammad taught about the importance of treating everyone equally in his final sermon. Therefore, Muslims believe they should treat a person of any faith in the same way.

3. Muslims believe it is important to educate others about religion rather than to treat people differently because they are of a different religion.

Situation ethics

This ethical theory states that the action that should be taken in moral situations is the one that is considered to be the most loving to the individual in the given situation. However, if humans are equal, they should all be treated the same. This could lead to problems when considering issues of prejudice and discrimination because situation ethics determines that each situation should be taken separately and, therefore, universal, absolute rules cannot be applied. This could result in people being treated differently, which seems to go against teachings such as the Qur'anic one above.

Now try this

Make sure you state three separate teachings.

Outline **three** Muslim teachings on prejudice and discrimination.

(3 marks)

Racial harmony

Islam teaches that all people are equal and, therefore, racial harmony is essential. All Muslims are part of the ummah – the worldwide Islamic community. Muslims encourage racial harmony with non-Muslim communities as well.

Muslims and racial harmony

Muslims from all around the world face Makkah when praying, attend Hajj and fast during the month of Ramadan.

Muslims from all around the world pray together in Arabic – a shared language of all Muslims.

Muhammad declared in his last sermon that 'there is no difference between Arabs and non-Arabs', which means that racism is wrong and people from all races are equal.

The Qur'an teaches that no race is better than any other.

There are Muslim organisations who campaign non-violently against racism, e.g. MuslimARC.

How Muslims work towards racial harmony

Why Muslims work towards racial harmony

Muslims believe Allah created all humans equally and, therefore, all humans should be treated the same, regardless of race.

There are examples of individual Muslims who campaigned/ campaign for racial equality, such as Muhammad Ali and Malcolm X.

All Muslims are part of the worldwide ummah and come from every race in the world.

Muhammad Ali and Malcolm X in 1964.

For more on Malcolm X, see page 129.

Muslim teachings on racial harmony

All mankind is descended from Adam and Eve, an Arab is not better than a non-Arab and a non-Arab is not better than an Arab; a white person is not better than a black person, nor is a black person better than a white person except by piety and good actions. Learn that every Muslim is the brother of every other Muslim and that Muslims form one brotherhood. (From the Final Sermon of Muhammad)

This teaching suggests that racial harmony is important in Islam.

The benefits of living in a multi-ethnic society

Encourages racial harmony – helps people of different cultures, races and religions to understand each other

Helps to reduce discrimination and race attacks

Brings together people with fresh new ideas – people can learn from those who have different faiths and ethnic backgrounds, as well as sharing their faith and individual ethnic backgrounds

Gives wider variety of music, food, clothes and culture and helps everyone to broaden their traditions and identify more with other people and the country they live in

Community centre, Keighley, West Yorkshire

Now try this

Make sure you give three different beliefs for this question.

Make sure you explain one benefit and then add a second sentence to develop it fully – this could be more explanation, an example or a quote.

1 Outline **three** reasons why Muslims work for racial harmony.   (3 marks)
2 Explain **two** benefits for Muslims of living in a multi-ethnic society.   (4 marks)

Racial discrimination

Discrimination on racial grounds is illegal in the UK. Muslim teachings support these laws to protect people from **racial discrimination**.

Racial discrimination and our society

Racial discrimination occurs when a person is treated differently, often negatively, because of their race, colour, descent, national or ethnic origin or immigrant status. This could include both positive and negative discrimination.

A march in Glasgow in 2015 in support of the International Day for the Elimination of Racial Discrimination

In the USA, signs such as these were legal until the Civil Rights Act of 1964 outlawed segregation. Use of the signs persisted illegally for some years after.

Muslim teachings about racial discrimination

1 Muslims believe everyone was made equal by Allah.

2 The Qur'an teaches: 'And of His signs is the creation of the heavens and the earth and the diversity of your languages and your colors. Indeed in that are signs for those of knowledge' (Surah 30:22). This suggests that Islam recognises there is diversity between people in terms of race, but they are all equal.

3 Muslims recognise that diversity between people can cause problems in society and lead to conflict.

O mankind, indeed We have created you from male and female and made you peoples and tribes that you may know one another. Indeed, the most noble of you in the sight of Allah is the most righteous of you. Indeed, Allah is Knowing and Acquainted. (Surah 49:13)

This quote promotes ideas of equality as it shows all humans were created as equal by Allah. Racial discrimination is wrong for Muslims as Islam recognises that one race is no different from another.

Malcolm X and divergent Muslim responses to racial discrimination

☑ Malcolm X was an African-American Muslim who campaigned for racial equality after his family.

☑ He became a minister for the radical Nation of Islam organisation to try to spread the message for a 'Black people only state'.

☑ In his speeches, Malcolm X said that his followers should not start violence but should defend themselves if attacked. Some Muslims today may share his view.

☑ Some Muslims today believe that equality should be achieved by entirely peaceful methods.

For more on Malcolm X, see page 128.

Now try this

1 Explain **two** Muslim beliefs on racial discrimination. **(4 marks)**

2 'We should all stand up to racial discrimination.'
Evaluate this statement considering arguments for and against. In your response you should:
- refer to Muslim teachings
- reach a justified conclusion.
(12 marks)

You are required to consider this statement from different points of view. Make sure you give a Muslim view and refer to their teachings. You could use Malcolm X as an example of a Muslim who was willing to use violence in certain circumstances.

Social justice

Justice in society is the equal distribution of wealth, opportunities and privileges.

Wealth and opportunity in the UK and world

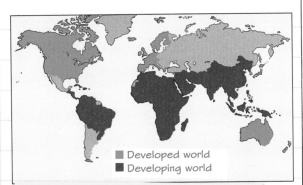

■ Developed world
■ Developing world

Wealth and opportunity are not distributed equally among people in the UK, nor in the rest of the world. Small numbers of people hold very large amounts of wealth, resulting in many people living in poverty. Wealth gives these people far greater opportunities in life than the majority of people worldwide.

Muslim teachings about social justice

Muslims believe:

☑ they have a duty to work for social justice

☑ Allah is always watching and they will be judged after death by Allah on their actions

☑ all humans are equal as they were made equal by Allah

☑ everyone is human and is entitled to human rights

☑ the Qur'an teaches Muslims they should work for social justice

☑ in Shari'ah law, which promotes social justice

☑ in the Five Pillars, which promote social justice – Zakah (charity) and Sawm (fasting) is done to sympathise with the poor in society

☑ that each situation should be taken individually and appropriate help given – this could be seen to be applying the ethical theory of situation ethics, which means the action taken in each individual situation is what is most loving.

The Qur'an and social justice

Those who follow the Messenger, the unlettered prophet, whom they find written in what they have of the Torah and the Gospel, who enjoins upon them what is right and forbids them what is wrong and makes lawful for them the good things and prohibits for them the evil and relieves them of their burden and the shackles which were upon them. So they who have believed in him, honored him, supported him and followed the light which was sent down with him – it is those who will be the successful. (Surah 7:157)

This quote talks of the importance of helping others through social justice in order to relieve the inequality within the world.

Worked example

Outline **three** ways in which Muslims work for social justice. **(3 marks)**

Muslims give Zakah (2.5%) to charity every year. Islamic charities such as Islamic Relief work for social justice. Muslims will try to educate others about social justice.

Other points you could include are the giving of sadaqah (voluntary charitable donations); helping others; and giving other examples of charities, such as Muslim Aid.

Now try this

Make sure you include a source of wisdom, such as a quote from the Qur'an or Hadith, within at least one of the reasons you explain.

Explain **two** reasons why Muslims work for social justice in the world. In your answer you must refer to a source of wisdom and authority. **(5 marks)**

Wealth and poverty

Poverty causes great suffering for many people in many countries around the world. The cause of poverty and its effects are of great concern for Muslims. Muslims believe wealth is a gift from Allah that should not be wasted but shared.

Nature of poverty

Poverty is the state of being extremely poor or lacking in basics. This could lead to a lack of food, safe drinking water, sanitation facilities, health, shelter, education or information.

Causes of poverty in the UK and world

Poverty is often caused by a number of combined factors. Some of the common causes of poverty are:

1. inequality in wages
2. lack of provision of benefits
3. population growth
4. war
5. unemployment
6. being made homeless
7. illness or injury.

Muslim teachings about wealth and poverty

Disapproval of greed and waste – all possessions belong to Allah

Expected to act responsibly and help those in need

Paying Zakah

> And be steadfast in prayer and regular in charity: and whatever good ye send forth for your souls before you, ye shall find it with Allah: for Allah sees well all that ye do. (Surah 2:110)

Choosing to give sadaqah

Disagreeing with gambling or lending money for profit

> Righteousness is not that you turn your faces toward the east or the west, but [true] righteousness is [in] one who believes in Allah, the Last Day, the angels, the Book, and the prophets and gives wealth, in spite of love for it, to relatives, orphans, the needy, the traveler, those who ask [for help], and for freeing slaves; [and who] establishes prayer and gives zakah; [those who] fulfill their promise when they promise; and [those who] are patient in poverty and hardship and during battle. Those are the ones who have been true, and it is those who are the righteous. (Surah 2:177)

Believing that every person needs to be treated as an individual and helped according to their needs

Giving to charities such as Muslim Aid and Islamic Relief

Explain each idea fully using evidence and examples to support what you write.

Now try this

Explain **two** reasons why Muslims believe it is important to share wealth with others. **(4 marks)**

The paper and (a) type questions

You take two exam papers from a choice of three areas of study. Each area of study must be on a different religion, e.g. Islam and Christianity.

- Paper 1 area of study 1: Religion and Ethics
- Paper 2 area of study 2: Religion, Peace and Conflict
- Paper 3 area of study 3: Religion, Philosophy and Social Justice

Each exam paper is separated into four sections (questions 1, 2, 3 and 4) and each question has four parts: (a), (b), (c) and (d). There are 102 marks available for each paper and you have 1 hour and 45 minutes to complete the paper, giving you 25 minutes to complete each section or 1 minute per mark.

(a) type questions

(a) type questions are worth 3 marks and ask you to outline or state three things. Aim to spend approximately 3 minutes answering each (a) type question. These may be beliefs, teachings, features, reasons or something else.

For example:

> (a) Outline **three** Muslim beliefs about the nature of Allah.   **(3 marks)**

> In this question you are asked to outline three separate beliefs. You must give three beliefs about what Muslims hold to be true about Allah. To be successful, you must give three accurate and factual ideas. Write a brief statement about the three things. You do not need to explain them, give examples (unless asked) or give extra quotes.

Worked example

> (a) Outline **three** Muslim beliefs about jihad.   **(3 marks)**
>
> One belief is that jihad is a striving every Muslim should make for Allah.
>
> Another belief is that greater jihad (personal struggle) is more important than lesser jihad (outer struggle).
>
> A third Muslim belief is that lesser jihad is understood as being a holy war.

> This answer is concise and offers three correct statements.

Worked example

> (a) Outline **three** Muslim beliefs about Akhirah.
>   **(3 marks)**
>
> One Muslim belief is that after death they will be judged by Allah.
>
> Also, they believe that if they are a good Muslim, they will be rewarded in paradise.

> This answer makes a good start and offers relevant and accurate information, but it is only a partial answer as it gives two beliefs instead of three.

Improved sample answer

> Muslims believe that after death they are judged by Allah.
>
> They believe good Muslims will go to paradise.
>
> They believe that people who have not been good will go to hell.

Remember:
- ✓ Make sure you state three things as required by this type of question.
- ✓ Write each idea in a separate sentence.
- ✓ Keep your answers short and to the point – you are **not** asked to explain the ideas, only state them.

> This answer is an improvement as it gives three separate beliefs, which is a requirement of the question.

(b) type questions

(b) type questions are worth 4 marks and require you to **describe** or **explain** two key areas within the Christian or Islamic faith. Aim to spend approximately 4 minutes answering each (b) type question. This could include beliefs, teachings, ideas, features, events or ways, to name a few.

Applying your skills

To do well on a (b) type question, you should:

- state **two** points, e.g. two beliefs, teachings or reasons for a Christian or Muslim view
- **develop** each point you give by adding a second sentence that explains the point you have given, adds new information that answers the question or offers an example to demonstrate your understanding. You can also include a quote that is relevant to an example.

Worked example

(b) Describe **two** ways in which prayer is different for Muslims and Christians. **(4 marks)**

One way that prayer is different for Muslims compared to Christians is that Muslims have set prayers (Salah). Although Christians are expected to pray every day to God, there is no set time.

Another way that prayer is different for Muslims is that they have a set of prayer positions, whereas Christians may sit, stand or kneel during prayer.

> Be aware that you could be asked to compare and contrast how ideas, beliefs or practices are different between one religion and another, as shown in this question.

> The two differences have been described, showing that the student clearly understands the practice of prayer and how it differs between Muslims and Christians. There is no need for development or explanation.

Worked example

(b) Explain **two** reasons why Muslims believe racial harmony is important. **(4 marks)**

The ummah shows that racial harmony is important. Muhammad spoke about it in his final sermon.

Improved sample answer

One Muslim belief is that the ummah shows racial harmony is important. The ummah includes all Muslims from every country and every race, showing that Islam teaches all Muslims are equal.

Also, Muhammad spoke about racial harmony in his final sermon. He spoke about there being no difference between Arabs or non-Arabs, showing that he taught all people of every race were equal.

> Although the student has offered **two** reasons, these are briefly stated and not developed. Neither one is fully explained, which is required by this type of question.

> This improved answer gives two different reasons and each one is developed by adding an explanation to show the student fully understands the reasons offered.

Remember:

✓ Make sure that the two reasons you give and develop in your answer are different from each other. You cannot include repetition in your reasons or development.

✓ Also make sure that the development you offer relates directly to both the question and the reason you have given.

(c) type questions

(c) type questions are worth 5 marks and require you to **explain** key areas within the Christian or Islamic faith. Aim to spend approximately 4 minutes answering each (c) type question. This could include beliefs, teachings, ideas, features, events or ways of worship.

Applying your skills

To do well on a (c) type question, you should:

* state **two** points, e.g. two beliefs, teachings or reasons for a Christian or Muslim view
* **develop** each point you give by adding a second sentence that explains the point you have given, adds new information which answers the question or offers an example to demonstrate your understanding
* add in a relevant **source of authority** for one of the two points given in your answer – this could be ,for example, a quotation from a relevant holy text, or writings and sayings of relevant leaders. This part is only worth 1 mark and can be a paraphrase, so do not worry if you can't remember the exact wording of the source.

Worked example

(c) Explain **two** reasons why some Muslims will not accept the use of contraception. In your answer you must refer to a source of wisdom and authority.   **(5 marks)**

Some Muslims believe that some forms of contraception actually cause an early abortion, which is considered murder.

Permanent contraception is used to intentionally lead a child-free life, which is against Muslim teachings about the importance of family and that only Allah, not people, should make decisions about life; as the Hadith states: 'No soul which Allah has destined to exist, but will surely come into existence'.

The two different ideas explained in this answer are both developed, adding further information to the first point made. The second reason has also been linked to a source of wisdom and authority. Remember that this can be from the Hadith, as this example shows.

Worked example

(c) Explain **two** reasons why forgiveness is important to Muslims. In your answer you must refer to a source of wisdom and authority.   **(5 marks)**

One belief is that Allah is forgiving: 'Allah is Forgiving and Merciful' (Surah 64:14).

Another is that they must follow the example of Muhammad who forgave others.

This student has offered two reasons but they are not developed, although one quote from a source of authority has been given to support the answer.

Improved sample answer

Muslims believe that Allah is forgiving, and so it is important for them to be forgiving in their own lives. As the Qur'an says: 'Allah is Forgiving and Merciful.' (Surah 64:14)

Muslims also believe that they must follow the example of Muhammad by forgiving others. If they don't, they cannot expect forgiveness from Allah.

This improved answer gives two different reasons and each one has been developed by adding new information. The first reason has also been successfully linked to a relevant source of wisdom and authority.

Remember:
The main difference between type (b) and type (c) questions is that (c) type questions have the added requirement of a reference to a source of wisdom and authority.

(d) type questions

(d) type questions are worth 12 marks and require you to **evaluate** a stimulus and consider different viewpoints about the significance of a particular aspect of belief. Aim to spend approximately 15 minutes answering each (d) type question.

Remember:

Questions 1 and 3 of the (d) type questions have 3 extra marks available for your use of **spelling, punctuation and grammar (SPaG)**, as well as your use of **specialist terminology**, making them worth 15 marks. Always go back to check your answers!

Applying your skills

To do well on a (d) type question, you should:

- consider a **range of viewpoints** on a given statement
- present **justified reasons** for those views within your answer
- try to **use examples** to illustrate the ideas you include
- **include teachings** – where possible, you could quote these within your answer
- **structure your answer** – make your point, develop it and give a source to support it
- use the arguments and reasons offered to create a **justified conclusion**.

Worked example

(d) 'Everyone should pay Zakah.'

Evaluate this statement considering arguments for and against.

In your response you should:
- refer to Muslim teachings
- refer to different Muslim points of view
- reach a justified conclusion.

(15 marks)

> Read the question carefully – you could be asked to refer to Muslim teachings, different Muslim points of view, non-religious points of view or even ethical theories. Make sure you check that you have met all the required elements.

Sunni Muslims would agree as they believe Zakah is a religious duty for every Muslim as it is one of the Five Pillars. The money is used to help the poor and needy, which the Qur'an includes when it lists the people – it is 'an obligation [imposed] by Allah' to help.

Caring for others and supporting the ummah (Muslim community) is seen as another duty. Zakah can be used to help all Muslims; therefore, everyone should pay it. As the Qur'an states: '[true] righteousness is [in] one who believes in Allah, the Last Day, the angels, the Book, and the prophets and gives wealth.'

Giving Zakah promotes social justice and equality. These are also important as this is how Muslims believe Allah wants them to live their lives.

> This answer offers a coherent argument of agreement, offering a number of reasons that are supported using appropriate quotes from a source of authority.

Some Shi'a Muslims may disagree, believing that Zakah is voluntary and a private decision. They place greater importance on khums as it is one of the Ten Obligatory Acts – Zakah is not the only way to help others. They may also point out that some Muslims are not expected to give Zakah and are exempt, e.g. due to poverty, so it is impossible for everyone to be expected to pay.

Finally, Zakah is a Muslim idea so non-Muslims would not be expected to give this money.

> Here, an alternative view is offered. The student has successfully referred to different Muslim points of view through offering the view of Shi'a Islam. A number of reasons have been given to disagree – each with developed evidence and ideas.

Overall, I think most Muslims would agree with this statement as they view Zakah as compulsory and a way of helping others. Even khums is used to help others, showing that Shi'a Muslims believe this idea is important. By paying Zakah, Muslims are showing submission to Allah – the central belief in Islam.

> Here, the student has made reasoned judgements that are supported by the evidence and the argument is brought together through the conclusion.

Answers

Unit 1 Christian beliefs

1 The Trinity

Award 1 mark for each point identified, up to a maximum of 3 marks.

- The Trinity is the idea of the Father, Son and Holy Spirit (1).
- Christians believe the Trinity helps them to understand that there is One God who is understood in three different ways (1).
- Christians believe that the three parts of the Trinity are equally important (1).
- The beliefs of the Trinity (Father, Son and Holy Spirit) are mentioned in Christian worship when Christians pray (1).
- The Trinity is mentioned as part of the Nicene Creed (1).

Accept any other valid response.

2 Interpretations of Creation

Award 1 mark for each way. Award a second mark for development of the way, up to a maximum of 4 marks.

- Literalist Christians believe the Creation story in the Bible is literally true (word for word) (1). They accept the world was created in six 24-hour 'days' and reject all science that conflicts with what the Bible says (1).
- Non-literalist Christians believe the Creation story in the Bible is true, but do not understand it as a factual account, rather a metaphorical one (1). They believe science and religion together explain how the universe was created (1).

Accept any other valid response.

3 The Incarnation

Award 1 mark for each point identified, up to a maximum of 3 marks. Answers could include any three from the following (or other relevant information):

- Christians believe Jesus is the Son of God, as shown in the Trinity (1).
- Christians believe Jesus was God in human form on Earth (1).
- Jesus is believed to be the Saviour of the world, as he came to redeem the sins of humanity (1).
- Christians believe Jesus was human and yet divine at the same time, as he took human form on Earth but was still one element of God seen in the Trinity (1).
- Jesus is believed to have performed miracles, so showing the power he had (1).

Accept any other valid response.

4 The last days of Jesus' life

Award 1 mark for each point identified, up to a maximum of 3 marks.

- Jesus shared a final meal with his disciples (known as the Last Supper) where they had bread and wine to represent the body and blood of Jesus (1).
- Jesus went with his disciples to the Garden of Gethsemane, where Judas betrayed him with a kiss to show the soldiers who to arrest (1).
- Jesus was put to death on a cross, having carried the cross himself (1).
- Three days after his crucifixion, Jesus was resurrected or brought back to life (1).
- Forty days after his resurrection, Jesus is believed to have ascended to heaven to be with God (1).

5 Salvation

Award 1 mark for providing a reason. Award a second mark for development of the reason, up to a maximum of 4 marks.

- Jesus died on the cross to atone for the sins of humanity and allow them to be saved (1). This means that Christians today believe they can also be rewarded in heaven and be with God (1).
- It is a crucial teaching in Christianity, seen through the importance given to Jesus and his actions (1). Many key practices and beliefs are related to Jesus so they are important today (1).
- Christians believe it allows them to get closer to God and develop their relationship with him (1). Understanding the sacrifice God made through giving his only son to the world to die on the cross helps them to understand that God loves them (1).

Accept any other valid response.

6 Life after death

Award 1 mark for each belief. Award a second mark for development of the belief, up to a maximum of 4 marks.

- Heaven is believed to be a reward for Christians who deserve it (1). It is for those who have performed good deeds and believe in God (1).
- Christians believe they will be judged by God after death to determine whether they deserve to achieve salvation in heaven (1). Christians believe the reward of heaven will be eternal life with God (1).
- Many Christians today do not believe heaven is a physical place (1). Heaven could be a spiritual place where those who deserve reward go after death to be with God (1).

Accept any other valid response.

7 Evil and suffering

Award 1 mark for providing a reason. Award a second mark for development of the reason, up to a maximum of 4 marks.

- Christians believe God is omnipotent, which means they believe he is all-powerful and can do anything, including stopping evil and suffering (1). Christians may question why an all-loving God allows his creation to suffer, especially focusing on why some people may suffer so much (1).
- Christians believe God is omniscient, which means he is all-knowing and would be aware of the suffering of his Creation (1). Christians may question how a God who knows everything would allow evil to happen and yet not do something to prevent it (1).
- Christians believe God is benevolent, which means they think he loves and cares for his creation so wouldn't want it to suffer (1). Christians may question why God, if he is all-powerful and loves his Creation, doesn't stop the evil (1).

Accept any other valid response.

8 Solutions to evil and suffering

Candidates must underpin their analysis and evaluation with knowledge and understanding. Candidates will be required to demonstrate thorough knowledge and understanding, as well as accuracy, of religion and belief when responding to the question and in meeting AO2 descriptors.

Arguments for the statement:

- There is too much evil and suffering and it makes it difficult to accept why God does nothing to stop it. It is the strongest argument used to prove that God does not exist.

- Some people suffer so much, either in the amount of suffering, the intensity of suffering or the many occurrences of suffering (e.g. the Holocaust, disease, etc.). Many people may question the justice and fairness of this, which may lead some to deny the existence of God.
- Some people are innocent yet still seem to suffer. Newborn babies or people who have done nothing wrong do not escape suffering. This can seem unfair and, at times, many people struggle to understand this suffering. This makes people turn away from accepting God.

Arguments against the statement:

- Perhaps suffering has a purpose and we just don't understand what it is (just as we don't fully understand all aspects of God). Many aspects of religion are not fully understood, but accepting faith means putting trust in things that are not always fully understood.
- The example of Job, in the Bible, suggests that evil and suffering could be a test of faith. Coping with suffering can make a person stronger, suggesting that perhaps evil and suffering have a purpose within the world.
- Christians believe that humans were given free will by God so that they could make their own decisions and be 'free'. Having this free will, however, means that humans can choose to do wrong and cause hurt to others, which perhaps explains some of the evil and suffering in the world, meaning God is not responsible, humans are.

Accept any other valid response.

Unit 2 Marriage and the family

9 Marriage

1 Award 1 mark for each reason. Award further marks for each development of the reason, up to a maximum of 4 marks. Award 1 further mark for any relevant source of wisdom or authority.

- Many Christians believe marriage is a sacrament (1). This means God is involved in the ceremony and blesses the union of the couple, so it is considered to be very important (1): 'But at the beginning of creation God made them male and female. For this reason a man will leave his father and mother and be united to his wife, and the two will become one flesh. So they are no longer two, but one flesh. Therefore what God has joined together, let no one separate.' (Mark 10:6–9) (1).
- Marriage is what Christians believe God intended (1) – it is considered to be the correct context for a couple to have a sexual relationship and children (1): 'That is why a man leaves his father and mother and is united to his wife, and they become one flesh.' (Genesis 2:24)
- Many Christians believe that marriage is an important form of commitment (1); it is seen to bring stability and security to society through the creation of a family unit (1): 'That is why a man leaves his father and mother and is united to his wife, and they become one flesh.' (Genesis 2:24)

Accept any other valid response.

10 Sexual relationships

Award 1 mark for providing a teaching. Award a second mark for development of the teaching, up to a maximum of 4 marks.

- Sexual relationships should take place within marriage and should be exclusive (1). The Ten Commandments states that a person 'should not commit adultery' (1).
- Sexual relationships should only be between a married couple for the purpose of having a child (1). This is what the Bible says is God's intention for humans (1).

Accept any other valid response.

11 Families

Award 1 mark for each point identified, up to a maximum of 3 marks.

- To provide stability and security within which children can be raised (1).
- To provide a place where children can be taught the difference between right and wrong (1).
- It is where a married couple can have children as God wanted (1).
- It is where children can be raised and introduced to the Christian faith (1).
- It provides the correct context for teaching children about the Christian religion (1).

Accept any other valid response.

12 Roles within the family

Candidates must underpin their analysis and evaluation with knowledge and understanding. Candidates will be required to demonstrate thorough knowledge and understanding, as well as accuracy, of religion and belief when responding to the question and in meeting AO2 descriptors.

Arguments for the statement:

- The Church teaches this is what God intended for a man and woman who are married. As it is what God intended, it is very important.
- It is where children can be taught the difference between right and wrong. It is where morals and teachings, which are very important, can be shared.
- It is where children can be raised as good Christians and introduced to the Christian faith. They can be involved within the Church and have Christian teachings shared and demonstrated so they too may choose to be part of the faith.

Arguments to disagree with the statement:

- Some people may not have a family so other things may be important to them. They may value friends or material things more due to their experiences.
- Some people may not want children and may be happy just being married. Some couples choose not to have children as they wish to focus on their career or just their relationship.
- Society today has changed, and families can take many different shapes and sizes. As family has changed, it may not hold as much importance as it once did.

Accept any other valid response.

13 The family in the local parish

1 Award 1 mark for each point identified, up to a maximum of 3 marks.

- By providing classes to support those expecting children (1).
- By organising family services to unite the family and special occasions to bring families together (1).
- By organising classes for children to attend as well as Sunday School (1).
- By organising rites of passage events such as christenings (1).
- By providing counselling where the vicar or professionals can help the family (1).

Accept any other valid response.

2 Award 1 mark for providing a reason. Award a second mark for development of the reason, up to a maximum of 4 marks.

- It is in line with Jesus' teachings on the importance of caring for others (1). Helping families in the local community can provide structure and stability to society (1).
- It is through the family that children can be introduced to Christianity (1). They can learn about their faith and the teachings in the Bible (1).

- It is through the family that children can be brought up correctly (1). They can be taught the difference between right and wrong and grow up to be good citizens (1).

Accept any other valid response.

14 The family in the parish today

Award 1 mark for each point identified, up to a maximum of 3 marks.
- The parish provides practical, emotional and spiritual support (1).
- The support of the parish demonstrates the love of God, as family was part of his intention for humanity (1).
- The parish provides a sense of Christian community and strengthens the Church and the people within it (1).
- The parish allows Christians to socialise with others who share their faith and beliefs (1).

Accept any other valid response.

15 Family planning

Award 1 mark for providing a reason. Award a second mark for development of the reason, up to a maximum of 4 marks.
- Christians may hold different views about the purpose of sex, which impacts on their views about contraception (1). Some may believe that sex is only for having children, meaning they won't use contraception, while others may believe that sex is also for pleasure, therefore they may use contraception (1).
- Some Christians can hold differing views about the various types of contraception (1). Some may only accept natural methods of contraception, while others will also accept artificial methods (1).
- In today's society there is the danger of sexually transmitted diseases (STDs), which may impact on beliefs about contraception (1). Some may believe using contraception is the lesser of two evils in preventing the spread of STDs (1).

Accept any other valid response.

16 Divorce

1 Award 1 mark for each point identified, up to a maximum of 3 marks.
- Marriage is intended to be for life (1).
- The marriage vows include the words 'till death us do part' (1).
- The marriage ring (an unbroken circle) shows that marriage should be eternal – for life (1).
- Divorce is seen to harm and threaten the family unit (1).
- Christians believe that marriage is intended to be for life, as it is a sacrament made with God (1).

Accept any other valid response.

2 Candidates must underpin their analysis and evaluation with knowledge and understanding. Candidates will be required to demonstrate thorough knowledge and understanding, as well as accuracy, of religion and belief when responding to the question and in meeting AO2 descriptors.

Arguments for the statement:
- Catholics would agree, as they believe marriage is a sacrament with God and cannot be broken. As this is the case, they do not accept or even recognise divorce.
- Most Christians would argue that marriage is intended to be for life and divorce, therefore, goes against this. The marriage vows say the words 'till death us do part', which show that marriage is intended to be for life.
- Many Christians view divorce and remarriage as adultery because of what the Bible teaches. They believe that a person can only be married once and, unless their husband/wife dies, the marriage cannot be broken.

Arguments against the statement:
- Some Christians believe that, although divorce is not ideal, it can be accepted as a last resort. They recognise that sometimes relationships go wrong and divorce should be an option.
- Some Christians believe that, as UK law allows divorce, it should be accepted in circumstances where the marriage has broken down.
- Some Christians believe that humans do make mistakes and God forgives, so divorce may sometimes be an acceptable option if all other options have failed.

Accept any other valid response.

17 Men and women in the family

Candidates must underpin their analysis and evaluation with knowledge and understanding. Candidates will be required to demonstrate thorough knowledge and understanding, as well as accuracy, of religion and belief when responding to the question and in meeting AO2 descriptors.

Arguments for the statement:
- Men and women are different but equal in all aspects of life, such as employment. If this is the case, there should also be equality within the family unit.
- Sexism (whereby men and women are treated differently) reflects outdated ideas. Although such views may have been relevant in the past, many people today would argue that they are out of date.
- Christians argue that men and women are both able to perform equal roles within the family. If this is the case, they should be viewed and treated equally.

Arguments against the statement:
- Men and women may be more suited to traditional roles within the family, as first promoted by Christians and described in the Bible. Men are seen as the providers and women the home-keepers.
- Although men and women are equal, they are not the same and therefore should have slightly different roles. The roles are seen to suit the gender and complement each other.
- Catholics accept that men and women were made equally by God but given different roles. In this way, they are the equal but not the same.

Accept any other valid response.

18 Gender prejudice and discrimination

Award 1 mark for providing a reason. Award a second mark for development of the reason, up to a maximum of 4 marks. Award 1 further mark for any relevant source of wisdom or authority.
- The Bible teaches that men and women are equal although suited to different roles (1). Christians believe God created men and women as equals but gave them complementary roles suited to the way they were made physically (1).
- The Bible teaches in Galatians 3:28 that all humans are equal, including men and women (1). If they are the same, they should be treated the same in all aspects of life (1).
- In the past the Christian Church has been accused of sexism, so many Christians feel it is important to engage with modern social views (1). For example, in some Christian denominations today, women can become vicars and bishops (1).

Accept any other valid response.

Unit 3 Living the Christian life

19 Christian worship

Award 1 mark for providing a way. Award a second mark for development of the way, up to a maximum of 4 marks.

- Liturgical worship (1) – this is where Christians have a set pattern of worship such as a Sunday service where they may use the Common Book of Prayer (1).
- Non-liturgical worship (1) – this is less formal and structured worship that may include clapping, singing or dancing (1).
- Personal prayer (1) – this is when an individual communicates with God on their own, perhaps kneeling and reciting prayers such as the Lord's Prayer or using their own words (1).

20 The role of sacraments

Candidates must underpin their analysis and evaluation with knowledge and understanding. Candidates will be required to demonstrate thorough knowledge and understanding, as well as accuracy, of religion and belief when responding to the question and in meeting AO2 descriptors.

Arguments for the statement:

- The Eucharist represents the body and blood of Jesus. Jesus' importance is central to the Christian faith, and Christians take the Eucharist in order to remember his sacrifice.
- The significance of Jesus' death and resurrection are central to Christianity and so the Eucharist underpins the daily beliefs and practices of being a Christian.
- The Eucharist is a key ceremony that is celebrated regularly in church and brings all Christians together.

Arguments against the statement:

- Baptism is a more important sacrament as it symbolises a person becoming a Christian.
- All the sacraments are equally important. None is more important than any other as they all have a key role within the Christian faith.
- Some denominations put more emphasis on different sacraments. The Eucharist and baptism are seen as particularly important to Protestants (they are the only two they recognise, whereas the Roman Catholic Church observes seven sacraments).

Accept any other valid response.

21 The nature and purpose of prayer

1 Award 1 mark for each point identified, up to a maximum of 3 marks.
- Set prayers – such as those found in the Book of Common Prayer (1).
- Informal prayers – praying privately alone (1).
- The Lord's Prayer – 'Our Father ...' (1).

Accept any other valid response.

2 Award 1 mark for providing a reason. Award a second mark for development of the reason, up to a maximum of 4 marks.
- The Bible says that Christians should pray (1); Christians believe prayer is a way of communicating and getting closer to God (1).
- Jesus told his followers to pray (1); he gave them the Lord's Prayer (1).
- It is regular communication with God (1); Christians believe this is important to develop a relationship with God (1).
- It provides hope that God is listening (1); Christians believe that God listens to their prayer and answers their needs (1).

Accept any other valid response.

22 Pilgrimage

1 Award 1 mark for each point identified, up to a maximum of 3 marks.
- To trace the roots of the religion (1).
- To remember important people and events in the religion (1).
- To get closer to God (1).
- To go on a spiritual journey (1).
- To share their faith with others (1).

2 Award 1 mark for providing a reason. Award a second mark for development of the reason, up to a maximum of 4 marks.
- Pilgrimage is a way of tracing the roots of the religion and understanding the history of the religion (1). For example, places such as Bethlehem and Jerusalem were very important in the life of Jesus. By visiting them pilgrims can understand the importance of Jesus within the Christian faith (1).
- Christians believe that pilgrimage can bring them closer to God (1) – spending extra time in reflection, study or prayer as well as focusing on special places can help them to understand the nature of God better (1).
- Pilgrimage can provide Christians with an opportunity to share their faith with others (1). By going on a spiritual journey, Christians can share their thoughts and reflections on spiritually and so come to understand their faith better (1).

Accept any other valid response.

23 Celebrations

1 Award 1 mark for providing a reason. Award a second mark for development of the reason, up to a maximum of 4 marks.
- Christmas celebrates the birth and incarnation of Jesus (1). Jesus' human birth is central to the Christian faith, as this enabled him to be sacrificed for the sins of the world (1).
- Christmas is a festival that brings families together (1). Christian ideas of sharing and spending time together are central to this festival (1).
- Christmas is a time to think of others (1). Helping others is a key teaching in Christianity, and Christians try to put this teaching into practice at Christmas (1).

Accept any other valid response.

2 Candidates must underpin their analysis and evaluation with knowledge and understanding. Candidates will be required to demonstrate thorough knowledge and understanding, as well as accuracy, of religion and belief when responding to the question and in meeting AO2 descriptors.

Arguments for the statement:

- Easter celebrates the resurrection of Jesus, which gives hope of an afterlife with God. Therefore, Easter is more important than Christmas as it gives evidence of life after death.
- The death of Jesus is remembered at Easter time; Jesus died for the sins of the whole world. This is a crucial event in the history of Christianity and is more relevant than Jesus' birth, which is celebrated at Christmas.
- The resurrection of Jesus is an essential event in the life of Christianity as it gives proof of his divinity as the son of God. It also provides hope and evidence of God's love for the world in sending his son to redeem the sins of humanity.

Arguments against the statement:

- Without the birth of Jesus there wouldn't be the death and resurrection of Jesus, so arguably Christmas is as important if not more important than Easter.

- More people celebrate Christmas than Easter, showing it has a wider social relevance than Easter and, therefore, is a more important Christian celebration.
- The birth of Jesus signifies the start of the religion of Christianity. Christians recognise the importance of tracing the roots of their religion, so this event would be important in achieving this and the celebration of the birth of Jesus is a way of marking this occasion.

Accept any other valid response.

24 The future of the Church

Award 1 mark for providing a way. Award a second mark for development of the way, up to a maximum of 4 marks.

- Churches can help their local area and bring the community together through evangelical work (1). They can tackle community projects, which can improve an area for all the people who live there (1).
- Education can be provided to help people understand their faith better (1). This can help them to gain a clearer understanding of their purpose in life and get closer to God (1).
- Evangelical work can bring practical help, especially in poorer areas and countries (1). Evangelical work can help with education or building projects that will serve communities for the future (1).

Accept any other valid response.

25 The church in the local community

1 Award 1 mark for each point identified, up to a maximum of 3 marks.
   - By holding parish activities such as coffee mornings and clubs for youngsters (1).
   - Through ecumenism – bringing those of different denominations together (1).
   - By holding special events and celebrating festivals (1).
   - By completing outreach work (1).

2 Candidates must underpin their analysis and evaluation with knowledge and understanding. Candidates will be required to demonstrate thorough knowledge and understanding, as well as accuracy, of religion and belief when responding to the question and in meeting AO2 descriptors.

Arguments for the statement:
   - The local church community helps to bring people together, both those of faith and those without faith. It can create a sense of belonging for all people.
   - The local church can put on activities to draw people into Christianity and create a sense of community. This brings people together and provides support for those within a local community, to ensure they feel that they belong.
   - The local church community can put Christian principles into action such as caring for others and helping them. It can provide support to the most vulnerable in the community such as the elderly and show compassion towards them; this reflects key teachings within Christianity.

Arguments against the statement:
   - Some people are not religious and do not want to be involved in religious events. It would not be right to force them.
   - There are still differences between people and sometimes even within a local community these are too great to conquer. It may not be right to try to bring some people together.
   - Some people do not have a local religious community or do not want to be part of a community. It may not be important to them.

Accept any other valid response.

26 The worldwide Church

Award 1 mark for each reason. Award further marks for each development of the reason, up to a maximum of 4 marks. Award 1 further mark for any relevant source of wisdom or authority.

- The Bible teaches the importance of caring for others (1); this could involve giving money to a charity such as Christian Aid or helping Christians around the world who may face persecution (1): 'A new command I give you: Love one another. As I have loved you, so you must love one another. By this all everyone will know that you are my disciples, if you love one another.' (John 13:34–35) (1).
- Charity and helping others is shown to be important in Christianity (1). Many Christians may give money, either through tithing or by giving it to a charity such as Christian Aid, in order to put Christian teachings from the Bible about charity into action (1): 'A new command I give you: Love one another. As I have loved you, so you must love one another. By this everyone will know that you are my disciples, if you love one another' (John 13:34–35) (1).
- There are many examples of Christian teachings about helping others and the worldwide Church achieves this (1). Christians work to reconcile others and break down barriers (1): 'Love your neighbor as yourself' (Mark 12:31) (1).

Unit 4 Matters of life and death

27 Origins and value of the universe

Award 1 mark for providing a way. Award a second mark for development of the way, up to a maximum of 4 marks.

- A literalist response would only accept what the Bible says (1). Literalists would reject all scientific discoveries, claiming that as they conflict with their source of authority (the Bible) they must be wrong (1).
- A non-literalist response would try to accept both science and Christian explanations (1). Non-literalists see science as explaining how the universe came to exist but Christianity explaining why (1).

Accept any other valid response.

28 Sanctity of life

Candidates must underpin their analysis and evaluation with knowledge and understanding. Candidates will be required to demonstrate thorough knowledge and understanding, as well as accuracy, of religion and belief when responding to the question and in meeting AO2 descriptors.

Arguments for the statement:
- Christians believe that life is special; the Bible says in Genesis 1:27 that God created man 'in his own image'. This suggests that human life was made to be different and this is an important belief for Christians.
- The Bible describes the human body as a 'temple'. As a temple is something special that should be looked after, this suggests that human life is sacred and should be treated as such.
- Christians believe that life is a gift from God and humans should make the most of it. This Bible teaching emphasises that life is special because God made it.

Arguments against the statement:
- Although many Christians would argue that life is special because God created it, they would also argue that life is special for other reasons too, such as because humans have the ability to communicate, think and feel.
- Many Christians would argue that life is special because humans have ambitions, want to succeed and aim to do well.
- Many non-religious people would claim that life is special and should be protected but they would not make any reference to God, instead claiming that life is special because you only get one life and should make the most of it.

Accept any other valid response.

29 Human origins

Award 1 mark for providing a way. Award a second mark for development of the way, up to a maximum of 4 marks.

- Some Christians may accept the theory of evolution and religious teachings (1). They may believe that the two complement each other and view evolution as part of God's plan in creating the world (1).
- Some Christians may reject all scientific explanations for human origins (1). They may view the Bible as the key source of authority, arguing that it is God's word and cannot therefore be wrong (1).

Accept any other valid response.

30 Christian attitudes to abortion

Award 1 mark for providing a reason. Award a second mark for development of the reason, up to a maximum of 4 marks.

- The Bible teaches that life is special as it was created by God (1), so having an abortion is seen as disrespecting God (1).
- The Bible teaches in the Ten Commandments 'you shall not murder' (1). Some Christians therefore view abortion as murder (1).
- Some Christians, such as Catholics, follow the pope's teachings on abortion, which is that abortion is wrong, and this view is supported by religious texts such as the *Humanae Vitae* (1). For many Christians, it is important that they accept and follow the teachings of a higher religious authority (1).

Accept any other valid response.

31 Life after death (1)

Award 1 mark for providing a reason. Award a second mark for development of the reason, up to a maximum of 4 marks.

- The resurrection of Jesus shows there is life after death (1). Jesus rose from the dead and showed the way that Christians too can achieve a reward in heaven (1).
- The Bible teaches that there is an afterlife (1). Passages such as Ephesians 2:6 talk of heaven (1).
- Christians believe in a just and loving God (1). The idea of being rewarded for the way you have lived seems fair and supports this view (1).

Accept any other valid response.

32 Life after death (2)

Award 1 mark for providing a reason. Award a second mark for development of the reason, up to a maximum of 4 marks.

- Christians maintain the Bible teaches them there is life after death (1). Passages such as 1 Peter 3:21–22 talk of Jesus being in heaven at the right hand of God (1).
- Christians argue that Jesus' resurrection is evidence of an afterlife (1). Jesus came back to life after death, which shows that non-religious arguments about there not being an afterlife are wrong (1).
- Being a Christian means to have faith in the teachings of God such as belief in an afterlife (1), and this means it is not necessary to have physical proof of life after death (1).

Accept any other valid response.

33 Euthanasia

1 Award 1 mark for each point identified, up to a maximum of 3 marks.

- Euthanasia is wrong (1).
- Some Christians view euthanasia as murder (1).
- Life is special as God created it (1).
- The Bible teaches that euthanasia is wrong (1).
- Hospices are an alternative to euthanasia (1).

2 Candidates must underpin their analysis and evaluation with knowledge and understanding. Candidates will be required to demonstrate thorough knowledge and understanding, as well as accuracy, of religion and belief when responding to the question and in meeting AO2 descriptors.

Arguments for the statement:

- Euthanasia can be seen as murder, which is forbidden in the Ten Commandments – 'You shall not murder'. This suggests that euthanasia is wrong.
- The Bible includes teachings about the sanctity of life – the idea that life is special as God created it. As life is special, this shows that euthanasia is wrong.
- Stories in the Bible, such as that of Job, illustrate that suffering may have a purpose and humans should not question it. Job faced many challenges to his faith but never doubted God. This suggests humans should not allow euthanasia, as suffering may have a spiritual purpose so they should not question it.

Arguments against the statement:

- Some Christians may argue that suffering is hard to accept – whether it is your suffering or that of a member of your family. The lesser of two evils may be to allow the person a painless death with dignity.
- Some non-religious individuals may feel that is it okay to allow euthanasia if a person requests it, as this shows respect for their ability to make their own decisions about their life.
- Some people may follow situation ethics principles, which state that we should make decisions based on each individual situation and that general rules of euthanasia being right or wrong shouldn't be applied.

Accept any other valid response.

34 Issues in the natural world

1 Award 1 mark for each point identified, up to a maximum of 3 marks.

- God created animals (1).
- Animals are not as important as humans (1).
- Humans have stewardship over animals (1).
- Humans have dominion over animals (1).
- Animals were not created with souls (1).

Accept any other valid response.

2 Award 1 mark for providing a reason. Award a second mark for development of the reason, up to a maximum of 4 marks.

- Christians believe they have the duty of stewardship over the Earth (1). This is a God-given responsibility to care for the world and everything within it (1).
- Christians believe the world was created by God as a gift and is special (1). They believe that after death they will be judged on how they took care of his creation (1).
- The Bible teaches Christians that they should care for the world (1). They believe that God wants them to preserve the world for future generations (1).

Accept any other valid response.

Unit 5 Crime and punishment

35 Justice

Award 1 mark for each reason. Award further marks for each development of the reason, up to a maximum of 4 marks. Award 1 further mark for any relevant source of wisdom or authority.

- Jesus taught about the importance of justice (1). He taught his followers the idea of treating others as you would like to be treated, meaning that everyone is treated in a just and fair way (1): 'Do to others as you would have them do to you.' (Luke 6:31) (1).

- The Bible teaches that God wants people to act in a just way (1). When God created the world, this is what he intended (1): 'He has shown you, O mortal, what is good. And what does the Lord require of you? To act justly and to love mercy and to walk humbly with your God.' (Micah 6:8) (1).
- There are rules from God in the Bible, which guide people in what is right and wrong (1). Examples include not killing or stealing, which are part of the Ten Commandments (1): 'You shall not murder .' (Exodus 20) (1).

Accept any other valid response.

36 Crime

1 Award 1 mark for each point identified, up to a maximum of 3 marks.
- The Bible teaches Christians the difference between right and wrong (1).
- The Ten Commandments are rules for Christians to follow (1).
- Christians believe all humans are able to sin (1).
- Christians believe following God will lead people away from crime (1).
- The Bible teaches that crime such as killing or stealing is wrong (1).

Accept any other valid response.

2 Award 1 mark for providing a reason. Award a second mark for development of the reason, up to a maximum of 4 marks.
- The Bible teaches that humans have a responsibility to help others (1). Christians feel they have a duty to help those in need, including criminals, in accordance with Christian teachings (1).
- God is believed to have made Christians stewards, which means helping others and society generally (1). It is important to Christians that they act in ways in the world that reflect God's intentions, and helping criminals is one way of doing this (1).

37 Good, evil and suffering

Award 1 mark for each point identified, up to a maximum of 3 marks.
- Christianity teaches that people who are good will be rewarded in the afterlife (1).
- Christianity teaches that people who are bad will be punished in the afterlife (1).
- Christianity teaches there is a purpose to suffering (1).
- The Parable of the Sheep and the Goats teaches Christians about good and evil. (1)
- Christians believe that God gave humans free will, which causes them to do good or bad (1).

Accept any other valid response.

38 Punishment

1 Award 1 mark for providing a reason. Award a second mark for development of the reason, up to a maximum of 4 marks.
- Punishment helps a person to learn that their behaviour is wrong (1). Christians teach the importance of forgiveness and giving people a chance to change, which is a key purpose of punishment (1).
- Punishment makes society feel safer (1). Christians believe God created the world with the intention of it being a just and fair place, so punishing those who have committed crimes helps to protect other people (1).
- Punishment can be seen as justice for Christians (1). They view God as just in the way he judges people, and a person being punished for what they have done wrong seems fair and reflects Christian ideas of reward and punishment (1).

Accept any other valid response.

2 Candidates must underpin their analysis and evaluation with knowledge and understanding. Candidates will be required to demonstrate thorough knowledge and understanding, as well as accuracy, of religion and belief when responding to the question and in meeting AO2 descriptors.

Arguments for the statement:
- Punishment is seen to protect society from the person who committed the crime. It makes people feel safer and shows that alongside forgiveness, punishment is needed.
- Christians believe that punishment helps to make the world fairer and more just. They believe this is what God intended for the world, so they think it is important that people are punished when they have done wrong.
- Christians believe that punishment will allow the person who has done wrong the opportunity to reflect on their behaviour and realise why it was wrong. Criminals can also be given the chance to change and be better people as a result of the punishment.

Arguments against the statement:
- Christians believe that the Bible teaches them the importance of forgiveness. They believe that all humans have the potential to sin and be tempted to do wrong and, therefore, forgiveness is following the example of Jesus and allowing people to move on with their lives.
- Forgiveness allows the criminal to realise that their behaviour is wrong and change their behaviour in order to be a better person. Christians believe God is merciful so in forgiving others they are following God's example.
- Christians believe that it would be hypocritical of them not to forgive, as they expect others and God to forgive them. The Lord's Prayer contains this idea and shows that forgiveness is a positive thing.

39 Aims of punishment

Award 1 mark for providing a reason. Award a second mark for development of the reason, up to a maximum of 4 marks.
- The aims of punishment seem to be in line with teachings from the Bible (1). For example, the aim of reformation is important to Christians, as it suggests ideas of forgiveness taught by Jesus in giving a person the chance to change their behaviour (1).
- The aims of punishment are needed to keep order in society (1). Protecting society is important, as it means people feel safe, and when God created the world he intended it to be a safe and just place (1).
- The aims of punishment seem fair and just (1). Christians believe justice is important, as God is just, and aims such as retribution – where the criminal is made to realise their behaviour is wrong – makes society a just place as God intended (1).

Accept any other valid response.

40 Forgiveness

Award 1 mark for each teaching. Award further marks for each development of the teaching, up to a maximum of 4 marks. Award 1 further mark for any relevant source of wisdom or authority.
- Christianity teaches it is important to forgive others (1). Christians believe this because the Lord's Prayer teaches that we should forgive others as God forgives our sins (1): 'For if you forgive other people when they sin against you, your heavenly Father will also forgive you. But if you do not forgive others their sins, your Father will not forgive your sins.' (Matthew 6:14–15) (1).
- Christianity teaches that Jesus forgave others and Christians want to follow his example (1). When Jesus was on the cross he forgave both the criminals for their sins and those who crucified him (1): 'Father, forgive them, for they do not know what they are doing.' (Luke 23:24) (1).

- The Bible teaches that people should forgive others (1). Bible passages such as Luke 6:37 show Christians the importance of forgiveness (1): 'Do not judge, and you will not be judged;. Do not condemn, and you will not be condemned. Forgive, and you will be forgiven.' (Luke 6:37) (1).

Accept any other valid response.

41 Treatment of criminals

Candidates must underpin their analysis and evaluation with knowledge and understanding. Candidates will be required to demonstrate thorough knowledge and understanding, as well as accuracy, of religion and belief when responding to the question and in meeting AO2 descriptors.

Arguments for the statement:
- Christians teach that all humans are equal and deserve equal treatment and dignity. Christians recognise that criminals have committed a crime and deserve punishment, which may mean removal of some human rights, but as human beings they still deserve respect.
- Most Christians believe it is wrong to torture a criminal, even though they have done something wrong. This is because they are human and God created them in the same way as other humans.
- Christians believe that a criminal has the right to a fair and unbiased trial by jury, so that an objective and unbiased decision can be made based on all the evidence. Teachings in the Bible support this.

Arguments against the statement:
- Some Christians may support the use of torture, as there are quotes in the Bible that appear to support this, e.g. '... handed over to the jailers to be tortured' (Matthew 18:34). If Christians follow this passage from the Bible, they may think it acceptable to torture a criminal.
- If situation ethics is applied to any given situation, it may be possible to justify not treating a criminal with respect. This may especially be true if that criminal has denied the human rights of another (e.g. if they have murdered someone) – then perhaps it can be argued their rights are no longer as important.
- Some Christians may feel that the rights of the victim are more important than the rights of the criminal. The Bible talks of protecting the innocent, and this may mean that criminals are not given the same level of respect and dignity as the victims of their crimes.

Accept any other valid response.

42 The death penalty

1 Award 1 mark for each point identified, up to a maximum of 3 marks.
- Many Christians disagree with the death penalty (1).
- Jesus taught that revenge was wrong (1).
- The Bible teaches 'You shall not murder' (1).
- Christianity teaches the importance of love and compassion, not killing (1).
- Many Christians have shown their lack of support for the death penalty by speaking out against it (1).

Accept any other valid response.

2 Award 1 mark for providing a reason. Award a second mark for development of the reason, up to a maximum of 4 marks.
- The Bible has many teachings that suggest killing is wrong (1). For example, the Ten Commandments says 'You shall not murder', showing the death penalty is wrong (1).
- Jesus taught about the importance of love and compassion (1). His teachings suggest the death penalty should not be supported, as it does not allow criminals the chance to repent and change for the better (1).

- The sanctity of life argument suggests that killing another is wrong (1). Life is special and sacred because God created it and so we should not end life (1).

Accept any other valid response.

Unit 6 Peace and conflict

43 Peace

Award 1 mark for each belief. Award a second mark for development of the belief, up to a maximum of 4 marks.
- Christians believe peace is important as Jesus promoted peace (1). Teachings such as the Beatitudes show that peace is what Christians should strive to achieve in the world (1).
- Christians believe peace is God's intention for the world (1), so this is how we should act and behave (1).
- Christians believe that peace in the world would help to achieve justice (1). They believe that people should live together in harmony, which would make the world fairer and more equal (1).

Accept any other valid response.

44 Peacemaking

Award 1 mark for each point identified, up to a maximum of 3 mark.
- They hold peace vigils (1).
- They try to educate others (1).
- They hold interfaith talks (1).
- They hold peace rallies (1).
- They take part in public demonstrations (1).

Accept any other valid response.

45 Conflict

1 Award 1 mark for providing a reason. Award a second mark for development of the reason, up to a maximum of 4 marks.
- Christians believe that God intended for the world to be a peaceful place where there is no conflict (1). Christians feel they have a duty to look after the world and this includes helping people to get on with each other (1).
- Christians follow the example of Jesus, who worked to end conflict (1). They believe that teachings such as 'treat others as you would want to be treated' demonstrate the idea of ending conflict between people (1).
- The Bible tells how Jesus condemned his disciples' use of violence when he was arrested (1). This shows how Jesus put his teachings into practice and helped others to create unity and end the causes of conflict (1).

Accept any other valid response.

2 Candidates must underpin their analysis and evaluation with knowledge and understanding. Candidates will be required to demonstrate thorough knowledge and understanding, as well as accuracy, of religion and belief when responding to the question and in meeting AO2 descriptors.

Arguments for the statement:
- Christians believe they have a duty to work to end the causes of conflict. They accept that God created a peaceful world, which they should support by ending conflict between people.
- Christians believe the teachings of Jesus show they should work with others and not be in conflict with them. Therefore, they feel that it is important to work to end conflict in the world by putting Jesus' teachings into action.
- Many non-religious people may believe it is important to end conflict in the world in order to create peace. They may accept that it is important to have unity and peace between people and that everyone shares in this responsibility.

Arguments against the statement:

- Many non-religious people may feel that they don't have any responsibility to help others achieve unity and work to end the causes of conflict. They may even believe that things such as religion cause conflict and should be removed from society.
- Many people, both religious and non-religious, may feel that working to end conflict in the world is dangerous and could lead to violence. Therefore, they may not feel that they have a responsibility to do this.
- Some people may feel that it is impossible to remove the causes of conflict in the world, as once one conflict ends, people find something else to be in conflict about. They may believe that the most we can do is reduce the impact of the causes of conflict.

Accept any other valid response.

46 Pacifism

Candidates must underpin their analysis and evaluation with knowledge and understanding. Candidates will be required to demonstrate thorough knowledge and understanding, as well as accuracy, of religion and belief when responding to the question and in meeting AO2 descriptors.

Arguments for the statement:

- Many Christians, such as Quakers, would agree because there are teachings in the Bible that seem to support pacifism: 'Put your sword back in its place. All who draw the sword will die by the sword' (Matthew 26:52) suggests that violence is not the answer.
- Many Christians believe Jesus taught about the importance of peace and that they should follow his example. He is known as the 'Prince of Peace' and gave teachings such as turning the other cheek when provoked: 'But I tell you, do not resist an evil person. If anyone slaps you on the right cheek, turn to them the other cheek also.' (Matthew 5:39)
- Many Christians follow the example of individuals such as Martin Luther King Jr, who was a pacifist and used non-violent methods to try to achieve his aim of equality for black Americans. King was involved in peaceful protests, including a bus boycott, petitions and rallies. Many Christians believe they can follow King's example to achieve peace without resorting to violence.

Arguments against the statement:

- Some Christians believe that if you are fighting for your country in war, the use of violence may not be wrong and therefore pacifism is not the correct way. They may believe that sometimes fighting is necessary in order to bring about peace in the world.
- Many Christians believe that you need to follow the laws of the country in which you belong, so if countries advocate conscription, this is sometimes acceptable.
- While some Christians do not accept violence as the way forward, they recognise that sometimes there is no other method available once all other methods have been tried.

Accept any other valid response.

47 The Just War theory

1 Award 1 mark for providing a reason. Award a second mark for development of the reason, up to a maximum of 4 marks.
- It is intended to provide a set of criteria designed to prevent war (1). Most Christians believe that the Bible teaches them that peace is what they should achieve not war (1).
- It has its history in the Christian tradition (1). Theologians such as St Augustine and St Thomas Aquinas developed the ideas of a just war to identify whether or not a war was justified (1).

- It allows authorities to decide whether or not to go to war and the conditions of a 'just' war (1). Christians are shown by the example of Jesus that they should obey sources of authority, including the government, to determine the correct action (1).

2 Candidates must underpin their analysis and evaluation with knowledge and understanding. Candidates will be required to demonstrate thorough knowledge and understanding, as well as accuracy, of religion and belief when responding to the question and in meeting AO2 descriptors.

Arguments for the statement:
- Some Christians may agree, believing that sources of authority such as the Bible and the example of Jesus teach that peace should be achieved and war is never the right answer.
- Many Christians agree that human life is sacred, as God created it. In times of war you cannot avoid harming innocents, as well as animals and the environment, so no war is ever just.
- Some Christians may agree that it is not possible to justify any war when there are other, more peaceful methods that could be used. Reconciliation, interfaith dialogue and working together to bring an end to conflict peacefully can help to avoid war.

Arguments against the statement:
- Some Christians may believe that if the Christian principles of the Just War theory are adopted, it is possible to avoid a war that it is unjustified. Although they recognise that it is intended to prevent war, they may believe that if these principles are applied, then war is more acceptable.
- Some Christians may accept that sometimes war is needed in order to bring an end to conflict and bring about peace. They recognise that some teachings in the Bible support this view.
- Both Christians and non-religious individuals may use ethical principles such as situation ethics to identify that in some circumstances the most acceptable action may be to go to war and, therefore, in such circumstances war is justified.

Accept any other valid response.

48 Holy War

Award 1 mark for each point identified, up to a maximum of 3 marks.
- The Bible teaches the importance of peace (1).
- The Bible teaches that those who take up a sword will die by the sword (1).
- The Bible teaches to love your enemies (1).
- Jesus taught, 'Blessed are the peacemakers'. (1).
- God seems to support vengeance in war in the Bible (1).

Accept any other valid response.

49 Weapons of mass destruction

Award 1 mark for each point identified, up to a maximum of 3 marks.
- WMD threaten human life, which Christians believe is sacred (1).
- WMD destroy the environment, which is God's creation (1).
- The Bible supports peace, not war and fighting (1).
- Jesus taught that peace should be achieved (1).
- WMD cause too much destruction (1).

Accept any other valid response.

50 Issues surrounding conflict

Candidates must underpin their analysis and evaluation with knowledge and understanding. Candidates will be required to demonstrate thorough knowledge and understanding, as well as accuracy, of religion and belief when responding to the question and in meeting AO2 descriptors.

Arguments for the statement:

- Christians believe they have a duty to protect God's creation, as this is their role as stewards. This would mean limiting or preventing the damage caused by modern violence and issues of conflict in the world.
- Christians believe that Jesus taught us to 'love our enemies' and not use violence against them. Christians believe this instructs them to find peaceful methods of solving conflict and avoid the use of violence.
- Non-religious individuals may share views with Christians that we all have a duty to stand up against violence in the world. They may believe that human rights and ideas of equality are important in bringing peace to the world.

Arguments against the statement:

- Some Christians may believe that working to bring about peace is everyone's responsibility, but sometimes this puts people in danger. They may argue that life is sacred as God created it and sometimes you do not have a choice, as you could be hurt.
- Some non-religious people may feel that authorities and governments have the power to overcome conflict in the world and individuals cannot do much to help.

Accept any other valid response.

Unit 7 Philosophy of religion

51 Revelation

Award 1 mark for each idea. Award further marks for each development of the idea, up to a maximum of 4 marks.

- Revelation shows that God is omnipotent (1). God's power is shown through his actions, e.g. his ability to bring a great flood in the example of Noah (1).
- Revelation shows that God is omniscient (1). God's ability to see everything is shown in the example of the covenant he makes with Abraham (1).
- Revelation shows that God is immanent (1). God acts within the world and knows what happens, which can be seen in examples such as that of Noah or Abraham (1).

Accept any other valid response.

52 Visions (1)

Award 1 mark for each point identified, up to a maximum of 3 marks.

- St Bernadette (1).
- Saul/St Paul (1).
- Joseph (1).
- Mary (1).
- Shepherds (1).

Accept any other valid response.

53 Visions (2)

Award 1 mark for providing a reason. Award a second mark for development of the reason, up to a maximum of 4 marks.

- Visions reveal the omnipotence (power) of God (1). This can be seen in the vision of Joseph, where in a dream it is revealed to him that he would be the earthly father of the Son of God (1).
- Visions reveal the benevolence that God has for the world (1). This can be seen in the experience of Saul being shown the true path of Christianity (1).

- Visions reveal the all-knowing nature of God and his wish to communicate with humanity (1). This can be seen in the vision of the Virgin Mary received by the child, Bernadette (1).

Accept any other valid response.

54 Miracles

1 Award 1 mark for each point identified, up to a maximum of 3 marks.

- Healing miracles in Lourdes (1).
- Jesus performing miracles such as the healing of a paralysed man (1).
- Jesus walking on water (1).
- Jesus turning water into wine (1).
- Resurrection of Jesus (1).

Accept any other valid response.

2 Award 1 mark for providing a reason. Award a second mark for development of the reason, up to a maximum of 4 marks.

- Non-religious individuals may not believe that miracles are real (1). They may offer scientific explanations for miracles rather than seeing them as God's miracles (1).
- Non-religious individuals may believe that there is uncertainty in the interpretation of miracles (1), as people can witness the same event and give differing accounts; this may be evidence that they are not really miracles (1).
- Even if a miracle occurs, non-religious individuals may believe that it is not God performing the miracle (1). The existence of God is not proven for non-religious people and, therefore, it cannot be claimed that God performed the miracles as there could be other explanations (1).

Accept any other valid response.

55 Religious experiences

Award 1 mark for providing a response. Award a second mark for development of the response, up to a maximum of 4 marks.

- Christians believe experiences are real to those who experience them (1). A person's relationship with God is personal and subjective, and religious experiences are a form of this sort of revelation (1).
- Christians believe that there are many ways of God revealing himself (1). Religious experiences are one example, alongside others such as through the teachings of Jesus and the Bible (1).
- Many Christians may respond by arguing that having faith in God means you do not need proof of God's existence (1). Religious experiences are a way of God communicating with humanity and strengthening the faith that religious people already have (1).

Accept any other valid response.

56 Prayers

1 Award 1 mark for providing a reason. Award a second mark for development of the reason, up to a maximum of 4 marks.

- Prayer is communication with God (1), which Christians teach is important in order to develop a closer relationship with him (1).
- Jesus taught that prayer was important (1) and he taught his disciples to pray to God (1).
- Prayer can bring comfort and hope (1) especially in times of trouble (1).

Accept any other valid response.

2 Candidates must underpin their analysis and evaluation with knowledge and understanding. Candidates will be required to demonstrate thorough knowledge and understanding, as well as accuracy, of religion and belief when responding to the question and in meeting AO2 descriptors.

Arguments for the statement:
- Many people believe prayers are answered and this is seen to provide evidence that God hears people's prayers and responds.
- Christianity teaches that regular prayer is important as a form of communication with God in order to develop a relationship with him. It also proves that he exists when God answers people's prayers.
- The Bible teaches about the importance of prayer and Christians believe they should follow this source of authority and guidance in order to please God. They follow the example of Jesus praying in their lives as it confirms that God exists.

Arguments against the statement:
- Many prayers are not answered, so prayer alone is not good evidence of God's existence. If God did hear people's prayers, why would be choose to answer some prayers and not others?
- There may be better evidence that God is real, such as visions or miracles. Some Christians feel that an experience of God is stronger evidence. Although some prayers are answered and prove God's existence, it is not the best evidence for God.
- Prayers that are answered could simply be down to luck or a coincidence. There is no scientific evidence that prayers are answered or that God exists, so many non-religious people claim there is no evidence of God's existence.

Accept any other valid response.

57 The design argument

1 Award 1 mark for each point identified, up to a maximum of 3 marks.
- It is based on the idea that there is design in the universe (1).
- It attempts to prove the existence of God (1).
- It can be seen as compatible with some scientific theories (1).
- It tries to prove that design in the universe is because of God (1).

2 Award 1 mark for providing a reason. Award a second mark for development of the reason, up to a maximum of 4 marks.
- It demonstrates the nature of God (1); it shows he is omnipotent, omnipresent and benevolent (1).
- It proves God must exist (1) – if God designed the universe, he must exist (1).
- It allows Christians today to accept scientific theories (1). For example, they can accept the theory of evolution as being God's design for humanity, so providing support for ideas in the Bible (1).

Accept any other valid response.

58 The cosmological argument

Candidates must underpin their analysis and evaluation with knowledge and understanding. Candidates will be required to demonstrate thorough knowledge and understanding, as well as accuracy, of religion and belief when responding to the question and in meeting AO2 descriptors.

Arguments for the statement:
- The cosmological argument confirms beliefs held by Christians in the Bible. It can be used as part of the Christian Creation story in Genesis to confirm that God created the universe and everything in it.
- The cosmological argument gives proof of God's existence, as the universe exists and is accepted as evidence.

- The cosmological argument helps to bring science and religion together and updates the Christian Creation story. It allows Christians to respond to modern-day scientific theories and still maintain their traditional beliefs that God created the universe.

Arguments against the statement:
- The cosmological argument is not successful in proving God's existence, as the Big Bang theory can explain where the universe comes from without reference to God.
- A problem with the argument is that the question can be asked: If everything is caused, what caused God?
- Non-religious people might claim that no argument can prove God's existence, as he does not exist. There is too much evidence against the existence of God and a philosophical argument doesn't change this.

Accept any other valid response.

59 Religious upbringing

1 Award 1 mark for each point identified, up to a maximum of 3 marks.
- Raising children to believe in God (1).
- Teaching children to understand the Bible (1).
- Attending church as a family (1).
- Attending Sunday School (1).
- Following rites of passage, such as confirmation (1).

Accept any other valid response.

2 Award 1 mark for each reason. Award further marks for each development of the reason, up to a maximum of 4 marks. Award 1 further mark for any source of wisdom or authority.
- Christians believe they have a duty given to them by God to raise their children within the Christian faith (1). This is stated in the Bible (1): 'Start children off on the way they should go, and even when they are old they will not turn from it'. (Proverbs 22:6)
- Christians believe that God wants them to bring their children up within the faith (1). They feel they should take them to church, show them how to be good Christians and live their life as God intended (1): 'Fathers, do not exasperate your children; instead, bring them up in the training and instruction of the Lord.' (Ephesians 6:4) (1).
- Christians believe all Christians will be rewarded in the afterlife (1). They believe God provides rules and guidance on how they should live their lives and raising their children as good Christians is part of this (1): 'Start children off on the way they should go, and even when they are old they will not turn from it.' (Proverbs 22:6)

Accept any other valid response.

Unit 8 Equality

60 Human rights

1 Award 1 mark for each reason. Award further marks for each development of the reason, up to a maximum of 4 marks. Award 1 further mark for any relevant source of wisdom or authority.
- Human rights are implied in religious teachings (1). The Bible contains many teachings about equality (1): 'God created mankind in his image.' (Genesis 1:27) (1).
- Human rights are demonstrated in the Bible through the example of Jesus (1). Jesus treated all people the same and with fairness, meaning Christians should follow his example (1): 'Do to others what you would have them to to you.' (Matthew 7:12) (1).

- The Christian Church teaches that human rights are important (1). Christians try to put these teachings into practice by helping those who need it, to ensure their human rights are respected (1): 'Whoever oppresses the poor shows contempt for their Maker, but whoever is kind to the needy honors God.' (Proverbs 14:31) (1).

Accept any other valid response.

2 Candidates must underpin their analysis and evaluation with knowledge and understanding. Candidates will be required to demonstrate thorough knowledge and understanding, as well as accuracy, of religion and belief when responding to the question and in meeting AO2 descriptors.

Arguments for the statement:
- Christianity teaches that God made all humans equal, which shows that all humans should be treated the same. Therefore, when human rights are denied, Christians feel they have a duty to work to address this.
- The Bible gives the example of Jesus treating all people the same, and Christians feel they should follow Jesus' example. In doing this, Christians may feel it is important to ensure everyone has their human rights.
- There are examples of Christians, such as Martin Luther King Jr and Desmond Tutu, who have stood up against injustice when human rights have been ignored. Christians believe they should follow their example.

Arguments against the statement:
- Some Christians may argue that, although human rights are important, sometimes it is too dangerous to stand up for them. For example, in the case of Martin Luther King Jr, he was assassinated, showing how dangerous making a stand can be.
- Some atheists may argue that, although human rights are important, only the people in authority such as the government have the power to help others and it is, therefore, not their duty to do so.
- Some people may feel that they themselves are just one person who can achieve very little by themselves, and that a group effort is needed in order to stand up for human rights and bring about change.

Accept any other valid response.

61 Equality

1 Award 1 mark for each point identified, up to a maximum of 3 marks.
- They believe they have a duty from God (1).
- It shows stewardship (1).
- They believe all humans are equal (1).
- They follow the example of Jesus (1).
- They believe it is how God intended them to live (1).

Accept any other valid response.

2 Award 1 mark for each way. Award a second mark for development of the way, up to a maximum of 4 marks.
- Individuals such as Martin Luther King Jr or Desmond Tutu have tried to promote equality (1). Martin Luther King Jr took part in peaceful protests to campaign for civil rights for black Americans (1).
- Many charities work to raise awareness of equality issues (1). For instance, Christian Aid works to raise awareness of gender inequality (1).
- Charity organisations offer practical help to those affected by inequality (1). For example, by providing aid after natural disasters or helping those people living in poverty in the world (1).

Accept any other valid response.

62 Religious freedom

Candidates must underpin their analysis and evaluation with knowledge and understanding. Candidates will be required to demonstrate thorough knowledge and understanding, as well as accuracy, of religion and belief when responding to the question and in meeting AO2 descriptors.

Arguments for the statement:
- Christians may agree with the statement, as some may believe that, although all religions hold some truth, only Christianity holds the complete truth. This will lead them to be able to use other religions to support some of their beliefs but retain the exclusive view of Christianity as providing the full answer.
- Non-religious individuals may agree with the statement, as they would not see any advantages to living in a multifaith society. They may believe that religious believers such as Christians are the only ones who may benefit.
- Some Christians may believe that people with no faith will not want to engage with religious teachings and, therefore, will not benefit from living in a multifaith society.

Arguments against the statement:
- Many religious believers including Christians believe there are many advantages to living in a multifaith society, including a better understanding of all religions – they believe that all people, religious and non-religious, can benefit.
- Christians may believe that the advantages of living in a multifaith society include new ideas about culture, which can be shared.
- Christians may believe that a multifaith society gives opportunity for improved tolerance and respect between people, which can benefit both Christians, other religious believers and non-religious people.

Accept any other valid response.

63 Prejudice and discrimination

Award 1 mark for each point identified, up to a maximum of 3 marks.
- The Bible teaches that prejudice and discrimination against religions are wrong (1).
- The example of Jesus shows that prejudice and discrimination are wrong (1).
- Stories such as the Good Samaritan illustrate that prejudice and discrimination are wrong (1).
- God made all humans to be equal (1).
- 'Treat others as you would want to be treated' is a Christian teaching that shows prejudice and discrimination against religions are wrong (1).

Accept any other valid response.

64 Racial harmony

1 Award 1 mark for each benefit. Award a second mark for development of the benefit, up to a maximum of 4 marks.
- Christians believe God created all people equal (1). Christians work for racial harmony, as they believe putting this teaching into practice means treating people from different races the same (1).
- The Bible teaches that there are no differences between people of different races (1). Christians believe they have a duty to put this teaching into practice and stand up for racial harmony (1).
- Christians follow teachings from the Bible, such as Jesus' teaching to 'Love one another' (1). Christians such as Archbishop Desmond Tutu have tried to put these teachings into action by campaigning for racial equality (1).

Accept any other valid response.

2 Award 1 mark for providing a reason. Award a second mark for development of the reason, up to a maximum of 4 marks.
- Living in a multi-ethnic society allows for racial harmony (1). Christians believe it is important to show that all humans are equal and this gives them the opportunity to do this (1).
- Living in a multi-ethnic society can help to reduce discrimination (1). Christians follow teachings such as Jesus' teaching to 'Love one another' and, if followed, this means people can be treated the same and with dignity (1).
- Living in a multi-ethnic society gives access to a wider variety of culture, food, music and tradition (1). Christians can learn from the example of others and come to appreciate the influence of other cultures in their lives (1).

Accept any other valid response.

65 Racial discrimination

Award 1 mark for providing a reason. Award a second mark for development of the reason, up to a maximum of 4 marks.
- Christians believe that God created all humans the same (1). Putting this teaching into practice means recognising that racial discrimination is wrong, as God created all races to be equal (1).
- The Bible teaches that racial discrimination is wrong (1). Galatians 3:28 teaches that all races are the same before God and, therefore, treating anyone different because of their race is wrong (1).
- The Bible describes how Jesus showed that racial discrimination is wrong through the stories (parables) he told (1). The Good Samaritan is one example of a parable that Jesus used to teach that all races should be treated the same (1).

Accept any other valid response.

66 Social justice

Candidates must underpin their analysis and evaluation with knowledge and understanding. Candidates will be required to demonstrate thorough knowledge and understanding, as well as accuracy, of religion and belief when responding to the question and in meeting AO2 descriptors.

Arguments for the statement:
- Christians believe every person in the world deserves respect and fair treatment, as God made all humanity. When people face difficulties in their lives, such as living in poverty or having their rights threatened, most Christians believe they have a duty to stand up for them and work for social justice.
- Many teachings in the Bible refer to examples of Jesus working for social justice or the belief that God wants his people to work for equality and social justice. Christians believe they have a duty to put these teachings into action and feel that as everyone is human, everyone should work for social justice.
- Situation ethics teaches us to do what is the most loving thing in the given situation. Christians feel that this means we should work to help others and bring social justice to the world. There are many Christian teachings that support this idea.

Arguments against the statement:
- Some Christians may feel that sometimes it is too dangerous to work for social justice and that they should not be involved in issues where authorities such as the government should be providing help.
- Some individuals may feel that, as only one person, they cannot make a big difference in the world. They may, therefore, feel that working for social justice should be left to those who can bring about change.

- Some people may feel that we should worry first about social justice issues where we live and not be concerned about issues all over the world.

Accept any other valid response.

67 Wealth and poverty

1 Award 1 mark for each point identified, up to a maximum of 3 marks.
- Low-paid work (1).
- Family issues such as health problems and divorce (1).
- Unemployment (1).
- War and political instability (1).
- National debt (1).

Accept any other valid response.

2 Award 1 mark for each reason given. Award a second mark for development of each reason, up to a maximum of 4 marks.
- Christians believe that the Bible teaches them to help other people (1). For example, 'Treat others as you would like to be treated' is a key Bible teaching that suggests helping others by sharing wealth is a good thing (1).
- There are many Christian charities that try to distribute wealth more evenly (1). Charities such as Christian Aid are trying to build a fairer society and help those in need (1).
- Christians believe God created all humans to be equal and that all humans deserve to be helped when they need support (1). Sharing wealth is seen as one way of doing this, and many Christians tithe, giving 10 per cent of their wages to help others (1).

Accept any other valid response.

Unit 1 Muslim beliefs

68 The Six Beliefs of Islam

Award 1 mark for each point identified, up to a maximum of 3 marks.
- During prayers – Salah or du'a (1).
- Through reading the Qu'ran (1).
- Through their actions and behaviour (1).
- Through the way they help others (1).
- Through the way they live their lives – e.g. following the Five Pillars, going to the mosque, etc. (1).

Accept any other valid response.

69 The five roots of 'Usul ad-Din in Shi'a Islam

Candidates must underpin their analysis and evaluation with knowledge and understanding. Candidates will be required to demonstrate thorough knowledge and understanding, as well as accuracy, of religion and belief when responding to the question and in meeting AO2 descriptors.

Augments for the statement:
- Tawhid (the belief in the oneness of Allah) is at the heart of the Islamic faith. Awareness of Allah affects every action a Muslim performs and their prayers are directed towards him.
- Many Muslims (Sunni and Shi'a) view Tawhid as underpinning all other beliefs, such as those found in the six Beliefs for Sunni Muslims and those found in the five roots of 'Usul ad-Din.
- When Muslims pray, perform the Five Pillars or go to the mosque, everything they do is directed towards Allah and they want to please him within their lives.

Arguments against the statement:
- There are many other beliefs in Islam that are equally important – Akhirah, risalah, etc.
- Islam is a religion of beliefs and practices. How a Muslim behaves and acts is just as important as what they believe.

- Muslims would argue that, although Allah is central to the faith, other beliefs have equally as much influence on their lives.

Accept any other valid response.

70 The nature of Allah

1 Award 1 mark for each way. Award a second mark for development of the way, up to a maximum of 4 marks.
   - Tawhid (1): Allah is one and has no start or end (1).
   - Transcendent (1): Allah is beyond human understanding (1).
   - Omnipotent (1): Allah is all-powerful and created the world (1).

Accept any other valid response.

2 Award 1 mark for each reason. Award further marks for each development of the reason, up to a maximum of 4 marks.
   - To help Muslims understand Allah better (1). They can relate to him and develop a more personal relationship (1).
   - To follow Allah (1). By using the characteristics Muslims can understand how he wants them to live their lives (1): 'And We certainly sent into every nation a messenger, [saying], "Worship Allah and avoid Taghut".' (Surah 16:36) (1).
   - They are given in the Qur'an (1). This is an important source of authority that Muslims follow (1): 'The most beautiful names belong to Allah: so call on him by them.' (Surah 7:180) (1).

Accept any other valid response.

71 Risalah

1 Award 1 mark for each point identified, up to a maximum of 3 marks.
   - They are messengers of Allah (1).
   - They are the channel of communication between Allah and humanity (1).
   - Some are rasuls, who are messengers who have had their message written down (1).
   - They have revealed truths to humanity (1).

Accept any other valid response.

2 Candidates must underpin their analysis and evaluation with knowledge and understanding. Candidates will be required to demonstrate thorough knowledge and understanding, as well as accuracy, of religion and belief when responding to the question and in meeting AO2 descriptors.

Arguments for the statement:
   - Without the prophets, Allah couldn't have communicated to humanity.
   - Without prophets such as Muhammad, holy books such as the Qur'an would not have been received.
   - Risalah is an important belief within the central teachings of Islam – Six Beliefs and five roots of 'Usul al-Din.

Arguments against the statement:
   - Tawhid is perhaps more important, as this is belief in one God – Allah.
   - Tawhid is seen to underpin all other beliefs including risalah, demonstrating its importance.
   - Actions may be more important than beliefs in Islam, as this is what Muslims believe they will be judged on after death.

Accept any other valid response.

72 Muslim holy books

1 Award 1 mark for each point identified, up to a maximum of 3 marks.
   - Revealed by Muhammad (1).
   - Main holy book for Muslims (1).
   - Contains teachings of Allah (1).
   - Muslims look to it for guidance in their lives (1).
   - Used within Muslim prayer (1).

Accept any other valid response.

2 Award 1 mark for providing a reason. Award a second mark for development of the reason, up to a maximum of 4 marks.
   - Other holy books are mentioned in the Qur'an (1), for example Tawrat, Zabur, etc. (1).
   - Muslims believe there were prophets who were messengers before Muhammad (1). They recognise messengers such as Ibrahim and Isa, who brought messages and holy books (1).
   - Muslims believe they are commanded to recognise other holy books (1) such as the Tawrah, as this was also revealed by Allah (1).

Accept any other valid response.

73 Malaikah

1 Award 1 mark for each point identified, up to a maximum of 3 marks.
   - Angels are called malaikah (1).
   - They are believed to be messengers from Allah (1).
   - They are not considered to have free will or physical bodies (1).
   - Some of the angels are Jibril, Mika'il and Izra'il (1).
   - They have been revealed to prophets (1).

Accept any other valid response.

2 Award 1 mark for each reason. Award further marks for each development of the reason, up to a maximum of 4 marks. Award 1 further mark for any relevant source of wisdom or authority.
   - They have brought messages to humanity (1), for example Jibril gave the Qur'an to Muhammad (1): ' ... then We sent her our angel, and he appeared before her as a man in all respects.' (Surah, 19 (Maryam):17)
   - They are mentioned in the Qur'an (1). Jibril, Mika'il and Izra'il are all mentioned as angels of significance (1): 'Whoever is an enemy to Gabriel – for he brings down the (revelation) to thy heart by Allah's will, a confirmation of what went before, and guidance and glad tidings for those who believe, – Whoever is an enemy to Allah and His angels and messengers, to Gabriel and Michael, – Lo! Allah is an enemy to those who reject Faith.' (Surah 2 (Al-Baqara):97–98)
   - Angels are given roles within Islam (1), for example Izra'il is the angel of death (1): 'The angel of death will take you who has been entrusted with you. Then to your Lord you will be returned.' (Surah 32:11)

Accept any other valid response.

74 Al-Qadr

Award 1 mark for each way. Award a second mark for development of the way, up to a maximum of 4 marks.
   - It affects their beliefs about the afterlife (1), so will have an impact on making them aware of how they act and behave in their lives (1).
   - Muslims will want to help others (1). Behaving in this way will gain them favour with Allah (1).
   - Muslims may read the Qur'an more often (1) to help them understand what Allah wants them to do (1).

Accept any other valid response.

75 Akhirah

Award 1 mark for each point identified, up to a maximum of 3 marks.

- Akhirah is the word for life after death in Islam (1).
- Muslims believe in the idea of reward and punishment (1).
- Muslims believe actions on Earth will determine their afterlife (1).
- Muslims believe Allah will judge them after death (1).
- The good will go to paradise and the bad to hell (1).

Accept any other valid response.

Unit 2 Marriage and the family

76 Marriage

Award 1 mark for each point identified, up to a maximum of 3 marks.

- To bring a man and woman together to have children (1).
- To share love and companionship (1).
- To follow what Allah wants (1).
- To create a family (1).
- To bring stability to society (1).

Accept any other valid response.

77 Sexual relationships

Candidates must underpin their analysis and evaluation with knowledge and understanding. Candidates will be required to demonstrate thorough knowledge and understanding, as well as accuracy, of religion and belief when responding to the question and in meeting AO2 descriptors.

Arguments for the statement:

- Muslims believe sex is a gift and it is what Allah intended for a married couple.
- Islam teaches that sex fulfils physical, emotional and spiritual needs.
- Islam teaches that sex is an act of worship.

Arguments against the statement:

- Society today is changing and some people may believe that the idea of sex being a gift from Allah is outdated.
- Many atheists and humanists may challenge this, believing that sex is a gift for procreation but has no religious basis.
- Some may disagree, arguing that sex is a way of deepening a relationship rather than being a gift from God just for children.

Accept any other valid response.

78 Families

Candidates must underpin their analysis and evaluation with knowledge and understanding. Candidates will be required to demonstrate thorough knowledge and understanding, as well as accuracy, of religion and belief when responding to the question and in meeting AO2 descriptors.

Arguments for the statement:

- A non-religious individual may agree if they have an unsupportive family or have had bad experiences of family.
- Some people may have different types of family in society today, which may impact on their opinion.
- Some people may prefer friends to family.

Arguments against the statement:

- Muslims would argue that family provides stability and structure to society – some non-religious individuals may agree.
- Family helps to strengthen the ummah in Islam.
- Family is where children are taught right and wrong and raised as good Muslims.

Accept any other valid response.

79 The family in the ummah

1 Award 1 mark for each point identified, up to a maximum of 3 marks.

- Worship (1).
- Rites of passage (1).
- Classes for parents (1).
- Groups for children (1).
- Counselling (1).

Accept any other valid response.

2 Award 1 mark for providing a reason. Award a second mark for development of the reason, up to a maximum of 4 marks.

- Children can be raised correctly (1) as good Muslims (1).
- Support can be given when facing personal problems (1), difficulties in the marriage or with raising the children (1).
- Strengthening the ummah (1) so all Muslims are united (1).

Accept any other valid response.

80 Contraception

Award 1 mark for providing a reason. Award a second mark for development of the reason, up to a maximum of 4 marks.

- Muslim authorities allow its use to preserve the life of the mother (1). If she could die through having another child, this would be a threat to her life and other children in the family (1).
- Some believe Muhammad supported the withdrawal method (1). This seems to be suggested in some Hadith (1).
- Some accept non-permanent methods for use by married couples (1). They can then plan when to have their family.

Accept any other valid response.

81 Divorce

Award 1 mark for each reason. Award further marks for each development of the reason, up to a maximum of 4 marks.

- Muhammad did not divorce (1). Muslims want to follow his example (1).
- Divorce is seen to threaten and damage the family unit (1). It can lead to problems in the family, which is not desirable as Muslims consider the family to bring stability to society (1).
- Muslims believe divorce is detestable (1). It is hated by Allah as it is disrespectful to him and the gift of marriage between the couple (1).

Accept any other valid response.

82 Men and women in the family

1 Award 1 mark for each way. Award a second mark for development of the way, up to a maximum of 4 marks.

- Men and women are seen to have contrasting roles (1). Men are the providers and women are the home keepers in charge of raising children (1).
- Men and women are seen to have equal responsibilities (1). They are both to raise their children as good Muslims (1).
- Men and women are completely equal (1). Both can go out and work and have a career (1).

Accept any other valid response.

2 Candidates must underpin their analysis and evaluation with knowledge and understanding. Candidates will be required to demonstrate thorough knowledge and understanding, as well as accuracy, of religion and belief when responding to the question and in meeting AO2 descriptors.

Arguments for the statement:

- Most Muslims believe men and women are equal in their roles within the family.
- Sources of authority suggest men and women are equal.
- Muslims believe men and women were created to be equal by Allah.

Arguments against the statement:

- Men and women are seen to have different roles in the family, suggesting inequality.
- Men and women are suited to different tasks, so should be treated this way.
- There are sources of authority that suggest inequality within Islam in terms of men and women and their roles.

Accept any other valid response.

83 Gender prejudice and discrimination

1 Award 1 mark for each point identified, up to a maximum of 3 marks.
- Gender prejudice and discrimination are wrong (1).
- Allah created all humans – men and women – as equal (1).
- Men and women were created from the same soul (1).
- Muslims believe they should fight against gender prejudice and discrimination (1).
- The Qur'an contains many teachings suggesting men and women are equal (1).

Accept any other valid response.

2 Award 1 mark for each way. Award a second mark for development of the way, up to a maximum of 4 marks.
- Malala Yousafzai (1) stood up for girls' education against the Taliban (1).
- Nadiya Hussain (1) inspired others through her own individual achievements in winning 'The Great British Bake Off competition' (1).
- Organisations such as Sisters in Islam (1) work to challenge gender inequality (1).

Accept any other valid response.

Unit 3 Living the Muslim life

84 The Ten Obligatory Acts of Shi'a Islam

Award 1 mark for providing a reason. Award a second mark for development of the reason, up to a maximum of 4 marks.
- They help them to worship Allah in their daily lives (1). By performing actions such as giving money to charity, fasting or praying Shi'a Muslims get closer to Allah (1).
- They provide guidance (1). The practices are seen to be commanded by Allah, which show Muslims how to act and behave (1).
- They help to identify key beliefs and practices (1). As they are mentioned in the Qur'an, it helps Shi'a Muslims to know what Allah wants them to do in their lives (1).

Accept any other valid response.

85 The Shahadah

Candidates must underpin their analysis and evaluation with knowledge and understanding. Candidates will be required to demonstrate thorough knowledge and understanding, as well as accuracy, of religion and belief when responding to the question and in meeting AO2 descriptors.

Arguments for the statement:
- The Shahadah is considered to underpin all other pillars, therefore, showing its importance as containing the central belief in Allah.
- The Shahadah is spoken daily, makes up part of the adhan (call to prayer), is whispered into the ears of newborn babies and should be spoken, if possible, before death, demonstrating the role it plays within the life of every Muslim and showing its central importance.
- The Shahadah is the first of the Five Pillars, which suggests it is the most important as it comes before all others.

Arguments against the statement:
- The pillars are all equally important as they are all considered to be duties and practices performed for Allah that all Muslims should perform within their lives.

- Salah (prayer) could be seen as more important as the Shahadah as this happens five times daily and is regular communication with Allah. Therefore, it is a practical way of developing a closer relationship with him.
- Zakah and Sawm are seen to be when Muslims can help others who are poor and needy and sympathise with their situation, so could be considered to have more of an impact in the world than the Shahadah, which is a personal proclamation of faith.

Accept any other valid response.

86 Salah

1 Award 1 mark for each point identified, up to a maximum of 3 marks.
- Regular communication with Allah (1).
- Commanded by Muhammad (1).
- One of the Five Pillars (1).
- Considered a duty to pray five times a day (1).
- Demonstrates equality between all members of the ummah (1).

Accept any other valid response.

2 Award 1 mark for each reason/belief. Award further marks for each development of the reason/belief, up to a maximum of 4 marks. Award 1 further mark for any relevant source of wisdom or authority.
- It is one of the Five Pillars (1). It is therefore considered compulsory, as it is a duty given to Muslims by Allah (1): 'So exalt [Allah] with praise of your Lord and be of those who prostrate [to Him]. And worship your Lord until there comes to you the certainty (death)'. (Surah 15:98–99) (1).
- It is communication with Allah (1). This is commanded in the Qur'an and demonstrates the key belief of Tawhid, which is at the centre of the Islamic faith (1): 'So exalt [Allah] with praise of your Lord and be of those who prostrate [to Him]. And worship your Lord until there comes to you the certainty (death)'. (Surah 15:98–99) (1).
- Salah was prescribed by Muhammad (1). Muhammad prayed to Allah regularly and taught his followers to do the same. It is in sources of authority (1): 'He said: "O Muhammad, they are five prayers each day and night, for every prayer there will be a tenfold (reward), and that is fifty prayers."' (Hadith Al-Bukhaari (349)) (1).

Accept any other valid response.

87 Sawm

Award 1 mark for providing a reason. Award a second mark for development of the reason, up to a maximum of 4 marks.
- If they are sick (1). It may affect their recovery and long-term health (1).
- If they are pregnant (1). They need to stay healthy so their unborn child gains nutrients to grow and develop (1).
- If they are travelling on long journeys (1). It may affect their ability to complete their journey or make them sick (1).

Accept any other valid response.

88 Zakah and khums

Award 1 mark for each benefit. Award a second mark for development of the benefit, up to a maximum of 4 marks.
- It can help the poorest and neediest in society (1). It is used to try to improve the conditions for many and make their lives more bearable (1).
- It reminds Muslims of the importance of all humans to Allah (1). Muslims believe Allah created all humans equally and this is a way of demonstrating equality.
- It shares and distributes wealth in the world (1). This is what Allah intended for his creation (1).

Accept any other valid response.

89 Hajj

1 Award 1 mark for each point identified, up to a maximum of 3 marks.
- Tawaf – circling of the Ka'bah seven times (1).
- Sa'y – running between the hills of Marwa and Safa (1).
- Mount Arafat – standing and praying or reading the Qur'an (1).
- Stoning of the devil at Mina – throwing stones at the pillars (1).
- Sacrifice of an animal (1).

Accept any other valid response.

2 Award 1 mark for each benefit. Award a second mark for development of the benefit, up to a maximum of 4 marks.
- It shows commitment to Allah (1) it is one of the Five Pillars of Islam and a duty all Muslims complete for Allah
- Completing Hajj strengthens the ummah (1) it unites all Muslims in their shared faith and belief in Allah as they all complete the same actions at the same time (1)
- It gives individual Muslims an opportunity to reflect on their belief and faith in Allah (1) they ask Allah for forgiveness and get closer to him (1)

Accept any other valid response.

90 Jihad

1 Award 1 mark for each point identified, up to a maximum of 3 marks.
- Fought for a just cause – to defend Islam or injustice (1).
- A last resort (1).
- Authorised by an accepted Muslim authority (1).
- Minimum amount of suffering is caused (1).
- Innocent civilians are not attacked (1).

Accept any other valid response.

2 Award 1 mark for providing a reason. Award a second mark for development of the reason, up to a maximum of 4 marks.
- Sources of authority have emphasised this (1). The Qur'an and Muhammad both stated this (1).
- It is viewed as an act of sacrifice to Allah (1). It is more important to overcome daily challenges rather than just go to war (1).

Accept any other valid response.

91 Celebrations and commemorations

Award 1 mark for each point identified, up to a maximum of 3 marks.
- Sacrifice of an animal (1).
- Sending of Id cards (1).
- Attending the mosque (1).
- Sharing a meal with friends and family (1).

Accept any other valid response.

Unit 4 Matters of life and death

92 Origins of the universe

Candidates must underpin their analysis and evaluation with knowledge and understanding. Candidates will be required to demonstrate thorough knowledge and understanding, as well as accuracy, of religion and belief when responding to the question and in meeting AO2 descriptors.

Arguments for the statement:
- The Qur'an says Allah created the universe – science says it was the Big Bang. These are different theories.
- Science seems to suggest the universe was created by chance, while the Qur'an suggests Allah planned and designed it.
- The Qur'an suggests a loving God, while science suggests no planning or designing from a loving God.

Arguments against the statement:
- Many Muslims believe that science helps to further explain teachings about creation in the Qur'an – it fills in the gaps.
- Several passages are seen by some Muslims to refer to the event known as the Big Bang.
- Many Muslims believe that science helps them to understand Allah better.

Accept any other valid response.

93 Sanctity of life

Award 1 mark for providing a reason. Award a second mark for development of the reason, up to a maximum of 4 marks.
- Life was created by Allah (1). Muslims believe that he created life to be holy and special, which is taught in the Qur'an (1).
- Muslims believe it is wrong to take life (1). All human life should be respected as a gift from Allah as he created it (1).
- Islam has many teachings about life being preserved (1). Muslims accept that abortion and euthanasia is wrong, as it means ending life created by Allah (1).

Accept any other valid response.

94 The origins of human life

Candidates must underpin their analysis and evaluation with knowledge and understanding. Candidates will be required to demonstrate thorough knowledge and understanding, as well as accuracy, of religion and belief when responding to the question and in meeting AO2 descriptors.

Arguments for the statement:
- Evolution does conflict with the Qur'an. Evolution suggests that life happened by chance as organisms adapted to their environments, whereas Qur'anic teachings suggest life was planned and intended by Allah.
- Evolution rests on the assumption that humans were created by the strongest characteristics surviving and the weakest ones dying out, making human life evolve from animals, whereas Muslim teachings reinforce the view that Allah loved his creation so much that he designed the world for human life to exist.
- There seems to be no common ground between Muslim teachings and scientific theories such as evolution, which leads some Muslims to reject modern theories offered by science and only accept the traditional teachings offered by the religion of Islam.

Arguments against the statement:
- Some Muslims believe that science can help to explain teachings that the Qur'an is not clear about. Although the Qur'an explains the origin of human life (Allah), evolution helps to explain his plan for how it was created within the world.
- Many Muslims believe that science and Islam can be brought together as they view evolution as part of Allah's plan, meaning that these teachings and ideas can work alongside each other rather than in conflict.
- Many Muslims believe that in today's modern, technological world you cannot deny scientific theories such as evolution, so you need to look for ways of making them work alongside traditional teachings. Muslims accept that evolution can help them to understand Allah and his ways better.

Accept any other valid response.

95 Muslim attitudes to abortion

Award 1 mark for each point identified, up to a maximum of 3 marks.
- The sanctity of life teaches that Allah created life and is holy, so abortion is wrong (1).

- Ensoulment means the soul is not believed to enter the body until 40 or even 120 days, so abortion could be seen as acceptable before this time as it is not killing life (1).
- The Qur'an contains teachings on the sanctity of life showing abortion is wrong as life is holy (1).
- Accepted reasons for abortion include the life of the mother being in danger (1).
- Islam teaches through the Qur'an that reasons not justified for abortion include a lack of money or a child born as the result of adultery (1).

Accept any other valid response.

96 Death and the afterlife (1)

Award 1 mark for providing a reason. Award a second mark for development of the reason, up to a maximum of 4 marks.

- Teachings from the Qur'an highlight the importance of life after death (1). They teach that life is a test in order that a person can be rewarded or punished after death (1).
- Islamic teachings reflect the importance of living life as Allah intended (1). This is connected to the afterlife as Muslims believe they will be judged by Allah after death on how they have lived their lives (1).
- Muslims teach that there is a connection between life and life after death (1). Living a good life will ensure a person is rewarded and not punished (1).

Accept any other valid response.

97 Death and the afterlife (2)

Award 1 mark for each reason/belief. Award further marks for each development of the reason/belief, up to a maximum of 4 marks. Award 1 further mark for any relevant source of wisdom or authority.

- Muslims reject humanist beliefs that there is no life after death by pointing to teachings in the Qur'an (1). They believe that the Qur'an teaches of an afterlife where people will be judged and rewarded or punished, therefore, it must exist (1). They say, '"There is not but our worldly life; we die and live, and nothing destroys us except time." And they have of that no knowledge; they are only assuming. And when Our verses are recited to them as clear evidences, their argument is only that they say, "Bring [back] our forefathers, if you should be truthful."' (Surah 45:24–25)
- Muslims reject arguments of social control as they believe there is a direct link between life and death (1). Islam teaches that how a person lives their life will determine how they are judged by Allah after death. This is taught in the Qur'an (1).

98 Euthanasia

1 Award 1 mark for each point identified, up to a maximum of 3 marks.
- Euthanasia is always wrong as it goes against the sanctity of life (1).
- Only Allah can give and take away life, so euthanasia is wrong (1).
- Muslims believe that human life has been given a purpose by Allah. To end it through euthanasia is wrong as this purpose is special and holy (1).
- Euthanasia is suicide, which is not allowed in Islam (1).
- The Qur'an teaches that no one dies 'unless Allah permits' (Surah 3:145), so euthanasia is wrong (1).

Accept any other valid response.

2 Award 1 mark for providing a reason. Award a second mark for development of the reason, up to a maximum of 4 marks.
- Muslims believe in the sanctity of life (1). As Allah gave life only he can take it away, meaning that euthanasia goes against this (1).

- Muslims believe that suffering in life has a purpose and euthanasia should not be used to take this away (1). They believe that Allah has a plan for every human life which should not be interfered with. People will be judged after death on how they acted in life, which may mean that someone who has had euthanasia may be punished (1).
- The Qur'an teaches that euthanasia is wrong (1). Muslims believe the Qur'an is the word of God and guides them on issues such as euthanasia. As it says that euthanasia is wrong, it should not happen (1).

Accept any other valid response.

99 Issues in the natural world

Candidates must underpin their analysis and evaluation with knowledge and understanding. Candidates will be required to demonstrate thorough knowledge and understanding, as well as accuracy, of religion and belief when responding to the question and in meeting AO2 descriptors.

Arguments for the statement:
- Muslims believe they have a duty of stewardship (khalifah) given to them by Allah, which means they should take care of the world.
- Muslims believe the world was created by Allah and given to humans as a gift, so they have a responsibility to look after it and take care of it.
- Islam teaches in the Qur'an that Muslims should not damage the world as it should be preserved for future generations.

Arguments against the statement:
- Some people without religious beliefs may claim that they do not have a responsibility to care for the world and, if they have not damaged it, they have no duty to help.
- Some people may believe that the people who did the damage should be the ones to work to save the world.
- Some people may believe that they are only one person and cannot make that big a difference to the world. They may believe that those in authority and with power should be the ones working to help the world.

Accept any other valid response.

Unit 5 Crime and punishment

100 Justice

Award 1 mark for each point identified, up to a maximum of 3 marks.
- Justice is what Allah intended for his creation (1).
- The Five Pillars of Islam demonstrate ideas of justice (1).
- Shari'ah law reinforces ideas of justice (1).
- Muslims believe that they will be judged in the afterlife on how just they have been in their lives (1).
- The Qur'an contains many teachings that reference ideas of justice (1).

Accept any other valid response.

101 Crime

1 Award 1 mark for each point identified, up to a maximum of 3 marks.
- Muslim individuals and organisations may work to try to reduce the impact, causes and effects of crime (1).
- They may teach about the importance of avoiding crime (1).
- They may reinforce the belief that Allah will judge Muslims after death on the way they have behaved in life (1).
- They may try to set an example of how a Muslim should live their life (1).
- They may refer to Qur'anic teachings to show that crime is wrong (1).

Accept any other valid response.

2 Award 1 mark for providing a reason. Award a second mark for development of the reason, up to a maximum of 4 marks.
- They believe they have a duty from Allah to care for others in society (1). Muslims believe Allah created all humans to be equal and this means they should support each other and try to make society just and fair (1).
- The ummah is important in Islam (1). One part of belonging to the ummah is supporting all Muslims all over the world, so working to reduce crime can benefit others (1).
- Muslims believe they should try to follow the example of Muhammad (1). Muslims believe Muhammad helped others and tried to improve their lives, so they should do the same for Allah (1).

Accept any other valid response.

102 Good, evil and suffering

Award 1 mark for each teaching. Award further marks for each development of the teaching, up to a maximum of 4 marks.
- Muslims believe that there is a reason why they suffer (1). It is part of Allah's plan, although Muslims do not know what this is (1).
- Muslims believe that suffering is a test of faith and character (1). Allah gave humans free will and they need to choose right or wrong actions in order to deserve reward in the afterlife (1).
- Muslims believe that some suffering is due to humans (1). For example, famine or war is the result of humans using free will, given to them by Allah, and choosing to hurt others (1).

Accept any other valid response.

103 Punishment

1 Award 1 mark for providing a reason. Award a second mark for development of the reason, up to a maximum of 4 marks.
- The Qur'an teaches the importance of punishment (1). Muslims believe a just society is what Allah intended and they should try to put this into action (1).
- Punishment is important in teaching people that some actions are wrong (1). Islam teaches that after death people will be rewarded if they have been good and punished if they have been evil, so punishment for any wrongdoing seems fair (1).
- Punishment creates a fair and just society (1). The Qur'an and the example of Muhammad shows that this is important in society (1).

Accept any other valid response.

2 Award 1 mark for each reason. Award further marks for each development of the reason, up to a maximum of 4 marks. Award 1 further mark for any relevant source of wisdom or authority.
- The Qur'an teaches the importance of justice and punishment is part of this (1). It teaches that Allah intended for a just and fair society, so punishment for a crime works to achieve this (1): 'And We ordained for them therein a life for a life, an eye for an eye, a nose for a nose, an ear for an ear, a tooth for a tooth, and for wounds is legal retribution.' (Surah 5:45) (1).
- Punishment maintains order and stability in society (1). Shari'ah law is based on the principles of justice, equality and order, and generates suitable punishments (1).
- Muslims believe the laws of the country should be followed (1). The Qur'an teaches this (1).

Accept any other valid response.

104 Aims of punishment

1 Award 1 mark for each point identified, up to a maximum of 3 marks.
- To protect society (1).
- To offer opportunity for the offender to reform (1).
- To deter other offenders from committing the same crime (1).
- To give retribution (1).

Accept any other valid response.

2 Candidates must underpin their analysis and evaluation with knowledge and understanding. Candidates will be required to demonstrate thorough knowledge and understanding, as well as accuracy, of religion and belief when responding to the question and in meeting AO2 descriptors.

Arguments for the statement:
- Muslims are taught that forgiveness and repentance are important. Following these teaching would mean giving the offender the opportunity to change their behaviour and become a better person.
- Muslims believe they have a responsibility from Allah to help people – an idea that is shown through the ummah. Helping offenders means giving them a second chance and an opportunity to reform.
- Criminals need time to be shown why their behaviour is wrong and this will have the biggest impact on society in bringing justice and fairness.

Arguments against the statement:
- The victim of the crime and their loves ones could be seen as more important than the offender. If their needs are put first, it would seem that perhaps retribution or protection is more important. The Qur'an has many teachings about justice being attained for the victim.
- Protection for others in society is more important as life is special and sacred. If others are not protected, they could be harmed.
- Muslims believe that justice is the most important aim of punishment as this is what Allah wants for society. In order to achieve this, everyone's needs must be taken into account – offender's and victim's.

Accept any other valid response.

105 Forgiveness

Award 1 mark for providing a reason. Award a second mark for development of the reason, up to a maximum of 4 marks.
- Forgiveness is a key teaching in Islam (1). The Qur'an teaches Muslims to forgive and they follow the example of Muhammad who was forgiving (1).
- Forgiving means everyone can move forward in their lives (1). It stops hatred and bad feeling between the offenders, which can have a negative impact on their lives (1).
- Islam teaches that Allah is compassionate and merciful and wants humans to be the same (1). By forgiving the offender, Muslims are demonstrating how Allah wants them to live and following his will (1).

Accept any other valid response.

106 Treatment of criminals

Award 1 mark for providing a reason. Award a second mark for development of the reason, up to a maximum of 4 marks.
- Allah is seen by Muslims as just and merciful and Muslims want to apply these characteristics to their lives (1). They believe that they will be judged after death by Allah on their actions, so acting fairly and in a just way towards others will help them to be rewarded.
- The Qur'an teaches that everyone should be treated equally and with fairness (1). Teachings such as this come from Allah and Muslims believe they should follow them in their lives (1).

- Muslims believe that all humans were created by Allah and deserve equal respect and dignity (1). They accept that all life is sacred and holy and, therefore, even if a person has done wrong, they deserve a level of respect in their treatment (1).

Accept any other valid response.

107 The death penalty

Award 1 mark for providing a reason. Award a second mark for development of the reason, up to a maximum of 4 marks.
- The Qur'an states that capital punishment is an option that can be considered in cases of punishment (1). For the most severe crimes, some Muslims may feel that this teaching should be applied (1).
- Shari'ah law agrees with the Qur'an about the use of capital punishment for the most serious crimes (1). This code of behaviour is referred to in law courts when considering what punishments to give, so capital punishment can be considered (1).
- Muhammad is sometimes seen to have supported the idea of capital punishment (1). There is some evidence that he sentenced people to death for committing murder (1).

Accept any other valid response.

Unit 6 Peace and conflict

108 Peace

Award 1 mark for each point identified, up to a maximum of 3 marks.
- It is what Allah wants (1).
- It is what the Qur'an teaches (1).
- The ummah demonstrates ideas of peace (1).
- Peace is important for justice in the world (1).
- Getting on with others and helping those around the world is a teaching in Islam (1).

Accept any other valid response.

109 Peacemaking

Candidates must underpin their analysis and evaluation with knowledge and understanding. Candidates will be required to demonstrate thorough knowledge and understanding, as well as accuracy, of religion and belief when responding to the question and in meeting AO2 descriptors.

Arguments for the statement:
- Islam teaches that Allah created the world to be a peaceful society. As Muslims believe this is what Allah wants and they will be judged on how they have behaved in this life for the afterlife, it is an important idea.
- The ummah demonstrates ideas of peace showing its importance. As the ummah is how Allah intended people to live their lives in harmony with others and caring for them, it is an important teaching.
- Muslims would argue that without peace in the world justice cannot be achieved. Justice is another key idea promoted in Islam through teachings in the Qur'an and taught by Muhammad.

Arguments against the statement:
- Although peace is important, other beliefs and teachings may be equally or more important. For example, belief in Allah and Muhammad as the prophet is central to the Islamic faith.
- Some practices within Islam might have more impact and achieve peace indirectly. Some of the Five Pillars, such as Zakah or Sawm, may help more people and work to achieve peace and justice within the world.
- Muslims believe that they have duties that they must perform and, through doing so, they work for peace.

Accept any other valid response.

110 Conflict

Award 1 mark for providing a reason. Award a second mark for development of the reason, up to a maximum of 4 marks.
- Islam teaches that all Muslims are part of the ummah and are equal, so should work to bring justice (1). Through educating others or resolving differences, they believe they can achieve peace and an end to conflict.
- Muslims believe Allah is merciful and compassionate and they should follow his example in bringing an end to conflict (1). They believe that Allah intended the world to be peaceful where people live in harmony, so they should work to achieve this (1).
- There are many examples of sayings from Muhammad on the importance of overcoming conflict (1). Muslims believe that they should follow the example of Muhammad in their lives in order that they may go to al-Jannah in the afterlife (1).

Accept any other valid response.

111 Pacifism

Award 1 mark for each condition. Award further marks for each development of the condition, up to a maximum of 4 marks.
- Muslims strive for justice and to resist oppression (1). It is a good thing if this can be achieved in a non-violent way, as this is putting the teachings into practice (1).
- Islam teaches the importance of peace and reconciliation, which could be achieved in a non-violent way (1). Working together to achieve peace through marching peacefully or writing letters can have an impact (1).
- Islam is often understood as 'submission to Allah', which suggests non-violence (1). These methods would be preferred by Muslims.

Accept any other valid response.

112 The Just War theory

1 Award 1 mark for each point identified, up to a maximum of 3 marks.
- Declared by a religious leader (1).
- Is a last resort (1).
- Will not threaten life (1).
- Is an act of defence (1).
- Will not harm the environment (1).

Accept any other valid response.

2 Award 1 mark for providing a reason. Award a second mark for development of the reason, up to a maximum of 4 marks.
- It must be a last resort (1). All peaceful methods of achieving peace should have been tried first before war is declared (1).
- It must not threaten human life (1). The war must be fought in such a way that innocent civilians are neither targeted nor accidently injured as a result of warfare (1).
- It should be an act of defence (1). It should be to defend Islam when the religion is attacked or to help people who are persecuted to escape their situation (1).

Accept any other valid response.

113 Holy war

Award 1 mark for providing a reason. Award a second mark for development of the reason, up to a maximum of 4 marks.
- The Qur'an seems to suggest that, in some situations war is acceptable (1). If it is to defend Islam, protect the freedom of Muslims or to strengthen the religion, holy war can be justified (1).
- There are examples that Muhammad was involved in fighting (1). Examples include the Battle of Badr, where he and his followers fought to defend Islam (1).

- Sometimes Muslims recognise that in order to achieve the end goal of peace, war is needed (1). This is a view reinforced in the Qu'ran and Hadith (1).

Accept any other valid response.

114 Weapons of mass destruction

Award 1 mark for each reason. Award further marks for each development of the reason, up to a maximum of 4 marks. Award 1 further mark for any relevant source of wisdom or authority.

- Muslims do not support the use of WMD as Islam has a set of rules that must be followed when considering war (1). One of the rules is that innocent life should not be threatened, which cannot be met if WMD are used (1): 'That if any one slew a person – unless it be for murder or for spreading mischief in the land – it would be as if he slew the whole people; and if any one saved a life, it would be as if he saved the life of the whole people …' (Surah 5:32) (1).
- Muslims would believe that the conditions of Just War theory wouldn't be met with the use of WMD (1). They indiscriminately affect innocent lives, which is not what Allah intended (1): 'That if any one slew a person – unless it be for murder or for spreading mischief in the land – it would be as if he slew the whole people; and if any one saved a life, it would be as if he saved the life of the whole people …' (Surah 5:32) (1).

Accept any other valid response.

115 Issues surrounding conflict

Candidates must underpin their analysis and evaluation with knowledge and understanding. Candidates will be required to demonstrate thorough knowledge and understanding, as well as accuracy, of religion and belief when responding to the question and in meeting AO2 descriptors.

Arguments for the statement:

- Conflict is a growing issue in the world and Islam's association with acts of terrorism has led to there being misconceptions about the religion. Better understanding of Islam is needed in order to be able to overcome the challenges of conflict.
- There have been many occurrences recently of a rise in the use of violence; both by Muslims and towards Muslims. This has led to a breakdown in relationships with Muslims, which is a big threat to all followers of the religion.
- From a non-religious point of view, the growing threat of conflict and violence in the world is due to religion; this has led to distrust and examples of aggression towards Muslims and those of other faiths.

Arguments against the statement:

- Although conflict is an issue facing Muslims, there are other issues such as the damage being caused to the universe, which Muslims believe is wrong because it is the creation of Allah; this could be the biggest threat as it could threaten human life and future generations.
- Conflict is not the biggest threat as the violence that Muslims are experiencing today through hate crimes is the worst challenge. There have been examples of damage to property, verbal abuse and even physical attacks; this is the greatest challenge Muslims are facing.
- Poverty and injustice in the world is considered to be an issue facing Muslims today – greater than the conflict they may face. Muslims feel they have a duty to help others as this is taught in the Qur'an and led in example through Muhammad. Facing this is the biggest threat in the world for Muslims.

Accept any other valid response.

Unit 7 Philosophy of religion

116 Revelation

Award 1 mark for each way. Award a second mark for development of the way, up to a maximum of 4 marks.

- Through direct revelation (1); this is where Allah communicates directly with humanity, for example through giving the world the Qur'an (1).
- Through messengers (1). Prophets such as Ibrahim, Musa and the 'Seal of the Prophets', Muhammad, brought messages from Allah, which is another way he reveals himself (1).
- Sources of authority such as the Qur'an demonstrate to Muslims what Allah is like (1). The Qur'an shows that he is benevolent and cares for his creation (1).

Accept any other valid response.

117 Visions

1 Award 1 mark for each point identified, up to a maximum of 3 marks.
  - They could be hallucinations (1).
  - They cannot always be verified scientifically (1).
  - Some people believe they are not real (1).
  - They may be illusions (1).
  - People could be mistaken (1).

  Accept any other valid response.

2 Award 1 mark for providing a reason. Award a second mark for development of the reason, up to a maximum of 4 marks.
  - Visions can help to strengthen belief in Allah (1). They confirm that he is real and examples such as Muhammad's vision prove that he is real (1).
  - Visions can provide evidence of the teachings of Islam and the nature of Allah (1). Allah revealing himself through a vision such as to Mary shows his power and benevolence he has for the world (1).
  - Visions can help Muslims to understand what Allah is like (1). It is a way of Allah communicating with humanity either directly or through prophets, which helps Muslims to understand him better (1).

  Accept any other valid response.

118 Miracles

Award 1 mark for providing a reason. Award a second mark for development of the reason, up to a maximum of 4 marks.

- There is no other explanation (1). Miracles such as the Night Journey, which Muhammad experienced, cannot be explained scientifically or in any other way other than Allah (1).
- Miracles are amazing events that prove the existence of Allah (1). They demonstrate what Allah is like and the characteristics he is believed to have, such as his power (1).
- They demonstrate that Allah is active within the world (1). They show that he loves his creation and wants to be close and involved with the world he created (1).

Accept any other valid response.

119 Religious experiences

Award 1 mark for each way. Award a second mark for development of the way, up to a maximum of 4 marks.

- Muslims may respond by arguing that religious experiences are real (1). Although some Muslims do not place great emphasis on them, they accept that Allah has the power to be able to communicate with humanity in this way (1).
- Muslims may respond by arguing that religious experience is a good way of Allah revealing himself (1). They believe that it is a way of Allah connecting with his creation and showing what he is like (for example, having power, being benevolent) (1).

- Muslims may respond by arguing that sources of authority such as the Qur'an give evidence of the truth of religious experience (1). There are examples such as the Night Journey of Muhammad, which shows that religious experience is real (1).

Accept any other valid response.

120 The design argument

1 Award 1 mark for providing a reason. Award a second mark for development of the reason, up to a maximum of 4 marks.
   - It seems to confirm and agree with teachings in the Qur'an (1). Surah 2:164 seems to mention the evidence of design in the world, so it strengthens previously held beliefs.
   - It seems to confirm the nature of Allah (1). The design argument suggest Allah is loving, cares for his creation and is all-powerful, which are ideas upheld by acceptance of the argument.
   - It uses evidence from within the world to prove its conclusion that Allah exists (1). This is evidence that can be seen, which supports previously held beliefs about Allah and strengthens belief in him (1).

Accept any other valid response.

2 Candidates must underpin their analysis and evaluation with knowledge and understanding. Candidates will be required to demonstrate thorough knowledge and understanding, as well as accuracy, of religion and belief when responding to the question and in meeting AO2 descriptors.

Arguments for the statement:
   - It confirms beliefs about the nature of Allah. It suggests that Allah cares for his creation and took time to plan and design it, as well as showing he has the power; therefore, it is good in reinforcing beliefs held by Muslims.
   - It offers an explanation for how the universe came to exist. It is important for Muslims to understand where the world came from and it confirms the beliefs and teachings within the Qur'an, showing that it is important.
   - Evidence from the world around us is used, which means it can be seen by Muslims. This means that it is good evidence of the existence of Allah as it is using his creation to prove that he exists.

Arguments against the statement:
   - Non-religious people may claim that the existence of the universe can be explained today by science and reference to Allah is not needed. The theory of evolution explains the apparent design in the world, which means that people do not need the explanations offered by Islam and the argument is not good evidence of the existence of Allah.
   - The argument cannot be 'proved' and, therefore, it means the existence of Allah also cannot be proved. This means it is not good evidence.
   - Many people argue that it is equally as valid to suggest that the universe came about by chance, which challenges belief in Allah. If this is the case, it is not sufficient evidence to confirm the existence of Allah.

Accept any other valid response.

121 The cosmological argument

Candidates must underpin their analysis and evaluation with knowledge and understanding. Candidates will be required to demonstrate thorough knowledge and understanding, as well as accuracy, of religion and belief when responding to the question and in meeting AO2 descriptors.

Arguments for the statement:
   - Non-religious individuals would agree. They offer criticisms such as the Big Bang theory being a more viable option to explain where the universe came from and, therefore, the argument cannot be used to prove the existence of Allah.
   - Some Muslims do not use this argument as they prefer to use religious sources of authority such as the Qur'an on which to base their beliefs and teachings. Although they may recognise the argument, they would not use it to try to prove the existence of Allah.
   - Some may argue that the cosmological argument only suggests that Allah exists and is not proof of this. As there are some criticisms, they may choose to not use this argument as proof of the existence of Allah.

Argument against the statement:
   - Some Muslims believe that the cosmological argument reinforces their beliefs held in the Qur'an. As it appears to agree with their source of authority, many Muslims would uphold the argument as good evidence for belief in the existence of Allah.
   - Al-Ghazali in the 12th century formulated his own Islamic version of this argument. As Islam has a proponent of the argument, many Muslims would point to this in showing its success at proving the existence of Allah.
   - Many Muslims believe the argument can respond to challenges such as that offered by the Big Bang by incorporating both into the explanation for the creation of the universe. If this is accepted, it could be seen as good evidence for belief in Allah.

Accept any other valid response.

122 The existence of suffering

Award 1 mark for each reason. Award further marks for each development of the reason, up to a maximum of 4 marks. Award 1 further mark for any relevant source of wisdom or authority.
   - It challenges the omnipotence of Allah (1). If he is forgiving and all-powerful, Muslims may question why he does not stop evil such as murder and killing (1): 'In the name of Allah, the Entirely Merciful, the Especially Merciful. [All] praise is [due] to Allah, Lord of the worlds – The Entirely Merciful, the Especially Merciful, Sovereign of the Day of Recompense. It is You we worship and You we ask for help. Guide us to the straight path – The path of those upon whom You have bestowed favour, not of those who have evoked [Your] anger or of those who are astray.' (Surah 1) (1).
   - It challenges whether he is all-loving, as the Qur'an suggests (1). Wouldn't a God who sees his creation suffering want to stop it? (1): 'In the name of Allah, the Entirely Merciful, the Especially Merciful. [All] praise is [due] to Allah, Lord of the worlds – The Entirely Merciful, the Especially Merciful, Sovereign of the Day of Recompense. It is You we worship and You we ask for help. Guide us to the straight path – The path of those upon whom You have bestowed favour, not of those who have evoked [Your] anger or of those who are astray.' (Surah 1) (1).
   - It challenges the very existence of Allah (1). If he is what the Qur'an claims he is, why doesn't he step in and prevent suffering in the world? (1): 'In the name of Allah, the Entirely Merciful, the Especially Merciful. [All] praise is [due] to Allah, Lord of the worlds – The Entirely Merciful, the Especially Merciful, Sovereign of the Day of Recompense. It is You we worship and You we ask for help. Guide us to the straight path – The path of those upon whom You have bestowed favour, not of those who have evoked [Your] anger or of those who are astray.' (Surah 1) (1).

Accept any other valid response.

123 Solutions to the problem of suffering

Award 1 mark for each point identified, up to a maximum of 3 marks.

- Pray for Allah to help them (1).
- Give money to charity (1).
- Volunteer or give time to help others through charity work (1).
- Share Islamic teachings with others about why they suffer (1).
- Remind people of the need to accept this life in order to achieve a good afterlife (1).

Accept any other valid response.

Unit 8 Equality

124 Human rights

1 Award 1 mark for each point identified up to a maximum of 3 marks.
- Islam teaches the importance of helping others (1).
- Islam teaches all humans were created as equal by Allah (1).
- Islam teaches that Muslims have a duty to stand up against injustice in the world (1).
- Muslims follow the example of Muhammad, who treated all people equally (1).
- The Qur'an supports all humans having human rights (1).

Accept any other valid response.

2 Award 1 mark for providing a reason. Award a second mark for development of the reason, up to a maximum of 4 marks.
- Islam teaches that all Muslims have a duty to help others (1). When human rights have been ignored, Muslims believe that they should stand up against these injustices (1).
- Muslims believe all humans were created as equal by Allah (1). This means that everyone is the same and deserves fair treatment. When this doesn't happen, others should stand up and help (1).
- Islam teaches Muslims to follow the example of Muhammad, who stood up for the human rights of others (1). He fought for equality for women and took care of the most vulnerable in society (1).

Accept any other valid response.

125 Equality

Award 1 mark for each way. Award a second mark for development of the way, up to a maximum of 4 marks.
- Through charity work (1). They can support charities such as Islamic Relief or Muslim Aid to help others all around the world facing inequality. For example, providing relief in emergency situations (1).
- They can educate others (1). This will help others to accept that all humans are equal as created by Allah and try to improve the quality and situation of the lives of others (1).
- They can give money in Zakah (1). This is one of the Five Pillars and money is given every year to support the most needy in society (1).

Accept any other valid response.

126 Religious freedom

Candidates must underpin their analysis and evaluation with knowledge and understanding. Candidates will be required to demonstrate thorough knowledge and understanding, as well as accuracy, of religion and belief when responding to the question and in meeting AO2 descriptors.

Arguments for the statement:
- Other people do not understand the Muslim faith and Muslims may face negativity and discrimination. It can be difficult for them to integrate and educate others making it problematic to live in a multifaith society.

- It may be difficult for Muslims to practise their faith and follow all aspects. This could be seen on a Friday which, traditionally, is a day of work in the UK, but which is the holy day for Muslims.
- Muslims may feel intimidated or excluded within society. After world events linking Islam to atrocities such as terrorism, all Muslims may feel they are stereotyped and treated differently.

Arguments against the statement:
- Many people today want to find out more about all religions in the UK. Muslims may value being open and honest about their faith, as well as learning about other faiths.
- There are many benefits from living in a multifaith society, including access to new cultures, foods, music and diversity.
- Muslims can help to bridge the gaps in understanding between different religions. There has been lots of work done between different religious groups in order to show the things they share in common, rather than their differences which could divide.

Accept any other valid response.

127 Prejudice and discrimination

Award 1 mark for each point identified, up to a maximum of 3 marks.
- Prejudice and discrimination is always wrong (1).
- Allah created all humans equally (1).
- Muhammad taught that all humans are equal (1).
- People should not be discriminated for their religion (1).
- Muslims should always work to help those facing discrimination (1).

Accept any other valid response.

128 Racial harmony

1 Award 1 mark for each point identified, up to a maximum of 3 marks.
- It is taught in the Qur'an (1).
- Muhammad preached about it (1).
- Muslims believe all humans were created equally by Allah (1).
- All races are believed to be equal (1).
- All Muslims believe they are part of the ummah, which demonstrates equality (1).

Accept any other valid response.

2 Award 1 mark for each benefit. Award a second mark for the development of the benefit, up to a maximum of 4 marks.
- Encourages racial harmony (1). All humans are recognised as being equal and should have fair treatment.
- Gives wider variety of cultural differences and influences (1). For example, food, music, clothing and shared understanding (1).
- Brings people together and helps improve communication between them (1). Helps to reduce inequality and discrimination (1).

Accept any other valid response.

129 Racial discrimination

1 Award 1 mark for each belief. Award a second mark for development of the belief, up to a maximum of 4 marks.
- Muslims believe Allah created everyone to be equal and racial discrimination is wrong (1). The Qur'an promotes this idea in Surah 49:13 (1).
- Muslims believe the ummah demonstrates equality (1). If all humans are equal, racial discrimination is wrong as races all deserve to be treated the same as promoted by Muhammad (1).

- Muslims recognise that people are different, but this does not make them unequal (1). All humans should be treated the same, as this is what Muhammad did and Muslims want to follow his example (1).

Accept any other valid response.

2 Candidates must underpin their analysis and evaluation with knowledge and understanding. Candidates will be required to demonstrate thorough knowledge and understanding, as well as accuracy, of religion and belief when responding to the question and in meeting AO2 descriptors.

Arguments for the statement:
- Muslims believe they have a duty to stand up against injustice in the world. They believe all humans were created equal by Allah and the Qur'an states that they should treat them equally.
- Muslims demonstrate racial equality through many of their religious practices. They believe the ummah demonstrates racial equality, and they have practices such as Zakah, Sawm and wearing white robes on Hajj, which demonstrate this belief.
- Muslims believe that Muhammad demonstrated that racial inequality is wrong and treated everyone the same. As he did this, Muslims feel that they should follow his example and behave in the same way.

Arguments against the statement:
- Some people may feel it is not their individual responsibility to stand up to racial discrimination. They may feel that this is what the law and government are there to do and enforce.
- There are examples of people standing up for racial equality and losing their lives as a result, for example Martin Luther King Jr, who was assassinated. It may be too dangerous to stand up to racial discrimination.
- Some people may argue that one person cannot make a big difference and it needs to be a majority group that can bring about change. They may feel that this issue needs all people to be united.

Accept any other valid response.

130 Social justice
Award 1 mark for each reason. Award further marks for each development of the reason, up to a maximum of 4 marks. Award 1 further mark for any relevant source of wisdom or authority.
- Muslims believe that they have a duty to help care for others (1). This is stated in many teachings within the Qur'an (1): 'Those who follow the Messenger, the unlettered prophet, whom they find written in what they have of the Torah and the Gospel, who enjoins upon them what is right and forbids them what is wrong and makes lawful for them the good things and prohibits for them the evil and relieves them of their burden and the shackles which were upon them. So they who have believed in him, honored him, supported him and followed the light which was sent down with him – it is those who will be the successful. (Surah 7:157) (1).
- Muslims believe that all humans are equal as they are created by Allah (1). If they are all created the same, they deserve equality and a fair life through equality in social justice (1): 'O mankind, indeed We have created you from male and female and made you peoples and tribes that you may know one another. Indeed, the most noble of you in the sight of Allah is the most righteous of you. Indeed, Allah is Knowing and Acquainted.' (Surah 49:13) (1).
- Shari'ah law promotes social equality (1). This code of behaviour argues the basic requirements every Muslim should have (1).

Accept any other valid response.

131 Wealth and poverty
Award 1 mark for providing a reason. Award a second mark for development of the reason, up to a maximum of 4 marks.
- Muslims disapprove of greed and waste (1). They believe possessions ultimately belong to Allah and should be shared (1).
- Muslims are expected to act responsibly and help those in need (1). Allah created all humans to be equal, and this should mean in what they have as well (1).
- Muslims give Zakah as part of the Five Pillars and sadaqah voluntarily (1). These are used to help the poor and are key ways of putting Islamic beliefs into practice to help others (1).

Accept any other valid response.

Notes

Notes

Notes

Notes

Notes